EDUCATION
IN A DEMOCRACY

EDUCATION

IN A DEMOCRACY

An Introduction to the Study of Education

ALONZO F. MYERS, Chairman, Department of Higher
Education, New York University

CLARENCE O. WILLIAMS
Professor of Education and Director of Education Extension, The
Pennsylvania State College

Third Edition

New York   ·   Prentice-Hall, Inc.   ·   Publishers

PRENTICE-HALL EDUCATION SERIES
E. George Payne, Editor

TO
Our Children

Preface

Education, broadly interpreted, comprises all the efforts, conscious and direct, or incidental and indirect, made by society to accomplish certain objectives that are considered desirable. These efforts may be put forth by organized society as a whole —a nation, for example—or by majority or minority groups, such as political parties or religious denominations. The goals, likewise, may be formulated either in the interests of society at large or by segments of society, which are sometimes self-seeking and selfish in their desires. The importance of education as an agency for modifying the attitudes and beliefs, and, consequently, the behavior of a people, has been increasing during the past four or five centuries.

The educational agencies have also been undergoing fundamental and far-reaching changes. First, the most noticeable change is in the number of agencies whose energies are devoted wholly or in part to educational effort. The school, the church, and the home must share the responsibility or the opportunity, depending upon one's point of view, with the press; the radio; the movies; innumerable social, civic, and fraternal organizations; and improved transportation facilities. Indeed, it may be said that the concrete highway is as much an educational agency as it is a scientific development. Second, the purposes and character and organization of these agencies are constantly changing. Before the invention of the printing press, it was almost impossible to make education universal. In the days of the town crier, governmental groups could release or withhold information at their discretion. Now, when a radio station is silenced by the Federal Radio Commission in this country, it is not difficult for the offending broadcaster to build a new station just across the border in Mexico and blanket the former area of his operations with signals much louder than before. Since many persons believe that the home and the church are relatively less influential as educative agencies than they were formerly, there have been increasing demands upon the school to assume a larger share of the responsibility.

No strong arguments are needed to show that the organized school is only one of society's educational agencies, but school people need to be reminded of the fact. While it is true that for three or four decades, in America, particularly, the responsibilities of the school have increased in number and complexity, still, it is doubtless true that in terms of total influence the school is relatively less potent in molding public opinion than it was in the past. The school can no longer be content merely to formulate its objectives and develop techniques for attaining them. It must constantly study its problems and results in terms of the objectives and efforts of all the other educational agencies.

Education, then, must be conceived as a social force, and the study of education consequently becomes a social study. To confine the study of education to the techniques and offerings of the school is grossly misleading to the student, whether he approaches the subject as a prospective teacher or whether he encounters it as one of the optional offerings of a broad cultural curriculum. Such restrictions will also make the attainment of the aims prescribed in the preceding paragraph increasingly difficult. Teachers and schools cannot effectively attack society's problems broadly and in coöperation with other institutions if, during the days of preparation, the prospective worker has his attention directed almost exclusively to skills and procedures and isolated objectives. Education needs to be studied in relation to the social sciences.

As a social science, education interests itself in the improvement of society. It does not confine itself to the teaching of a limited compact body of subject matter. Results take precedence over procedures; changes in individuals become more important than subject matter and the activities of students eclipse the activities of the teacher. This conception of education necessitates a better understanding of the basic sciences that explain changes in human behavior, notably biology and psychology. It will also demand

a fuller appreciation of the social, economic, and political forces
at work in society.

All individuals are "consumers" of education or of the products
of an educational system, in a threefold sense. First, as students
and learners, we are on the receiving end of the educational process.
Second, in adult life, we are employees or employers, and the relationships existing between these two groups are conditioned by
the type of education each experiences. Third, as individuals we
are subject to the environmental conditions surrounding us, which
have in part been determined by educational forces. The status
of an individual is directly affected by the educational advantages
available to him. It is in that sense that all are "consumers." On
the other hand, the teachers and other educational workers are the
"producers" in the process.

This book is written as much for the consumer as for the producer; for the student interested in social forces as much as for
the prospective teacher. It may be used as a textbook for those
who are studying education as a social science, or it may serve as
a syllabus for a professional course, perhaps the first of a series of
courses, in the curriculum for persons preparing for teaching. It
will provide a useful vocational try-out experience for students
who are uncertain as to whether or not they wish to engage in
educational work.

In preparing this volume the authors had in mind the course
commonly called "Introduction to Education," an orientation
course that aims to give the student a broad overview of the educational system and of the necessary steps in preparing for a
career as a teacher. It has been their intention to prepare a
treatment that differed significantly from other textbooks designed
for introductory courses in education, in point of view and procedure, as follows:

1. The major emphasis is placed upon the function of education in society, whether the student be a professional or a non-pro-
fessional student. Attention is, therefore, given to the educational implications of contemporary social, economic, and political
problems.

2. Education is given a broad interpretation; it is not confined to formal instruction. The schools are studied in relation to the many non-school educative agencies.

3. The best use of the book calls for extensive reading to discover points of view of many authors, instead of intensive study of a limited amount of text material. Rather complete reference lists are provided.

4. All topics are approached with the idea of raising questions concerning the fundamental issues involved.

5. The students will be encouraged to develop attitudes and express opinions, these objectives taking precedence over the acquisition of information in the customary preparing-for-examination manner.

The material is organized into units instead of chapters. The units are more or less interrelated, but they are sufficiently differentiated to be considered comprehensive subdivisions. This organization will lend itself to a contract- or unit-type procedure, with emphasis upon the broader implications rather than upon lesson assignments and recitations. Abundant opportunities are provided to encourage a student to work inedependently along some line of special interest. A complete outline of each unit is presented, to enable the instructor to furnish the students with an overview of the topic under consideration.

It has been the author's hope that this book may be used in a manner that will reduce the emphasis upon lesson learning and reciting or lecturing by the instructor and place a higher premium upon independent study by the students. To the end that the methods used might encourage students to develop efficient habits of library study and thought-provoking attitudes of inquiry and investigation, each unit has been concluded with a number of problems and references that should serve as a guide to the instructors and students in planning the out-of-class work. This collateral material is classified under two headings:

1. *Problems for Students.* Here there has been presented a number of typical problems or projects or topics for independent study or class discussion. These may be assigned to individuals

or to groups of students and may be made the basis of special reports in class or of term papers.   Many other problems that have
particular local significance should be used to supplement these.

2. *Selected References.*   These do not comprise an exhaustive
list by any means, but they are representative.   The books will
provide an opportunity for the students to become acquainted
with the best-known authorities in the field, and the magazine
articles will inform them concerning current developments.   These
lists have been prepared to accompany each of the major divisions
of each unit.

The authors are indebted to several of their colleagues for valuable suggestions concerning the contents and organization of this
volume and for their critical reading of many portions of the
manuscript.   They desire to express appreciation for the cour-
tesies extended by a number of authors and publishers of books
and periodicals in granting permission to reprint copyrighted
materials.   Acknowledgment is made, particularly, to New York
University for extending permission to publish in this volume the
material contained in a doctor's dissertation written by one of the
authors under the supervision of a member of its faculty.

✓   ✓   ✓

We believe the basic idea for this book as originally written in
1936 is fundamentally sound; consequently the book has not been
greatly altered in this, the third edition.   It has, however, been
brought into harmony with the facts and necessities of the present
time.   The authors have had in mind the necessity for coping with
certain major changes that have occurred in the world, in the
United States, and in the American public school system.   We have
tried to take into account the fact that democracy has been, and
continues to be, challenged.   Three distinct outcomes are sought:

First, the study of education as a career, the Vocational emphasis.   It is hoped that students and readers will be assisted in
answering the question, "Shall I become a Teacher?" developed in
Unit One.

Second, an understanding of our American school systems, the

Professional emphasis. The prospective worker in education needs to get this broad overview of the structure of school systems in the United States. This objective is accomplished largely in Units Two, Three, Six, and Seven.

Third, the function of education in society, the Social emphasis. The student is challenged to realize the importance and significance of education in society. The school as a social agency, with the peculiar obligation to serve the ends of society, receives major emphasis in Units Four and Five.

The Vocational or career emphasis may be taken up at any point in the course. In the original edition we put this material in Unit Seven. In this new edition, that material has been made Unit One. The instructor will have his own methods for determining the location of this part of the study.

Alonzo F. Myers
Clarence O. Williams

Editor's Foreword

No one seems to question the fact that we are passing through a period of more or less fundamental readjustment in our community and national life, and for this reason we are facing the necessity of vital reconstruction of our institutions and social processes and a new emphasis in education. As a matter of fact, fundamental changes in a variety of institutions and social processes have already taken place. Because their significance is not clear to many thinkers, educators often find themselves bewildered, and there is therefore a demand that we re-examine our social processes, our social institutions, and the operation of social forces in our complex life, and that we discover the nature and function of education in its relation to them. It is absolutely necessary that the student entering the field of education get a general view of the school and other educational institutions and agencies in relation to the complex social processes and forces.

Moreover, in spite of the fact that we have discussed the facts of social change *ad nauseam,* the student about to enter the long period of study, preparation, and apprenticeship for the profession of teaching must face the problems of social change and consequent readjustment in order to define for himself his place and function in the educational world. Furthermore, he should face this task early in his career of preparation in order that he may not muddle along without a clear understanding of the importance of the educator and the educational function in bringing order out of our educational and social chaos.

It is significant to note that altogether too much emphasis in the education of teachers has been placed upon the techniques of school management and instruction, with the result that teachers, supervisors, and superintendents have been skilled artisans in the handling of a conventional school program, but have failed adequately to envisage this program in its relation to the major forces of

American life. Thus the schools in their hands have lagged behind social progress and in many instances have retarded social progress. There is no reason why this condition should continue if educators cease to be mere peddlers of a conventional educational pabulum, and instead become leaders in educational reconstruction and progress. The attainment of a position of leadership hinges upon the degree to which they can comprehend the forces of our social life and the place of education among them.

The authors of this book have been keenly alive to the new educational demands. They have visioned a new school, a new teacher, and a new school administrator, and the student who masters this text cannot be an educator in the conventional sense, nor will he be satisfied with our laggard schools. He will become a new social force in our educational advance.

E. George Payne

Contents

xv

Unit Six

NECESSARY AND IMPENDING CHANGES IN AMERICAN EDUCATION   Page 271

Unit Seven

PROMISING EDUCATIONAL ACTIVITIES TODAY   Page 307

Tables and Figures

TABLES

xix

FIGURES

Shall I Become a Teacher?

The question that serves as a title for this unit is a pertinent one for a very large proportion of the students who will be using this book as a text or reference. The unit places emphasis upon one of the three major outcomes expected from a study of the book, namely, upon the consideration of teaching as a career. The question might be stated in another way as, "Is there a job in education for me?" or more broadly, "Do I want to engage in any kind of work that is primarily educational in nature?" This discussion is intended to help the reader decide whether he wishes to apply his talents and abilities to the development of any part of our far-reaching educational structure.

A wiser choice will undoubtedly be made if the individual understands the possibilities and limitations of any particular type of work and is fully appreciative of his own fitness and aptitude, or lack of them, for the job. There are many types of positions in the educational field other than classroom teaching. (We should hasten to add that the best basic preparation for any type of speciality in education is a typical experience as a classroom teacher.) We shall enumerate some of the specialities and indicate the type of preparation that is desirable for each. But in no sense is this discussion to be considered a sales talk or argument for entering educational work. If well-qualified young people are encouraged to become educational workers as a result of this study, then these pages will have served a useful purpose. By the same token, if an occasional person becomes doubtful about the educational world as a suitable field of endeavor for himself, a similarly useful service will have been rendered because a group of

1

children somewhere will not become the victims of an unhappy, frustrated teacher. It is the hope of the authors that study of this unit will assist many young persons in answering the question, "Shall I become a teacher?"

TABLE 1

Number of Teachers in the United States, 1939–40[1]

	Men	Women	Total
Kindergarten and Elementary Schools	71,011	569,036	640,047
Secondary Schools	140,352	193,776	334,128
Higher Education	86,247	30,570	116,817
Miscellaneous	3,295	7,696	10,991
Total	330,905	801,078	1,101,983

A. Society's Critical Need for Teachers

1. Importance of Teaching

Teaching is an important function in any society. It is probably a more important function in a democratic society than in any other. That public education is the proving ground for the young members in a democracy has long been an accepted principle in this country. The writings of our colonial leaders make frequent reference to the significance of common schools open to all the children of all the people.

The teacher is the most important factor in the democratic school. Though there be well-organized schools, with good administrative leaders, operating in modern, comfortable buildings, · the educational objectives of a democratic society cannot be attained without the stimulation and guidance of teachers imbued

---

[1] Benjamin W. Frazier, "Teaching as a Profession," U S. Office of Education Pamphlet No. 95, 1944.

with that society's ideals. From the earliest days in this country the preparation and certification of teachers have been recognized as a state responsibility. This fact underlines the principle that society selects and educates teachers, and delegates certain significant responsibilities to them for the direct purpose of having them serve society. This book has been written to lay stress upon the importance of education as an agency in society. In this unit the major portion of that stress is placed upon the importance of the teacher.

2. Great Need for Superior Teachers

The determination of who shall teach should not be left to chance nor to control by any faction or minority group. The best minds, the ablest citizens, and the firmest believers in democratic ideals should be the delegated representatives of society in the schools. Factors such as wealth, social position, location of residence, or availability should not be permitted to operate as major considerations in the selection of teachers. Society, through its constituted agencies made up of educational leaders and representative citizens, should seek out the most able of our young people and encourage them to engage in one of the most important tasks that a democratic society shares with its constituents. Positive, systematic programs of selection are needed. These must be accompanied by rewards and by recognition on the part of society of such character that interest in the professional work will be genuine and more or less permanent. Some of the factors that enter into this selective process will be discussed later in this unit.

3. Selection of Candidates for Teaching

The two most important steps in the process of selecting teachers are: first, recognition by the individual himself that he has a genuine interest in teaching; and second, observation by his teachers and co-workers of the extent to which he possesses the qualities of leadership and professional attitudes needed in educational work. Of these two, the most important is the first. It is probably true that the most important single factor contributing to success in any occupation is a sincere interest in that occupation and an inner urge or drive to be successful at it. That generalization is probably even more true of teaching and other social occupations. When this genuine interest and drive are lacking, many pitfalls and frustrations are certain to be encountered. It is the responsibility of guidance counselors and school officials to provide opportunities and experiences for young people to test themselves out with respect to their interests. At the same time machinery needs to be set in motion that will systematically collect and record for high school and college students observations of the personal and social qualities that contribute to success in educational work. This objective appraisal, coupled with the student's self-evaluation, should enable us to find the young people who give promise of being successful teachers and happy, challenging workers in the educational field.

B.   Types of Educational Positions

1.   Classroom Teaching

The front-line positions in the educational world are in the classrooms. The classroom teacher is the fundamental unit in the educational structure. The apprenticeship, so to speak, for any type of work in education is served as a regular teacher in a typical classroom. Specialists of one kind or another and administrative and supervisory officials are more successful in working with their colleagues if they themselves have spent a few years as classroom teachers. Even those who would teach in a college or university should begin their careers in the public elementary or secondary schools before they complete their graduate studies. In the following paragraphs we shall outline briefly some of the opportunities and responsibilities of classroom teachers at different age levels.

a. *Pre-school education.* In this area we find nursery schools and kindergartens. The former are almost always private or proprietary enterprises, not a part of the public school system. Whether kindergartens are public or private depends in large measure upon the part of the country under consideration or the traditional background in the community. There are indications of increasing demands for persons trained to do this kind of work, and it offers many possibilities for those who are primarily interested in little children. In these schools the chief emphasis is placed on the social and personality development of the pupils. The best training consists of a firm foundation study in child psychology and development, mental hygiene, sociology, and family relationships.

b. *Elementary education.* The first six grades (in many places the first eight) offer some of the best opportunities in educational work, particularly in terms of the demand for elementary teachers at the present time. Elementary school enrollments declined during the thirties but are due to begin a rapid increase because of the acceleration in the birth rate since 1940. No matter what the economic situation is in this country for the next few years, there will be a continuing demand for good elementary teachers for two reasons: first, the number of children will necessitate more teachers; second, for several years the number of college students preparing for elementary teaching has been far below that needed annually for replacements in the schools. Coupled with this demand for mere numbers is the urgent need at the present time for men in the elementary schools. A young man of superior abilities and good personality who will equip himself for elementary teaching, obtain some experience on that level, and prepare himself further by means of graduate study for either administrative work or college teaching can very nearly write the specifications for his own career. Elementary education offers unusual opportunities to men as well as women, a fact frequently overlooked by students themselves and by guidance counselors.

Two factors have operated to make teaching in the elementary schools more attractive: first, the establishment of a college degree as a basic requirement, as it is, generally, for secondary teachers; and second, the payment of equal salaries for equal experience and preparation no matter what the level of teaching. The trend in recent years has definitely been toward a uniform level of preparation and single salary schedules throughout the school system. Numerous cities and several states now guarantee the same starting salaries and the same annual salary increments for teachers at all levels. The broader, more extensive basic preparation has proved more attractive to young people with scholarly interests than the old system under which elementary teachers studied principally the subjects that were taught in the elementary grades. Not so long ago it was necessary for teachers to leave the elementary school and move upward into the secondary school in order to make progress professionally, on the salary scale, or in social prestige. That is no longer the case. The public is coming very definitely to recognize the principle that all teachers are important and that work at all levels should be equally rewarded.

For one who is contemplating teaching in the elementary schools, an inherent interest in children is the first requisite because the teacher needs to be able to deal with the children on their own level. Many teachers think this latter fact leads to a certain stereotyping of their reactions; they miss the challenge and stimulation of contacts with adult intellects and activities. This lack is particularly felt where teachers are limited in their social and recreational activities. On the other hand, one frequently hears teachers say that daily contacts with children help to keep them youthful in spirit. Although it is exceedingly difficult to get this point of view accepted by all the persons concerned, it is undoubtedly true that the elementary school should attach greatest importance, not to the subject matter that is taught, but to the child's growth in the use of the skills and knowledge comprising the subject matter. Preparation for elementary teaching has been done traditionally in a two- or three-year normal school course, but best practices are rapidly moving toward a four-year curriculum leading to a college degree as a minimum program. Without doubt, the elementary teacher of the future will need to be more broadly educated than in the past.

c. *Secondary education.* The prospective teacher needs to remember that secondary education now embraces the junior high school and includes all the work through grades seven to twelve.

The majority of positions open to secondary teachers are at the junior high school level. Students of education are cautioned to keep this fact in mind in selecting their college courses. Beginning science teachers are more likely to teach general science for a few years than chemistry or physics; and the mathematics teachers, arithmetic rather than geometry or trigonometry.

Splendid opportunities for persons who like to work with early adolescents and who are not primarily interested in becoming subject matter specialists are afforded by the junior high schools. Since this unit is essentially a tryout period, teachers with broad sympathies and a wide variety of interests and experiences will be able to render the most effective service. Minimum preparation should consist of a college degree without too much emphasis upon narrow specialization. The foremost requirement is love and sympathy for the bubbling, effervescent, enthusiastic boys and girls who are seeking their places in the social group and in many cases struggling to be emancipated from the restraints of the home. Teaching procedures need to be adjusted to the interests and capacities of the students during the transition stages of early adolescence.

Teaching in the senior high schools differs only slightly from junior high school teaching in so far as relations with the pupils are concerned, but it does offer opportunities to deal with subject matter more nearly like that encountered in college. It is a serious mistake, however, for any secondary school teacher to regard his work as that of a scholar interested in intense specialization in a field of knowledge. In all phases of secondary education the social and personal development of children is of far more importance than subject matter objectives. Anyone who does not enjoy the social, athletic, and extracurricular life of the high school should regard that as a significant symptom; he probably would not be very happy teaching on that level. A college degree is an almost universal requirement for high school teaching, and, in many areas, particularly certain cities, a master's degree or its equivalent is considered the minimum preparation. At the time of this writing there is a serious shortage of high school teachers, especially in mathematics, science, physical education, vocational education, and home economics.

d. *The junior college.* It would be quite appropriate to include this with the units of the public school system because there is abundant evidence that we are moving in that direction. As a rule, a master's degree is considered minimum preparation for teaching on this level. It may be regarded as a good stepping-stone to college teaching and is just the place for high school teachers who have a scholarly interest in subject matter and who wish to specialize to a greater extent than teaching in many high schools makes possible.

All the evidence points to an expansion of the junior college program in this country. In many states junior colleges are extending the public education offering to include the thirteenth and fourteenth years and are making the first two years of college work almost as easily attainable as is a high school education. One of the results of the war, by virtue of the benefits of the GI Bill of Rights, will be the establishment of junior colleges, many of them at public expense, within fairly easy reach of high school graduates in most sections of the country. The subsequent increased enrollment is certain to bring an accompanying demand for teachers. Young people contemplating a career in education would do well to look ahead to the possibilities of teaching on the junior college level after they have secured the necessary graduate training and, perhaps, a few years of teaching experience in the secondary school.

e. *College and university teaching.* If we regard the college or university as the repository of the world's accumulated knowledge and scholarship, then we may rightfully regard the college professor as the guardian of that heritage. He is a specialist in his field. His duties consist either of instruction or research, or a combination of both. He usually enjoys a large measure of economic security, long tenure, and comparatively high rank in the cultural, social, and civic life of the community. Opportunities for writing, lecturing, and experimentation are commensurate with one's abilities and aptitudes.

The tremendous increase in college and university enrollments has created an unusual demand for instructors. It seems clearly indicated that the enrollments will remain at high levels for many years to come and that, consequently, the demand for college teachers will continue. Many young persons who think they would like teaching and who have high scholarly interests and the ability and inclination to do graduate study might very profitably look forward to teaching on this level. Three suggestions are offered to young people with such ambitions. First, let them include professional preparation in teaching techniques and guidance in the college degree curriculum; second, get a few years of teaching in either the elementary or secondary schools; and third, map out a program of graduate studies that will lead to the doctor's degree. One word of caution with regard to this last step in the process is to avoid too narrow specialization. A college teacher must be recognized as a scholar in his field but he must also be interested in the student he is to teach. Particularly at the freshman and sophomore level he must have a wide interest in all subjects.

The leaders in higher education are giving much thought to the selection of instructors and currently a great deal of emphasis is being placed upon ability to teach. Because a person holds a degree in a given field is no guarantee that he will be a good teacher —he might be a better research worker. Likewise an interest in students and a desire to counsel them must take at least equal rank with interest in scholarly pursuits. There are good opportunities in college teaching, particularly for those who have systematically prepared themselves for such a career.

2. School Administration and Supervision

a. *The superintendent of schools.* The superintendent occupies ne of the most attractive educational positions because of its income and its place of leadership and prominence in the community. He is also in the most precarious position, as his tenure is less secure than that of teachers. A superintendent's decisions establish policies and affect the personal welfare of individuals.

He is the professional representative of the board of education and is most susceptible to changing policies and shifting control in that body. Young people with vision, courage, tact, leadership, and a vision of community service may well aspire to such a position but only after thorough preparation and a rich experience in teaching at all levels of the school system. The superintendent, or supervising principal, as he is called in smaller communities, is rapidly becoming a leader with influence second to none in the community, as is the case in the schools of Europe. He takes his place at the council table with the business, civic, and professional leaders of the community and is in a position to place the schools on a high plane of social service if he has the tact, courage and social philosophy that will command the respect of his associates in and out of the profession. Such a position of leadership demands the broadest kind of preparation. The superintendent of schools is in a genuine sense a combination business man and educator, because education today is a big business.

b. *The supervising principal.* In many states the smaller school districts employ an official legally known as a supervising principal. In nearly all respects he has the same duties as a superintendent of schools. He is the local professional leader, and the difference in title is about the only distinction that one can find. It is he who interviews prospective teachers, confers with the board of school directors, and assumes practically all the prerogatives of a superintendent. Men in these positions are the most frequent sources of recruitment for superintendents for the larger districts.

c. *The school principal.* The principal, of either the elementary or secondary school, is certainly one of the most influential persons in a school system. His duties are almost wholly professional. That is, he is concerned primarily with educational problems, dealing with teachers, pupils, and parents. The business affairs of the school are largely taken care of by the superintendent's office. Principals are the responsible leaders of their schools; it is to them that superintendents delegate the educational problems, including organization and administration of the school buildings, and usually the supervision of instruction. They are usually recruited from the ranks of teachers. In some states they must attain certain standards required for principal's certificates. These are attractive positions, paying good salaries and not subject to the dangers and difficulties of the superintendency. The elementary school principalship, particularly, offers many opportunities to young men who are qualified.

d. *Supervision.* This service, a type that has come into schools during the last few decades, offers opportunities to ambitious and superior classroom teachers. Their duties consist largely of observing classes and conferring with teachers with the view of improving instruction. It is the instruction they are supervising, not the teachers or the pupils. To these supervising persons the superintendents delegate the responsibility for the instructional program, in coöperation with the principals. Supervisors are of many types. There are elementary school supervisors who are responsible for all elementary instruction, coördination of the work of all teachers, and safeguarding the standards and interests of pupils. On the high school level this work is usually done by heads of departments or directors of the several subjects, English or social studies, for example. Then there are supervisors of special subjects, including music, art, physical education, penmanship, and the like, although it should be noted that with the better all-round preparation of teachers in recent years there has come a lessened need for special subject supervision. Such persons are usually recruited from among the teachers who have exhibited qualities of leadership and have made special preparation for the positions.

3. Specialized Services in Education

In addition to the top positions for administrators and supervisors there is a great variety of specialized jobs in educational institutions to which teachers can look forward. Usually the accompanying salary is somewhat higher, but so are the responsibilities. This fact does not mean that the specialists work harder or are necessarily worth more money. They frequently put in more time during the year, however, serving on an eleven- or twelve-month basis rather than for the teacher's nine- or ten-month term. They have larger responsibilities throughout the school district, as well, and their training is usually more extensive. All of these things together justify the higher salaries paid them. As was indicated in an earlier discussion in this unit, any specialized job in education should be sought only after a brief period as a teacher. Practically all the jobs as a specialist are related to the classroom in one way or another. The specialist who has himself been a classroom teacher is better able to understand the problems of teachers and, particularly, to work with the latter in solving them. We cannot name all the specialized services here, but we shall mention a few of them to indicate some of the opportunities ahead for the more ambitious teachers less inclined to remain in a classroom.

a. *Guidance and personnel work.* A comparatively new type of service in public schools is that rendered by guidance counselors, deans of girls or advisers of boys. The prime requisite is ready access to the confidence of young people and sympathy for and interest in their problems. Since so many of their problems are of a very personal nature, counselors must be straightforward and trustworthy and motivated by a desire to render service while being objective and analytical in their dealings. Pupils' problems frequently involve educational and occupational adjustments necessitating broad interests and wide contacts and experiences on the part of the counselor. It would be a serious mistake for a young person to think of counseling as an occupation until after several years of successful teaching and graduate study in guidance and personnel work. To this should be added as many contacts as possible with the world of work.

b. *School psychologist.* City schools have found it profitable to employ school psychologists to diagnose the learning difficulties of unadjusted pupils and to take charge of the entire program of testing in the schools. Rural areas also need such expert technical service and will in time be able to employ such persons through consolidation or coöperative efforts among districts. Such skilled service calls for technical preparation in psychology and should also include experience in teaching.

c. *School health service.* Here we have a type of service that has become indispensable in recent years. School nurses have performed a service of incalculable value in discovering and controlling contagious diseases and in preventing serious losses in time and efficiency among pupils. Countless lives have been saved or lengthened through the efforts of these people. As a result of the follow-up contacts in the homes, school nurses have brought the home and the school into closer relationship in the urgent problem of community health and in many other important educational situations. This position combines the splendid opportunities for service of nursing and teaching. A minimum of professional study beyond the requirements for nurses' training is required for certification. Dental hygienists have performed a similar service in locating dental defects and in carrying on a corrective and follow-up program through the schools.

d. *Recreation director.* Another promising field of activity is that of recreation. A number of factors are operating to encourage communities to support the provision of recreation by public funds. Such programs call for trained leadership, which means a great deal more than merely supervising playgrounds. The recreation program of the future will include arts and crafts, music, dramatics, and dancing, as well as sports and games. Because school facilities will be used frequently and because the support of the program will sometimes be tied in with school funds, it is advisable for young people interested in recreation to secure a teacher's certificate and even to do some teaching. The demand for recreation directors is increasing now, and as more people become qualified to operate recreation programs, more and more communities will establish such programs. Closely related to the work of the recreation director is that of directing school camps, a new activity in public education that shows great promise for the future.

e. *Teaching exceptional children.* In Unit Six there is a discussion of the necessity for providing for exceptional children, those who are mentally retarded or superior, or children with physical handicaps. At the present time there are not nearly so

many teachers for such classes as are needed.   Less than a year's
specialized work is required for special class certification and salaries are usually higher than those paid other teachers.   Teachers
with a particular interest in the underprivileged would find this
area of specialization attractive.

f. *Speech correctionist.*   Another rewarding type of special
study is that of speech education.   Stutterers and stammerers and
children with other types of speech defects usually respond readily
to clinical treatment under the care of persons trained in that work.
About a year of graduate study is necessary for certification.
The number of school districts seeking speech correctionists far
exceeds the number of qualified specialists available.

g. *Numerous other opportunities.*   Many other positions in the
educational field might have been enumerated, such as special instruction of many types, adult education, college administration,
statistician, librarian, and athletic coaching.   What we have tried
to do was to list the more frequent opportunities for employment.
In connection with all of them we should like to stress the value—
indeed, the necessity—of actual teaching experience, regardless of
the type of position ultimately desired.   Instruction is the primary
business of the school, and any auxiliary program calls for full understanding of the aims, objectives, and problems of the instructional staff.   We need also to stress the importance of broad, general training before entering upon any type of educational work.
The tendencies indicate that in the near future all members of the
school staff, even the elementary teachers, will be required to secure a bachelor's degree as the minimum requirement for certification.   In these days when so much stress is being placed upon
integration of subject matter and upon controversial issues that
involve a good understanding of current social and economic problems, anyone working in any capacity in the educational field needs
to be broadly educated and trained in the habit of making critical
evaluations.

C.   An Appraisal of Education as a Career

In making a decision concerning an occupation or a life career,
an individual should make a careful and critical analysis of two

very important aspects of the problem: first, an analysis of the occupation with particular reference to its opportunities and limitations; and second, an appraisal of his own qualifications in terms of the demands of the occupation. This analysis is a more complex problem in the case of a profession because of the relatively long period of preparation, which is expensive and time-consuming. A man wants to consider his decision carefully because he does not want to make a mistake in his first choice. The young lady who says, "I certainly don't want to be a stenographer and I don't think I would make a good nurse; I guess I'll have to be a teacher," would most assuredly be making an important decision on an entirely wrong basis. We shall, therefore, mention a few of the important considerations concerning educational work as a career.

1. Teaching Is Social-civic Service

Probably the most significant question concerning any occupation is, What kind of work is it? Where does it fit into the occupational picture? Teaching is public service. It is a form of social service, but not in the sense that the teacher needs to be a reformer or a missionary. As used here, the term means that the teacher is a servant of society, attempting to render service that will make a contribution to the welfare of society. It is civic service in the sense that public educational workers are in the employ of organized society. The school district is an integral unit in society, a subdivision of the government. Possibly the term *social-civic* more accurately describes the type of work expected of the teacher. To persons who are motivated by a high ideal of service, educational work offers a fine opportunity. Such persons get a great deal of satisfaction from knowing that they are doing useful work that, on the whole, is much appreciated. This is not to say, however, that teachers need to be imbued with any missionary spirit or possessed of a Messianic urge to save the world.

Some people would be most unhappy in such service. They would be irritated and disturbed by the very fact that, as public servants, they are subject to the whims and fancies of a fickle public and occasionally under the domination of scheming, small-town politicians. One brilliant young high school teacher, holding a

doctor's degree, remarked in disgust, "Why should I take orders
from a school board made up of blundering politicians, some of
whom can't read or write?" Because the teachers are regarded
as the employees of the community and since their relationships
touch virtually every home in the locality, they are placed on a
pedestal and looked up to as examples of decorum and good taste.
The parents of the school children take such an interest in the
teachers that the social activities of the latter are closely scrutin-
ized and frequently very narrowly circumscribed. Such attitudes
on the part of the community would be regarded by many as an encroachment on their liberties and would irritate them beyond the
point of endurance. Educational work will prove an unhappy
berth for persons not willing to submerge themselves and their activities in the community or public interest. Although it is true
that the school is no place for the individualist or the person lacking in a social philosophy, it is also true that some localities make
unreasonable demands of their teachers. Communities should be
encouraged to treat their teachers as people and to expect them
in their social and personal activities to behave as other decent
citizens of the community do, rather than to expect them to live
differently from the rest of the world. A ridiculous example of
this unreasonable attitude is seen in the following extract from
the teacher's contract in a small North Carolina town.[2]

I PROMISE to take a vital interest in all phases of Sunday School
work, donating of my time, service and money without stint, for the
benefit and uplift of the community.

I PROMISE to abstain from all dancing, immodest dressing, and
any other conduct unbecoming a teacher and a lady.

I PROMISE not to go out with any young men except in so far as it
may be necessary to stimulate Sunday School work.

I PROMISE not to fall in love, to become engaged or secretly married.

I PROMISE to remain in the dormitory or on the school grounds
when not actively engaged in school or church work elsewhere.

_____

[2] Quoted in *Social Frontier*, 2:158, February, 1936.

I PROMISE not to encourage or tolerate the least familiarity on the part of any of my boy pupils.

I PROMISE to sleep at least eight hours each night, to eat carefully, to take every precaution to keep in the best of health and spirits in order that I may be better able to render efficient service to my pupils.

I PROMISE to remember that I owe a duty to the townspeople who are paying me my wages, that I owe respect to the school board and to the superintendent who hired me, and that I shall consider myself at all times the willing servant of the school board, and the townspeople, and that I shall coöperate with them to the limit of my ability in any movement aimed at the betterment of the town, the pupils or the school.

2. Remuneration

Education does not offer too much promise to the person seeking material reward. The income is steady and regular, but except in a negligible minority of cases it is never very large. In Table 2 will be found summaries of teachers' salaries on a nation-wide basis. These figures represent average salaries. Salaries paid to teachers increased markedly following World War I. Similar increases have been taking place since the close of World War II.

During the years 1945–46 and 1946–47 the National Education Association with the assistance of numerous other agencies in the country were most successful in calling to the attention of the public the comparatively low incomes of teachers. One direct result of these efforts was a definite upturn in the level of average salaries. With the great rise in the cost of living, however, teachers as a professional group have not been able to keep pace with other employed persons, not even government workers. A number of states have been able to secure state-wide salary schedules with comparatively high minimums for professionally prepared teachers with college degrees, as, for example, $2,000 in New York, Pennsylvania, and Delaware; $2,200 in Maryland; and $2,400 in California, Washington, and Indiana. Teachers in many states and communities may reasonably look forward to maximum salaries of from $4,500 to $5,000.

The net result of all the agitation and the legislation promises to the young college graduate a beginning income that compares favorably with that received by his classmates in other occupations. Since teachers are public employees, however, their salaries are paid from funds raised by taxes; consequently maximum salaries are usually not so high as those received by the most successful workers in other lines. There is increasing evidence that the public wants teaching to be well supported financially and there is good reason to believe that this trend will continue. Probably very few workers in any line expect to find all their satisfactions in the pay envelope. Certainly that is not true of teachers. A good share of the compensation of the teacher comes from the satisfaction found in the work and the expressed appreciation of grateful students.

A Teacher's Satisfaction [3]

Nobody likes to be misunderstood and no intelligent person enjoys being regarded as crazy. But we teachers find ourselves frequently in one or the other of these situations. . . . In prosperous times, even our friends wonder what can be the matter with us that we don't quit teaching and make some money. . . .

If one may venture to express it (without speaking for others) he hazards the guess that the development which a teacher sees in his students from year to year and their making good after leaving his classroom is the greatest joy which a teacher can experience. This is the incentive which keeps him at his task; this is the goal which he is ever striving to reach. . . .

One type of man is happy by his own successes; the teacher—possibly a higher type—is happy over the success of others—those whom he has taught.

One of the unfortunate traditions in our school system fixes salaries for high school teachers considerably in excess of those of elementary teachers, even though the latter might have equal or better preparation and experience. It is unfortunate that in most school districts teachers may make progress up the salary scale only by transferring to the secondary school level, a situation that

---

[3] Wendell S. Brooks, in *School and Society,* 44:142–3, August 1, 1936.

attracts many people away from the field of labor for which they are best fitted by training and inclination.

TABLE 2

Median Salaries Paid Educational Workers
of Different Types During 1946–47 [4]

Educational Position	Population Groups [a]				
	2,500 to 5,000	5,000 to 10,000	10,000 to 30,000	30,000 to 100,000	Over 100,000
A. Teachers:					
1. Elementary	$1,864	$1,948	$2,118	$2,288	$2,897
2. Junior High	2,087	2,155	2,354	2,546	3,075
3. High School	2,274	2,375	2,595	2,774	3,593
B. Principals:					
1. Elementary:					
Teaching	2,071	2,214	2,382	2,576	2,815
Supervising	2,900	2,948	3,031	3,328	4,334
2. Junior High	2,625	2,965	3,425	4,016	4,953
3. High School	3,197	3,496	4,071	4,700	5,741
C. Supervisors:					
1. Vocational Education	3,300	3,233	3,550	3,900	4,663
2. Physical Education ..	2,400	2,706	2,976	3,467	4,206
3. Art	2,150	2,327	2,532	3,127	3,975
4. Music	2,196	2,480	2,708	3,127	3,902
5. Industrial Arts	2,600	2,557	2,943	3,583	4,250
6. Home Economics	2,038	2,067	2,358	3,100	4,200
7. School Library	2,138	2,175	2,350	2,675	3,575
D. Superintendents	4,225	4,719	5,856	7,307	10,000
E. Janitors	1,875	1,843	1,977	2,794 [b]	3,850 [b]
F. Nurses	2,021	2,091	2,235	2,309	2,313
G. Attendance Officers	2,050	1,811	2,144	2,204	2,832

[a] Population classification of 1,897 cities reporting.
[b] Head Janitors.

[4] National Education Association, *Research Bulletin*, Vol. XXV, No. 1, February, 1947.

This tradition, fortunately, is rapidly disappearing. A few years ago we should have been able to cite only a few cities with so-called single salary schedules, those providing equal pay for equal service and preparation regardless of the grade level in the school system. There is a pronounced trend now toward the adoption of the single salary schedule everywhere. A number of states have passed laws providing for this type of recognition of all the teachers on a state-wide basis.

3.   Hours of Labor

This feature of the teacher's work is likely to turn out to be a mirage to an unsuspecting prospective teacher. To the outsider unfamiliar with the details, the six-hour day and the five-day week look most alluring. "What a soft job you have, nine to four, five days a week," is frequently heard. Don't be misled. With the crowded classrooms and heavy teaching loads of the present day, most of a teacher's preparation for classes must be carried on outside the regular school hours. In addition there are many extra duties and civic and community responsibilities that are time-consuming, and a teacher finds little time that he can call his own. The long summer vacation looks attractive too, and is a desirable feature when the yearly income, if distributed over twelve months, enables the teacher to maintain a standard of living in harmony with his tastes and interests. We need to remind ourselves, however, that while the teacher ordinarily works only nine or ten months a year, he must live twelve months. For those who can find other summer employment, or leisure pursuits that are interesting and profitable, the long summer vacation is an attraction.

4.   Economic and Social Security

In an earlier unit we mentioned longer tenure and more security for teachers as one of the needed changes in our school organizations. The prospective teacher needs to consider this matter carefully. Teachers do not have the benefit of Federal Social Security legislation. In the majority of states teachers now receive the benefits of state-wide retirement systems, which, coupled with guaranteed minimum salaries, provide reassuring guarantees of security and an accompanying peace of mind. The majority of teachers, however, do not have tenure, and in many sections teachers are subject to rather rapid turnover and unwarranted dismissal. Such occurrences are tragic, indeed, to those who have given many years of service and may possibly have a considerable equity in a retirement pension.

5. Social Position

As a rule teachers enjoy social standing and position that make them respected and appreciated in the community. Because of their intimate contacts with children, in many communities they are received into the best of homes and taken into confidence by all classes in society. Few workers of any other occupation are more highly regarded or are privileged to enter more freely into the social, civic, or cultural activities of the community. It should be noted, however, that in some circles teachers, as a group, are regarded as a rather self-satisfied, complacent, self-centered lot. It may be interesting to some to learn that in early colonial days in Virginia and neighboring states the teachers were debentured servants or sometimes exiled prisoners given a bit of freedom in return for the menial service of teaching. Some people find all the intellectual and cultural urge they desire among teachers as associates, while others find them dull and uninteresting. There is just as much variation in this regard among teachers as among other workers. There are all types of teachers as there are all types of people, and it would be unsafe to generalize about all teachers in terms of the personal attributes or qualities of a few representatives of the profession. Personality of the teacher is an important factor in the classroom, but it would be most unfortunate if we attempted to develop a "teaching personality" that was stereotyped and uniform.

6. Teaching Is Hard Work

Teaching as an occupation may look attractive to young people seeking a white collar job. It has much to commend it in this

regard. The work is done amid pleasant surroundings, usually
among congenial associates, and the teacher enjoys a degree of
independence not found in many occupations. All this may lead
one to think that it is easy work. No evaluation could be more
erroneous. To be sure, there is little of manual physical labor.
The hours are not long, but they are strenuous. Most teachers
work under a severe mental and nervous strain that takes its toll
in vitality and energy. There are few moments of relaxation during the day, and the necessary out-of-school preparation makes it
difficult to secure the needed recreation and rest at home. It is
not merely the teacher's work that necessitates effort, but the responsibility for securing satisfactory achievement on the part of
thirty to two hundred children. This responsibility produces
nerve strain that more than offsets the minimum of strenuous
physical exertion. It is true that teachers as a class are considered good risks by casualty and life insurance companies, but
this circumstance is due, in part, to the fact that there are few
occupational hazards. Let no one be deceived into thinking that
teaching is easy work. It is a hard, steady, strenuous grind, and
the work is never finished. Some workers can leave their work
at the shop or office; but much of the teacher's work, and in many
respects the most important part of it, is done during what the
layman would consider as the teacher's leisure time.

D. Qualities Contributing to Success in Teaching

Many persons have attempted to enumerate and evaluate the
qualities that contribute to the success of the teacher. Others
have made frequency tabulations of the personal traits and characteristics that have been considered essential attributes by superintendents employing teachers, or institutions selecting students.
We shall present a few of the generalizations from these studies to
give the student some notion of the bases on which he will be judged.
In addition, there are several even more subjective characteristics
that contribute largely to the personal satisfaction that comes
from educational work: "job satisfaction," the personnel workers
call it. It is undoubtedly true that success in any job in large

measure is conditioned by the personal satisfaction one finds in it. Occasionally one hears of a superintendent or community that holds very narrow views concerning the qualities and personal attributes demanded of teachers, as evidenced by restrictions on social life or living arrangements. These are mere incidental matters that have little or nothing to do with success. We wish to call attention to several more vital and significant attributes of teachers.

1. Interest in Children

This is probably the first requisite for success and satisfaction in teaching. It is inconceivable that anyone could be happy in the classroom unless he was motivated by an abiding interest in children and deep sympathy for their problems. That is the reason for the distinction we made earlier between a scholarly interest in subject matter and a friendly interest in boys and girls. Interest in the growth and development of the students must take priority over everything else in the classroom.

2. Interest in People and Events

The teacher cannot live the life of a hermit or recluse, either figuratively or literally. He must be a part of the life and times surrounding him and his pupils. Communities are justified in asking that teachers live in the community and participate in its activities, although there are dangerous tendencies in the refusal in recent years to employ any except home town "products." If the schools are to bring the pupils into a fuller appreciation of their places in society, the teachers themselves must possess a genuine interest in people and their doings. People whose inclination is to work with things and materials will find the close personal contacts and relationships of the school irritating and disturbing. It is true that great scientists or technicians or artists, whose whole interest is in their laboratory or shop or studio, attract students in large numbers, but it is usually on the graduate school or adult level. The public school teacher will find that relations with people and participation in events pay the biggest dividends.

3. A Sound Social Philosophy

The teacher cannot be an individualist if he is to make the maximum contribution to society. He must be motivated by a sound social philosophy that endeavors to place the welfare of society above the rights of individuals. This factor is difficult to define and impossible to measure, but is none the less important. The teacher must commit himself to a life of service, else his success will be limited and his enjoyment greatly reduced. He must be a socially-minded individual; his goals and objectives must be in harmony with those that lead to improvement of conditions in society. The school cannot contribute to social betterment unless it is staffed by socially-minded individuals.

4. Studious Attitudes and Habits

The work of the teacher involves study, the preparation of lessons, and the evaluation of the mental efforts of other people. It is essentially mental effort; it is primarily the work of a student. The teacher lives in a world of words, too much so at times. A person who has never found joy and satisfaction in study, in mental labor, will find little satisfaction in teaching. This is not to say that the teacher must wear an honor society key or be a *cum laude* graduate, and we have purposely avoided saying that only persons of very superior intelligence should become teachers. In truth, there is considerable evidence that the most adaptable and successful teachers are found among those possessing somewhat better than average mentality and wide interests, rather than among the near-genius types with their highly specialized interests. But there is no denying that the teacher should be a student. If he is not, he will neither work with the fullest measure of success, nor will he find satisfaction in tracing references and in locating, organizing, and interpreting subject matter. The day is past when the teacher could consider his preparation sufficient when he was a couple of jumps in advance of the students or when he had read a lesson or two in advance in the textbook.

5. Originality and Creative Power

These are necessary qualities of a successful teacher. He must be original in the sense that he should not be a blind follower of a textbook or course of study. These are merely instruments that serve as guides. Classroom situations call for adapting subject matter to the level and interests of students. The individual who lacks initiative and originality will find himself hopelessly at sea in many classroom situations, and the tragic part of it is that the students will realize it before he does. Creative power is what he needs: that sense of security and confidence that comes from being master of the situation, being able to control and direct activities constructively. His work is not creative in the sense that he takes the children as raw material and fashions or molds them according to a model or pattern. His problem is to create the total classroom atmosphere that contributes to learning, growth, and development on the part of children. Teaching is not a mechanical operation or routine job. It calls for a high order of originality and initiative. It is creative because the situation as it is found must be directed into a challenging, constructive, wholesome learning environment.

6. An Objective, Analytical Attitude

This is a possession that will save the teacher much difficulty and nerve strain. He must be quick at sizing up a situation and alert in meeting its demands. He must be objective because he will carry on close personal dealings with persons in whom he will develop a lively interest and for whom he will have great sympathy and affection, but he must do it impersonally and analytically and without being emotionally disturbed by the results or consequences. His dealings must be on an intellectual rather than on an emotional plane. Eventually he must evaluate the efforts of the students, and he will do it objectively and analytically only if he reduces the personal element to the minimum. One reason why parents have difficulty in managing their own children is that they are not able to view them objectively; their emotional reactions take precedence over their intellectual judgments.

7.   Sense of Humor

There is probably no other characteristic that serves so well for a safety valve as does a good sense of humor.   Pent-up feelings and overwrought nerves can be so easily relaxed if the teacher can take advantage of the humor of the situation.   Nothing else will save many situations that arise in the classroom.   This fact does not mean, of course, that the teacher must be a clown and wisecracker.   Quite the reverse.   The teacher needs to be able to see

By Harry Haenigsen

Courtesy of *Philadelphia Inquirer*

Fig. 1.—Where Would This Teacher Be Without a Sense of Humor and a Sympathetic Understanding of Children?

the humor in many relationships that would be unbearable otherwise. A good laugh during a tense moment is the best means of bringing a group into coöperative and harmonious relationships. The classroom has no room for the confirmed pessimist and long-faced, sour-visaged, humorless grouch. The classroom needs to be a happy place, and it cannot be that without a good-natured teacher in charge. One superintendent said that he would not employ a teacher who could not smile—not the synthetic smile that is flashed when the desired effect seems to demand it, but the genuine, natural, pleasant smile that expresses good cheer.

8. Professional Standards

At its annual meeting in Buffalo, New York, in 1946, the National Education Association created a new commission of nine members to be called, "The Commission on Teacher Education and Professional Standards." The commission is charged with the responsibility of carrying forward a continuing program for the organized profession in matters of recruitment, selection, preparation, certification, and advancement of professional standards, including standards for institutions that prepare teachers. The "Goals for Action" presented officially by this new commission are reprinted here in order to acquaint the young student of education with the expressed objectives and professional standards of the profession.

    a. Immediate elimination of emergency permits, but in no case by the lowering of regular certification standards.

    b. Raising of certification requirements for new teachers in every state to a minimum of four years of thorough professional preparation; continued progress in advanced states by the adoption of a minimum requirement of five to six years of professional training.

    c. Minimum *beginning* salaries of $2,400 per year for four-year college graduates professionally prepared to teach.

    d. Annual salary increases starting with the second year of service and continuing with additional experience and training to a level of at least $4,000 per year for college-trained teachers with ten years of service, with salaries of $5,000 to $6,000 per year for teachers of long experience and demonstrated efficiency.

  e. A maximum class size of 25–30 pupils, with teachers in high
     schools and other departmentalized schools dealing with a maxi-
     mum of 100 pupils per day in four, or at most five, classes per day.
  f. Refusal by colleges and universities to admit students of low
     ability into teacher preparation curriculums.
  g. Liberal scholarships to attract the most competent young people
     into teacher preparation courses.
  h. Increase of $2,000,000,000 in financial support for public schools
     from local, state, and federal sources.
  i. Financial support of teacher preparation institutions by an
     amount per student equal at least to the average expenditure per
     student for other types of general and professional higher edu-
     cation.
  j. Effective tenure, retirement, and tax legislation extended to all
     states and institutions.
  k. Coöperative in-service education programs for teachers, with ade-
     quate financial support.
  l. The same degree of professional and personal freedom and com-
     munity respect as that accorded to physicians and other competent
     professionals.

9. Summary of Traits for Success in Teaching

The Research Division of the National Education Association
has made an exhaustive study of publications dealing with success
in teaching and has summarized under the captions presented below
those qualities mentioned most frequently as contributing to success.

  a. *Vigorous health.* The teacher's work is exhausting. Well
     done, it demands both physical and mental effort, and if the
     teacher's health fails he soon finds that his work suffers.
     Even temporary fatigue may affect his work.
  b. *Intelligence.* This is one basic factor in success in school
     and college. However, brilliance is not necessary for it has
     been impossible among teachers, who represent a fairly well-
     selected group intellectually, to demonstrate a high correla-
     tion between intelligence and teaching effectiveness. Ob-
     viously, the teacher needs enough to complete his training.
  c. *Liking for study.* The teacher is usually one who was a
     good student in high school and at least average in college.

As he must always do some studying, he should enjoy it. Evidence for this is seen in his selection of the "harder courses."

d. *Emotional maturity and balance.* This is a somewhat inclusive term. It comprises such traits as poise, self-confidence, self-control, persistence (at whatever he undertakes to do), patience, and decisiveness. A great part of a person's adjustment to others depends on the degree of his emotional maturity.

e. *Love of children.* If a person does not thoroughly enjoy children, especially of the age he intends to teach, and get along with them, he should try another profession.

f. *Sympathy (or social intelligence).* By this is not meant sentimentality, but the ability imaginatively to put one's self in the other person's place—and act accordingly. Other desirable qualities stem from it, such as leadership—not dominance—of the sort that persuades others to do what is for their own good and the good of those around them, and like it.

g. *Interest in and liking for teaching.* Perhaps this should have been mentioned sooner. The teacher should enjoy his work and the associations it furnishes, and be proud of the services he can render. The teacher with a critical and disparaging attitude toward his profession is not so likely to be successful.

h. *Cheerfulness and sense of humor.* Pupils in school, no less than others, enjoy a cheerful teacher and one who can see a joke even at his own expense. In a sense, both are evidences of emotional maturity, for the really mature person does not take himself too seriously.

i. *Friendliness.* The aloof person should not teach, since so large a part of the teacher's work is bound up in personal relationships. The teacher should like people and welcome friendship from all quarters.

j. *Good work habits.* The teacher has to work hard at a variety of tasks. He should be able to plan them and carry them out quickly and accurately. Also, where initiative, originality, and resourcefulness are called for by the work, he should be able to meet the demand.

k. *Coöperativeness.* The teacher must be able to work with others and be willing to do so.

l. *Breadth of interest.* Teachers with many different kinds of interests succeed; some with narrow interests succeed. Yet to appeal to the varied interests of pupils the teacher must be sincerely interested in many things. Pupils are quick to detect and dislike sham.

"Miss Haskins, how can a smart young chick like you bury herself in a grind like this?"

Reproduced by permission of Boris Drucker and Collier's Magazine.

Fig. 2.—A Blow at a Popular Fallacy with Respect to the Teaching Profession. The day is past when the public wants to pay high salaries to unattractive personalities who haven't the ability to hold a good position in some other occupation. It is the "smart young chick" that is needed in our schools and the evidence indicates that we shall get more and more of them into the classroom in the future.

m. *Tolerance.* This is probably an outcome of sympathy. The teacher who is prejudiced against different customs, kinds of people, religions, and so forth, loses pupil respect and influence.

n. *Good judgment.* Many of the teacher's difficulties stem from his use of poor judgment as to the sensible, kind, and suitable course to take.

o. *Sense of justice.* It must be applied to the treatment of people and the organization of the work (tests should cover fairly what was taught).

p. *Good appearance and voice.* These seem to be less important than many have thought, but failure in either respect can affect the teacher's work unfavorably even if pupils and others cannot put a finger on what is wrong. (Especially true of voice.)

q. *Ability to explain clearly.* With pupils this trait ranks very near the top. It probably results from the interaction of general intelligence, breadth of interest, and good training in methods of teaching.

r. *Personality* is the total of these traits and others.

10. A Layman's Appraisal

A newspaper columnist recently highlighted the observable qualities in teachers in a most interesting fashion. Some teachers might object to his characterization, but the authors believe that this point of view, presented by one whose business it is to observe workers of all kinds, represents a fine tribute and a high compliment to teachers and the teaching profession. With the columnist's permission we are extracting a few paragraphs from his column written on the occasion of the attendance of a large number of teachers at a public hearing in support of school legislation at a state capitol. We think this brief statement describes that "indefinable something" that makes teachers proud of their profession better than many of our educational leaders' pronouncements.

There is something about a lady schoolteacher which distinguishes her from other professional workers, from stenographers and clerks and the like. Just what it is would be difficult to say with exactness. Still, there is about her a certain air, if that's the word, that enables one to spot her at a glance.

It can't be age, for the dames we saw galavanting around were, in some instances, ripe with years. Others were as young and fresh-looking as the last class out of a teachers' college. And all the years and ages in between were represented, too.

It can't be their dress, for they are as smart and as up-to-date in their attire as Mary Sachs herself and Mary is about as sharp as they come in this or any other town.

Oh, well we give up! There's something about a schoolteacher just as there's something about a soldier and that's as far as we are prepared to go at this stage of the game, Mr. Editor.[5]

This teacher-appraisal is a large order, we admit, and it might appear that under this system we should be able to recruit our teachers only from a race of supermen. Not so. We do not expect the impossible, but we do wish to call to the attention of the prospective teacher some of the requirements of the job. We frequently hear discussions as to whether teaching is an art or science. Dr. Bagley suggests that the teacher is at times an artist (using creative effort), an applied scientist (employing technical knowledge), and a tradesman (a routine worker) as well. It is not too much to say that the teacher needs to be a salesman, actor, judge, diplomat, and detective, all in one combination.

It is impossible, adequately, to summarize in a brief statement the requisites for successful teaching. Henry Van Dyke attempted it in a tribute to what he termed the "Unknown Teacher":

And what of Teaching? Ah, there you have the worst paid and the best rewarded of all the vocations. Dare not enter into it unless you love it. For the vast majority of men and women it has no promise of wealth or fame, but they, to whom it is dear for its own sake, are among the nobility of mankind.[6]

---

[5] John M. Cummings, "Teachers Win Acclaim for Conduct at Hearing," column in *Philadelphia Inquirer*, April 25, 1947.

[6] Quoted in *Pennsylvania School Journal*, 85:15, September, 1936.

E.   Preparation and Certification for Teaching

It is rather generally accepted that teachers are servants of the state and that the preparation and certification of teachers are a state function.   There is a wide variety in the form of certificates or licenses and in the manner of issuing them.   In recent years there has been a strong tendency toward more highly centralized state control of this function.   Practices range from granting a one-year certificate to people who take an examination under the supervision of the county superintendent after completing the eighth grade, to granting a life certificate upon the completion of a four-year college course.   There is every conceivable variation between these two extremes.   In some states different types of certificates are provided for by legislative enactment, while in others the details are determined entirely by regulations of the state department.   In spite of the great variation in practice, there are certain generalizations that may be made.   In general, four aspects of a teacher's preparation have come to be recognized as necessary: academic preparation, subject-matter specialization, professional preparation, and social or personal development.

1.   Academic Preparation

Under this caption we refer to the general or cultural development provided by a college course leading to a bachelor's degree, which is a minimum requirement for high school teachers and seems destined to become a minimum also for elementary teachers.   This preparation is expected to provide for the intellectual and cultural growth of the teacher and is considered a basic or foundational requirement.   In some institutions this type of study precedes professional study, being confined largely to the first two years, sometimes called the lower division.   In others it parallels the specific teacher preparation throughout the four years.

2.   Subject-matter Specialization

In this category we find the specific requirements for securing a license to teach a given subject, such as history or music or manual arts. In some states this requirement specifies a minimum number of college credits that must be submitted in a given field to secure a license to teach that subject. This is sometimes as low as six semester hours and in a few states as high as thirty. Some states provide blanket certification, which permits the teaching of almost any subject in the curriculum. State departments of public instruction will supply circulars that will tell the student the minimum requirements for teaching each subject at any level.

3. Professional Preparation

This requirement is the cause of much contention and argument among people who are concerned with the problem of teacher preparation or placement. Specifically, it refers to courses and credits in education and psychology. It comprises the technical training for the specific job of teaching. It is called professional preparation because it aims to prepare for the profession of teaching. Arguments and contention grow out of the fact that one group, those with an academic background, insist that what one knows one can teach; that one does not have to learn to teach. The other group, those with a background of professional preparation in education, contend that mere knowledge does not guarantee teaching ability, that one needs to give attention to methods and procedures while learning the subject matter. The certification requirements of state education departments are, of course, a compromise between these two groups, each of which would go to extremes if not checked. The requirements in this category vary considerably, also, both as to the minimum number of credits and as to the specific courses required. The variations range from six to twenty-four professional credits and usually include educational or child psychology, principles or technique of teaching, and practice teaching. The last-named requirement is usually provided for, in part at least, by a campus training school or laboratory or demonstration school. In institutions where it is possible, very close coördination exists between the theory courses of the college classrooms and the practical work of the training school. It is at this point that we find the chief cause for the quarrel between the teachers' colleges or normal schools and the liberal arts colleges.

The former insist that the colleges cannot do justice to the task of preparing teachers because as a rule they are entirely lacking in these essential training school facilities. The liberal arts college people retort that such training is not the most essential feature, that it is thorough knowledge of subject matter that is most important.

4. Social and Personal Development

The foregoing requirements are all quantitative; so many credits in this or that field may be written into the regulations. But under this heading we have an exceedingly important factor in the success of a teacher, and there is no sure way of doing a very satisfactory job of preparing teachers on this basis. Nor can we be sure of the best ways of selecting teachers in terms of social qualities and personality traits. All are convinced that the personality of the teacher is of prime importance in the classroom. About the best we can do is to provide wholesome social and recreational experiences for the students who are preparing to teach, and to admit to professional study only those persons whose social and cultural backgrounds are satisfactory and whose personalities are desirable from the point of view of the demands of the teaching service.

The difficulty lies in the mystery surrounding this whole question of personality. There are many people who believe that an individual has a pleasing personality or that he has not, and that nothing can be done about it. There is considerable support now for the belief that much can be done toward improving one's personality, even though it is rather generally believed that the development of personality traits begins in early childhood. This point of view can be more readily accepted if we define personality as the interaction of the personal qualities and traits of two or more individuals. That is, it is not something static, fixed and unchangeable like eye color, but rather the result of the stimuli in the environment. The problem in connection with improving one's personality is really threefold: First, the individual must know what kind of improvement is needed; second, he must have the desire to improve; third, he must know how to go about the improvement. We can readily see that it is the first and third statements that present the problem. Most of us would be quite willing to improve if we only knew what improvement was needed or how to go about it. That is why teacher-preparing institutions see values in the efforts of skillful, tactful social directors who assist in organizing and carrying on a rich and varied program of social and student-life activities designed to bring out the potentialities of individuals. This is also one of the principal justifications for providing dormitories and social and recreational facilities in teacher-preparing institutions. As a result of interviews, conferences, and careful study of the students, each one will be encouraged to participate in the experiences that will be the most profitable. It is in social contacts that personality is developed. As one student expressed it, "That certainly is true; I discovered that I was not friendly when I met people, so I went to work to correct that defect in my personality."

5. Certification Machinery

Most teacher licenses are state certificates, issued by a bureau of teacher certification in the state department of education, although there are many states that issue county certificates. The state department of education publishes regulations prescribing the minimum requirements for each type of certificate, such as two or three years of work in a normal school or teachers' college for elementary teaching and a bachelor's degree for secondary school teaching. The number of college credits required for teaching each subject and the number of professional credits are specified; also, certain institutions are approved to prepare teachers for certain fields of work. The first certificate issued is usually a temporary or provisional certificate, good for a limited number of years. After a specified number of years of teaching, during which, in some states, the candidate must have pursued additional study, the license is renewed or made permanent. In addition to the foregoing, certain cities require the candidates, even though holders of state certificates, to take a series of examinations to determine their eligibility for appointment. Thus, it is seen that the state

education department is vested with considerable power and authority in teacher preparation.   It determines minimum requirements,
approves the institutions eligible to offer various types of work,
and establishes policies concerning the education of teachers
throughout the state.

6.   Current Tendencies in Teacher Education

a. *Better selection of candidates for teaching.*   With the return
to more nearly normal conditions following the war we are seeing
a renewed emphasis upon selection of candidates for teaching.
(During the war it was necessary to accept such persons as could
be obtained.)   The new NEA Commission on Teacher Education and Professional Standards will continue to stress selection of
superior young people; and other agencies in the profession will
contribute to this process.

b. *Longer period for pre-service preparation.*   There are un-
mistakable signs that point in the direction of a longer period of
pre-service preparation for teaching.   Just what the ultimate program will be or how rapidly the changes will occur no one can predict.   The indications are that four years of college work for
elementary teachers and five years for secondary teachers will soon
be recognized as the standard minimum pre-service preparation.
Several states now impose these requirements, although in many
parts of the country the standards are much lower.   There are
still a few states that issue certificates as a result of a high school
training course.   There are several reasons for this tendency
toward more pre-service preparation: (a) A richer, fuller curriculum requires better educated teachers.   (b) A surplus of
teachers encourages more ambitious teachers to secure better
preparation as an added assurance of a position.   (c) Higher education has become exceedingly popular during the last twenty
years, and teachers have just naturally risen to higher preparation levels.   (d) Better salaries, longer tenure, and retirement
systems have proved an incentive to more able people and justified
more preparation.   We are safe in saying today that no one should
think of entering educational work with less than four years of

preparation, and secondary school teachers should look forward to completing work equivalent to that required for a master's degree.

c. *Increasing emphasis on in-service preparation.* Another tendency that has been most noticeable during the past ten or fifteen years is the increasing emphasis on the improvement of teachers in service. In spite of the tendency toward a longer pre-service period of preparation, the indications are that we shall see more attention paid to individual and group study by teachers. These in-service education programs take many forms, which may be classified more or less as follows: supervision by helping teachers or supervisors, internship, summer school study, extension classes, correspondence study, school visitations, workshops, seminars, and travel.

d. *Broad, general education minimizes specialization.* Teachers should be more broadly educated than, as a rule, they are. This narrowness of range has been characteristic of both elementary and secondary teachers, but the most serious offenders have been the teachers of special subjects, such as commercial subjects, home economics, physical education, industrial arts, music, and the like. The plan providing for a wider scope does not recommend that the teacher should not specialize in a certain area, but only that in addition thereto the teacher education curriculum should be based on a broad, general foundation.

e. *Discontinuance of permanent certificate.* The next few years may see the passing of permanent or life certificates. Many school authorities think that permanent certificates stand in the way of progressive improvement of school staffs, particularly in places where teachers enjoy permanent tenure.

F.   Problems and References for Collateral Study

Problems for Students

1. Write a carefully prepared statement in answer to the question, "Shall I become a teacher?"
2. Prepare a rather exhaustive digest of published material dealing with teaching in some field in which you are interested.

3. Compare in some detail teaching as a career with other professions, considering preparation, possibilities, and limitations.

4. Compare the codes of ethics formulated by teachers' organizations with those of other professions.

5. In parallel columns compare the attributes and characteristics of your good and poor teachers.

6. Make an extended survey of student opinion relative to the qualities they like and dislike in teachers.

7. What are the arguments for and against the same salary schedule for elementary and secondary school teachers?

8. Attack or defend the proposition that all elementary school teachers should have four years and all secondary teachers five years of post-high-school preparation.

Selected References

Barr, A. S., *Characteristic Differences of Good and Poor Teachers.* Bloomington, Ill.: Public School Publishing Company, 1929.

Chamberlain, L. M., *The Teacher and School Organization.* New York: Prentice-Hall, 1940.

Cole, L. W., *Background for College Teaching.* New York: Farrar and Rinehart, 1940.

————, *Teaching in the Elementary School.* New York: Farrar and Rinehart, 1939.

Commission on Teacher Education, American Council on Education:
Evaluation in Teacher Education, 1945.
Teacher Education in Service, 1945.
Teachers for Our Times, 1945.
The College and Teacher Education, 1945.
The Improvement of Teacher Education, 1946.

Ellsbree, Willard, *The American Teacher.* New York: American Book, 1939.

John Dewey Society, *Teachers for Democracy.* New York: Appleton-Century, 1940.

Kyte, G. C., *The Principal at Work.* Boston: Ginn, 1941.

Mursell, James L., *Successful Teaching: Its Psychological Principles.* New York: McGraw-Hill, 1945.

NEA Commission on Teacher Education and Professional Standards, 1201 16th Street, Washington, D. C.:
Summary of Activities and Plans, 1946–47.
America's Children Deserve Capable Teachers (Materials on teacher selection), 1947.

Reaves, W. C., and Jacobson, P. B., *Duties of School Principals.* New
York: Prentice-Hall, 1940.
Slacks, J. R., *Rural Teacher's Work.* Boston: Ginn, 1938.

Books by Teachers and about Teachers

Chase, Mary Ellen, *A Goodly Fellowship.* New York: Macmillan,
1939.
Crabtree, J. W., *What Counted Most.* Lincoln, Neb.: University
Publishing Co., 1935.
Duncan, Kunigunde, and Nichols, D. F., *Mentor Graham: The Man
Who Taught Lincoln.* Chicago: University of Chicago Press, 1944.
Fenner, Mildred S., and Fishburn, Eleanor, *Pioneer American Edu-
cators.* NEA, 1944.
Flexner, Abraham, *I Remember.* New York: Simon and Schuster,
1940.
Holt, Rackam, *George Washington Carver.* New York: Doubleday,
Doran, 1943.
Kennedy, Millard Filmore, and Harlow, Alvin F., *Schoolmaster of
Yesterday.* New York: McGraw-Hill, 1940.
James, Henry, *Charles W. Eliot.* Boston: Houghton Mifflin, 1930.
Leidecker, K. F., *Yankee Teacher: The Life of William Torrey Harris.*
New York: Philosophical Library, 1946.
Lutes, Della, *Country School Ma'am.* Boston: Little, Brown, 1941.
Lutz, Alma, *Emma Willard, Daughter of Democracy.* Boston: Hough-
ton Mifflin, 1929.
Mann, Mary P., *Life of Horace Mann.* NEA, 1937.
Mayo, Bernard, ed., *Jefferson Himself.* Boston: Houghton Mifflin,
1942.
Minnich, H. C., *William Holmes McGuffey and His Readers.* New
York: American Book, 1936.
Morgan, Joy Elmer, *Horace Mann: His Ideas and Ideals.* NEA,
1936.
Palmer, George H., *Autobiography of a Philosopher.* Boston: Hough-
ton Mifflin, 1930.
————, *Life of Alice Freeman Palmer.* Boston: Houghton Mifflin,
1924.
Perry, Bliss, *And Gladly Teach.* Boston: Houghton Mifflin, 1935.
Phelps, William Lyon, *Autobiography.* New York: Oxford Univer-
sity Press, 1939.
Shepard, Odell, *Pedlar's Progress: the Life of Bronson Alcott.*
Boston: Little, Brown, 1937.

Van Doren, Carl, *Benjamin Franklin*. New York: Viking Press, 1938.
Warfel, Harry F., *Noah Webster*. New York: Macmillan, 1936.
Winslow, Ella, and Harlow, Alvin F., *Schoolhouse in the Foothills*. New York: Simon and Schuster, 1935.

Our American School System

In the preface to this book for college students, it was pointed out to the reader that the authors had a three-fold purpose in writing it: vocational, professional, and social. The second of these objectives—the professional—will be treated in Units II and III. By the professional approach we mean a study of the schools as they are today, the current tendencies in educational practices, and the influences affecting our schools. When pursuing the social objectives (Units IV and V), we shall endeavor to determine the function of schools in society and the relations between the schools and other educational agencies. In the present unit the student is furnished with an opportunity to study the structure of our American school system as a basis for understanding the relationships among the various educational enterprises in society. One major division is devoted to current tendencies in American education. The direction in which schools are moving and the influences furnishing the motive for change will provide clues to the function of education as a social force.

A. How Our Schools Are Organized

Paradoxical as it may sound, it can truthfully be said that there is an American school system, but no national system of schools. ⌈There are forty-nine school systems, one in each of the forty-eight states and in the District of Columbia.

The schools of the United States present a study in contradiction when compared with the educational structure of the countries of Europe. First, although there is no national school system, there is more uniformity in organization and curriculum when

43

comparisons are made from one state to another than one would expect to find. Second, there is no centralized authority for education in the Federal Government, and yet there is quite general acceptance throughout the country of the same ideas about education and the operation of the schools. The Federal Constitution makes no mention of education, but practical application of constitutional and statutory provisions among the states have resulted in almost identical school organization and procedure.

It is really a remarkable tribute to the functioning of democratic processes that American schools have achieved such a uniformly high standard of excellence from one section of the country to another. The absence of any official agency in Washington directing our educational policies makes it difficult for advanced students of education in other countries to understand how the schools of the several states happen to be so much alike. The fact is that this uniformity did not just happen. There are perhaps four reasons for it. First, instead of an authoritative agency in Washington issuing pronouncements about education, we have a multitude of national organizations and committees made up of all kinds of educational leaders and, in many instances, of leaders in other occupations. These groups prepare reports, which are developed democratically and which have wide circulation among all the people, educators and laymen, who are responsible for education. Second, the people of the United States enjoy about as free dissemination of published materials on all subjects as is to be found anywhere in the world. By virtue of the wide coverage of the press, periodicals, innumerable conventions and conferences, and more recently the radio, it would be practically impossible for one bit of good practice to remain a secret or become the property or vested right of a provincial group. Third, there is great mobility among the people of our country; consequently, good practices in education are carried from one locality to another. Fourth, and most important of all, since the original source of authority for all school matters rests with the people of a community, the high degree of uniformity throughout

the nation attests to the almost universal acceptance and application of the democratic ideal.

This study of contradiction may be further illustrated. The
educational unit covered by the term elementary school, or
more popularly the "grade school," is generally understood, even
though there are great variations in the procedure of various
elementary schools, in the offering, and in the number of years in
the course. The length of the elementary school course varies
from six years in many places to seven and eight years in other
communities. The term high school is almost universally understood to include certain grades offering certain subjects, even
though a high school may vary from a one-teacher, two-year
school, in a sparsely settled rural community, to a mammoth
metropolitan organization of ten thousand pupils. On the other
hand the terms college and university are used so indiscriminately
that no one can tell from the name of an institution what type of
school it is, what it offers, or what relation it bears to other institutions. The so-called universities of commerce and business
colleges, which frequently admit pupils who have not finished
elementary school, are almost without standing in collegiate circles.
Occasionally large shops that train barbers are called "barber
colleges." Many institutions that are called universities make
no pretense of being more than liberal arts colleges offering only
general curricula or at most a few pre-professional courses. On
the contrary, some institutions called colleges are in effect important universities comprising many professional and technical
schools. The land grant colleges in many states are good illustrations of the latter type. In spite of all this confusion there is
in the mind of the American public a fairly distinct understanding
of what a college is like and what it attempts to do. And in more
recent years the term junior college has likewise come to be fairly
clearly understood.

1. Divisions of Our School System

a. *Our "graded ladder" organization.* The organization of the
American school system may be characterized as a "graded lad-

der." That is, our educational structure consists of a one-track
system, one grade being built on top of the preceding one. If
represented pictorially, the units would resemble the rungs of a
ladder. This scalar organization is perhaps the most distinctive
feature of the American school system. During the time our
school system was developing, no other nation had attempted to
provide universal free public education throughout the elementary
and secondary grades. Even now, there are few countries in
which the organization pattern is a vertical graded ladder scheme,
each unit being completely articulated with those above and below it, and all levels being integrated into one continuous program
open to all children.

This graded ladder arrangement in the United States developed
during the latter half of the last century. Since 1900 it has been
modified to its present form, in which the rungs of the ladder may
be appropriately labeled as follows:

HIGHER EDUCATION
    University
    Professional
    College—Technical
SECONDARY EDUCATION
    Junior College   (Grades 13–14)
    Senior High School (Grades 10–12)
    Junior High School (Grades 7– 9)
ELEMENTARY EDUCATION
    Intermediate Grades (Grades 4– 6)
    Primary Grades   (Grades 1– 3)
PRE-SCHOOL EDUCATION
    Kindergarten
    Nursery School

The designations "primary" and "intermediate" grades are in
common use, and properly so, but the term "grammar" grades is
definitely outmoded. "Elementary school" is the currently accepted designation for the first six grades and "elementary education" the more general label for the first major division of our
school system. Likewise, the term "secondary education" is used

to indicate what is popularly called the "high school" and now embraces all education in grades seven to twelve, whether organized as three-year junior or senior high schools, as six-year junior-senior high schools, or as four-year high schools. In fact, the seventh and eighth grades are commonly referred to as junior high school, even when housed in an elementary school building. Furthermore, there is a growing tendency to include the junior college years in the secondary school classification.

The modifications that have gradually appeared in the organization pattern of our schools are shown in Figure 3, which exhibits clearly the graded ladder arrangement. There are no separate schools for the classes and for the masses, as in many European nations. Differentiation is not found until the later years of the secondary school period, and then it takes the form of different curricula, but there is nothing fixed or immutable about them. There are, of course, selective factors at work in the American schools, but they are not due to the type of organization, as they are in many European schools. American schools constitute a one-track system to which the children of all the people are admitted.

Column C in Figure 3 shows the organization generally found throughout the United States at the opening of the twentieth century. It is now generally referred to as the 8–4 system. When people spoke then of the common schools, they were thinking of the eight years of the elementary school. The high school was universally understood to embrace a four-year course, and this conception persists today in spite of the changes indicated in columns D and E.

About 1910 the 6–3–3 system began to replace the 8–4 plan. The elementary school course was shortened, and the secondary school course extended downward to embrace the seventh and eighth grades, the so-called grammar grades. At first, the reorganization was found in cities where separate junior high schools were formed, and the tenth, eleventh, and twelfth grades were left as a senior high school. As the movement spread to smaller communities, the reorganization took the form of a combined junior-

senior high school, which resulted in what is now referred to as the
6–6 plan.   Several cities, notably Cleveland and Pittsburgh, have
also organized six-year schools.

Thus, it is seen that the first change in the American school system brought about the junior high school.   Column *E* indicates
the next change, the addition of the junior college to the public
school system, a 6–3–3–2 or a 6–6–2 plan.   Although junior colleges had been increasing in number steadily for two decades, it
was not until the early twenties that the movement gained headway in the public schools.   The depression of the early thirties
probably checked the normal development of the program in most
places, but it was also the cause of the introduction of junior
colleges in some cities and states that had not previously established them.   The Emergency Education Division of the Works
Progress Administration encouraged the organization of junior
colleges, or freshman colleges, as they were called, and reported
in August, 1936, that 215 centers had been established in sixteen
states, enrolling 8,232 students and employing 754 teachers.[1]

The results from this emergency junior college program were
just beginning to be seen when World War II disrupted many educational institutions.   Now, following the war, we are seeing a
revival of interest in junior colleges.   Because of the educational
benefits furnished by the Veterans Administration, millions of men
and women are seeking an education.   Many of them might not
have been attracted to college work without such assistance.   It
now appears that the emergency centers established in many states
to take care of this great rush of students may result in the establishment of more or less permanent institutions, many of which will
be organized as junior colleges.

A projection of this plan into the future or a forecast of what
may happen is shown in column *F* of Figure 3.   There is much
speculation concerning a 6–4–4 system, which represents a lengthening of the junior high school to include the tenth grade.   The
remaining two years of the senior high school would then be merged

---

[1] From a press release from the office of L. R. Alderman, Director, Education Division, Works Progress Administration.

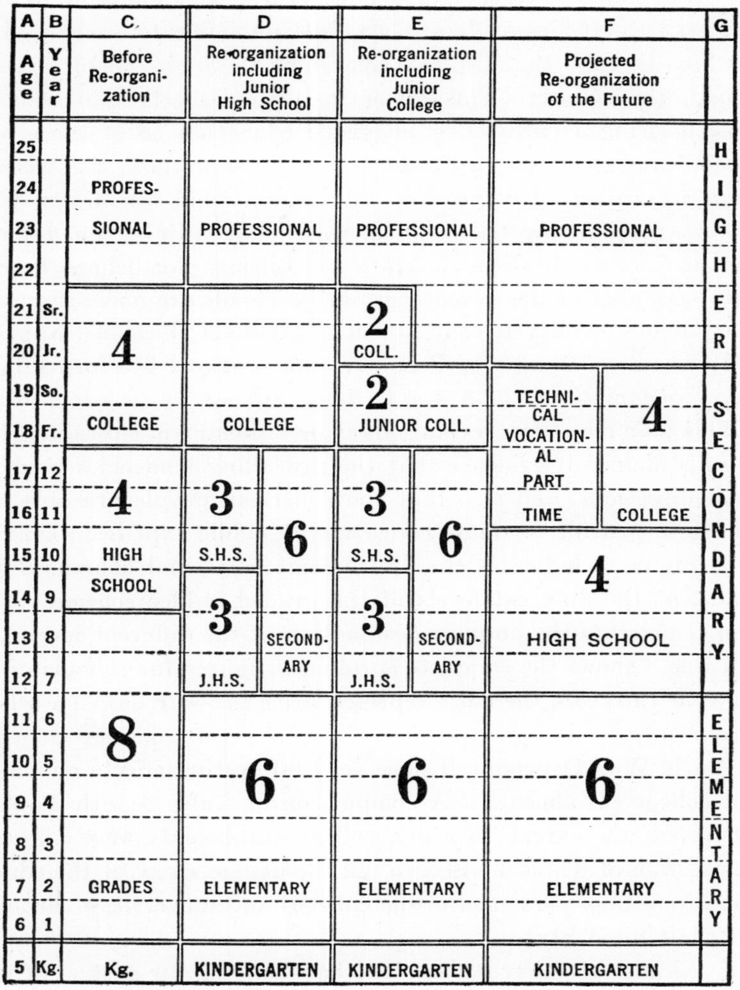

A	B	C.	D	E	F	G
Age	Year	Before Re-organi-zation	Re-organization including Junior High School	Re-organization including Junior College	Projected Re-organization of the Future	
25						H
24		PROFES-				I
23		SIONAL	PROFESSIONAL	PROFESSIONAL	PROFESSIONAL	G
22						H
21	Sr.	**4**		**2** COLL.		E
20	Jr.					R
19	So.			**2**	TECHNI-CAL	S
18	Fr.	COLLEGE	COLLEGE	JUNIOR COLL.	VOCATION-AL	E
17	12	**4**	**3**	**3**	PART	C
16	11				TIME / COLLEGE	O
15	10	HIGH	S.H.S. **6**	S.H.S. **6**		N
14	9	SCHOOL			**4**	D
13	8		**3** SECOND-ARY	**3** SECOND-ARY	HIGH SCHOOL	A
12	7		J.H.S.	J.H.S.		R Y
11	6	**8**				E L
10	5		**6**	**6**	**6**	E M
9	4					E N
8	3					T
7	2	GRADES	ELEMENTARY	ELEMENTARY	ELEMENTARY	A R
6	1					Y
5	Kg.	Kg.	KINDERGARTEN	KINDERGARTEN	KINDERGARTEN	

Column C—Until about 1910
Column D—Changes beginning about 1910
Column E—The Junior College in the Graded Ladder
Column F—A Forecast for the Future

Fig. 3.—Chart Showing Changes in the Organization of the Schools of the United States.

with the junior college. Robert M. Hutchins, Chancellor of the University of Chicago, has given wide publicity to such a plan, in which he calls the first four-year unit the high school and the second, the college. This latter institution meets the needs of those desiring a cultural or academic education or of those who expect later to pursue professional study. For those who wish to make an earlier adjustment in the occupational world, the plan makes provision for technical or vocational training on a part-time or full-time basis in separate institutions paralleling the college, beginning at the eleventh grade as schools are now organized. The public school systems in Moberly, Missouri; Parsons, Kansas; and Pasadena, Compton, Pomona, and Ventura, California have been reorganized on the 6–4–4 basis.

This plan may seem revolutionary or visionary in character, but there is abundant evidence that the prevailing tendencies point in those directions, and also that the American people are able and willing to provide for more education at public expense. Column A in Figure 3 indicates the approximate age, and column B the grade, at the different levels of the graded ladder scheme. Column G presents the popular designation of the different levels.

Table 3 shows the complete enrollment figures for schools of all types in 1937–38, the most representative pre-war data on school enrollment.

World War II produced some very interesting effects on school and college enrollments. A comparison of Table 4 with Table 3 will reveal the extent to which college enrollments were affected. One section of Table 4 will also tell the unique story of the education of military personnel in the colleges and universities throughout the United States.

b. *Elementary education.* The backbone of our system of universal free public education is the elementary school. It is in this division of our schools that a student receives his first instruction in citizenship, thus fulfilling the first objective of elementary education.

Throughout the lower grades much stress is placed upon the individual's privileges and responsibilities as a citizen. It is here

TABLE 3

*Number of Students and Teachers in Schools and Colleges
of Different Types, 1937–38* [2]

Type of School	Schools		Enrollment		Teachers	
	Public	Private	Public	Private	Public	Private
Elementary ...	222,042	b 9,992	19,842,744	2,240,894	594,793	67,139
Secondary a ...	25,467	b 3,327	6,269,723	b 415,435	282,473	25,239
Universities, colleges and independent professional schools	138	806	469,774	613,972	43,158	59,490
Junior colleges	209	244				
Teachers colleges	160	14	82,041 125,114	39,469 5,162	4,407 9,694	4,693 585
Normal schools	93	26	12,554	2,819	1,231	419
Total	248,109	14,409	26,801,500	3,317,751	935,756	157,565

a Includes junior high schools.
b 1936 data.

that efforts are made to get all the pupils to think together about common problems; to develop the qualities desired in good citizens; to foster patriotism and loyalty. Professor Briggs [3] expresses this objective aptly and succinctly: "To integrate the future citizens of a democracy." There are many who charge that this patriotism has been of a blind and unthinking sort, and there is some truth in this criticism. Still, it must be admitted that the elementary school has always been and continues to be a great democratizing influence, bringing together as it does in daily association the children of all the people, with a limitless variety of social, economic, and racial backgrounds and creeds. For example, the class rolls of one county in an Eastern state listed thirty-seven nationalities during one school term. The founders of our nation saw clearly the need for an enlightened and informed citizenry as the bulwark of our democracy. In its formation we find the first objective of elementary education.

[2] *Biennial Survey of Education*, 1937–38, United States Office of Education, Washington, D. C.
[3] T. H. Briggs, *The Junior High School* (Boston: Houghton Mifflin, 1918), p. 26.

Table 4

Enrollment and Number of Teachers in Schools and Colleges, 1943-44 [4]

Type of school	Schools		Enrollments		Teachers	
	Public	Private	Public	Private	Public	Private
Elementary	169,905	10,285 [a]	17,750,941	2,078,959	538,936	65,512 [a]
Secondary	28,973	3,011 [a]	5,576,339	444,551	290,130	34,060 [a]
Universities, colleges, and independent professional schools [b]	156	825	296,665	421,857	34,271	59,985
Junior colleges [b]	210	203	56,439	28,177	3,945	3,869
Teachers' colleges [b]	175	23	67,599	5,074	8,782	276
Normal schools [b]	48	10	1,249	457	714	139
Total	199,467	14,357	23,749,282	2,979,075	876,778	163,841

[a] 1941–42 data.

[b] Enrollments in institutions of higher education include only civilian students. In addition there were 277,755 full-time, regular session military students distributed by type of institution as follows:

Publicly controlled	149,454
Universities, colleges, and professional schools	133,486
Teachers' colleges	11,474
Normal schools	49
Junior colleges	4,445
Privately controlled	128,301
Universities, colleges, and professional schools	128,154
Junior colleges	147

[4] *Biennial Survey of Education, 1943–44*, United States Office of Education, Washington, D. C.

Photo from Black Star

Fig. 4.—Developing Individual Tastes and Aptitudes Through Art.

This first objective of elementary education really consists of two rather separate but related functions. Initially the school must concern itself with the growth and development of the children, their health and physical well-being, their emotional maturing, and their social adaptation. Each child must be provided with experiences that will furnish him with a basis for discovering and understanding his own potentialities, capacities, and abilities. Ultimately the school must create an environment in which each child will find satisfaction in participation in group living. Out of these experiences will develop an understanding and appreciation of the democratic processes at work.

An interesting illustration of this expanding concept of the program of the elementary school is found in a recent publication of the Pennsylvania Department of Public Instruction. This bulletin states the responsibilities of the school in such a manner as to indicate clearly the recent shift of emphasis from subject matter to child development. The school's responsibilities, then, consist in:

1. Developing a social living program, which is conceived as the area including the traditional subjects, history, geography, natural science, and civics.

2. Developing physical well-being, which includes great responsibility in mental as well as physical health.

3. Developing a skills program, which is seen as including skills in the use of numbers, in the use of oral and written language, in reading, in control of the body, and in the skills of living in a democracy.

4. Developing personal tastes and abilities, which is seen as development through literature, music, use of form, line and color, rhythmics, and the like.[5]

The second objective of elementary education is no less important and contributes much to the accomplishment of the first; namely, the teaching of the fundamental skills necessary to further progress as a learner or as an active, intelligent citizen. These skills are frequently referred to as the tool subjects and include reading, language, spelling, writing, and arithmetic. The schools have been noted throughout their history for their stress upon the "three R's" but in late years there has been a considerable shift in emphasis, which may be summarized as follows:

1. In reading, the shift has been from oral to silent reading. In addition to drill and practice on the mechanics of reading, greater interest is shown in the pupil's choice of reading material. In addition to mastering one reader, pupils today are encouraged to read widely in a variety of books. A typical first or second grade pupil today will read ten or twelve books, instead of rereading a single reader four or five times, as in former years.

2. Stress is placed upon oral and written speech habits. Formerly the major instruction in English was left to the upper grades; hence the name "grammar" grades, since chief emphasis was placed upon formal grammar.

3. Instruction in spelling is based upon the words in common use instead of words of the "demon" type, on which our forebears gained their reputations in the famous spelling bees.

---

[5] Pennsylvania Department of Public Instruction, "Improving the Elementary Curriculum," *Bulletin* No. 233A, 1946, Harrisburg, Pennsylvania, page 3.

4. Perfection in writing as a goal for all has been replaced by legibility in writing. Good schools no longer require all the left-handed pupils to write with their right hands nor do they insist upon the perfect letter formation of some particular system. It is legibility that counts.

5. Arithmetic is almost a "backslider" among the original triumvirate. Social and practical values receive first emphasis, and the brain-testing drill of ciphering matches is almost a memory. There is serious questioning by many today whether arithmetic should be taught at all in the elementary school. One superintendent [6] has told of an experimental postponement of the forward study of arithmetic until the seventh grade.

An even more noticeable modification of the elementary school program is seen in the expansion of the curriculum. This expansion took place more or less gradually, but in two fairly distinct steps. First, the tool subjects were enriched by the addition of content subjects, such as history, geography, and literature; and second, these were augmented by the introduction of what have come to be called "expression subjects" or "creative experiences." The latter include music, art, physical education, home economics, and manual arts. A pupil in a good elementary school today comes into contact with as varied a sample of the world's knowledge as did a high school student of a generation or two ago.

A committee of teachers from New York City schools demonstrated this new alignment of the subject-matter areas of the elementary school in a different manner:

Pupil Participation: routines and housekeeping responsibilities, planning, personal management, social behavior and responsibility, exploring school and community, practices of democracy, school and community activities and services.

Health: health instruction, guidance, and services; safety education; emotional adjustment within self and within group; physical activities, rest, recreation, and play; nutrition.

Art: manipulation, experimentation, use of materials and tools, con-

---

[6] L. P. Benezet, "The Story of an Experiment," *NEA Journal*, November, 1935, pp. 241–3.

struction; expression through painting, modeling, textile work, and other processes; practical applications.

Music: vocal, instrumental, and rhythmic; for enjoyment, expression, and understanding.

Language Arts: reading, literature, use of library; composition, spelling, penmanship, correct usage; speech, listening, dramatization.

Social Studies: history, geography, civics; character, family relationships, consumer problems, intercultural education, citizenship, concepts and attitudes of democracy.

Science: nature study (weather, plants and soils, animals, earth and sky), food and water, instruments, simple machine and electrical devices, flightcraft.

Arithmetic: size, shape, space, distance, time, weight, position, concepts, meanings, relationships, computation, problem-solving.[7]

The length of the elementary course is now quite generally regarded as six years, although not even half the schools have abandoned the 8–4 organization. The 6–6 plan is the pattern that serves as a guide to school administrators preparing to reorganize their schools. The elementary schools are not attempting and accomplishing less, but they are striving to attain their goals in six years instead of eight. In former days there was much drill and repetition in the seventh and eighth grades. It is now considered better to work for more thorough mastery in the first six years and, in the seventh and eighth grades, to furnish the pupil with a forward look, through exploratory and try-out experiences. But the number of years is not considered the important factor. Goals are being stated in terms of functions and accomplishments.

The schools of Rochester, New York, have embarked upon a program that allows the superior pupils to proceed more rapidly, but the slower ones to complete the kindergarten and first six grades in nine years without being stigmatized as failures. This new program, known as the Continuous Progress Plan, may be seen at a glance in Figure 5.

---

[7] Board of Education of the City of New York, "Curriculum Development in the Elementary Schools," *Curriculum Bulletin* No. 1, 1945–1946 Series.

Some schools, of which those in Bronxville, New York, and Winnetka, Illinois, are good examples, stress individual instruction without the usual promotion.   One superintendent said, "We do not like to admit that we have grades," meaning that the grade placement of a pupil was considered less important than the pupil's actual growth and development.

Grades	Rapid Group	Normal Group	Slow Group
Sixth Grade Fifth Grade Fourth Grade	2½ years	3 years	4 years
Third Grade Second Grade First Grade Kindergarten	3½ years	4 years	5 years

Fig. 5.—Chart Showing Operation of Continuous Progress. Plan in Rochester, N. Y.

These paragraphs have been presented to give the reader a snapshot picture of the elementary school as one of the steps in the graded ladder organization.   In a subsequent division of this unit we shall present a discussion of current tendencies in American education.   The attention of the reader is directed to that section for a more complete picture of the program of a good elementary school today.   (See page 82.)

c. *Secondary education.*   Someone once said, "the American secondary school is America's Youth Movement."   That statement probably epitomizes the most fruitful efforts of our secondary schools, which provide outlets for the social and recreational impulses of adolescent boys and girls while they continue their systematic education in preparation for more advanced study, or for taking their places in the occupational world.   This education of the whole child is accomplished, in part, by means of socialized school activities, generally referred to as extracurricular activities, but which in modern secondary school practices are now regarded as among the most important aspects of the curriculum. These include musical and dramatic organizations, intramural and inter-scholastic athletics, participation in the government of the school or in the preparation of school publications, and countless other experiences that challenge the interests and occupy the time of the students. In addition, the classwork offers them a great variety of vicarious experiences that serve to take up the slack in their surplus energy and to provide for the wanderlust tendencies of youth. This feature also characterizes the Youth Movements in Europe, to some extent. The fact that about seventy per cent of the young people of secondary school age are in school attests to the popularity and appeal of such a program. In Table 5 we see the tremendous gains in school enrollment compared with the changes in population. The ratio of the elementary school enroll-

TABLE 5

Public School Enrollments Compared with Population Changes, 1870-1945 [8]

Year	Population	Elementary Enrollment		Secondary Enrollment	
		Number	Per cent of Population	Number	Per cent of Population
1870	38,558,371	6,791,295	17.6	80,227	.2
1880	50,155,783	9,957,228	19.9	110,277	.2
1890	62,947,714	12,519,518	19.9	202,963	.3
1900	75,994,575	14,983,859	19.7	519,251	.7
1905	84,219,378	15,788,598	18.7	679,702	.8
1910	91,972,266	16,898,791	18.4	915,061	1.0
1915	91,342,625	18,375,225	20.1	1,328,984	1.5
1920	105,710,620	19,378,927	18.3	2,200,389	2.1
1925	114,867,141	20,999,388	18.3	3,650,903	3.2
1930	122,775,046	21,278,593	17.3	4,399,422	3.6
1935	126,425,000	20,829,789	16.5	5,669,156	4.5
1940	131,891,632	17,961,029	13.6	6,601,444	5.1
1945	138,083,449	17,665,594	12.9	5,560,190	4.0

---

[8] Taken from "Biennial Surveys of Education," United States Office of Education and Census Bureau *Reports*.

ment to the total population has steadily declined since 1900, even though the total enrollment increased until 1930. The secondary school enrollments continued to increase until about 1940, there being nearly thirty times as many high school students then as in 1890. It will be noted that the secondary school enrollment practically doubled every decade from 1870 to 1930, owing, in part, to the increases in population, but also to the more attractive secondary school program, and to the economic and industrial changes.

This enriched and challenging program found its way into the public high school about 1900 and is generally referred to as the reorganized secondary school. It brought with it the junior high school, which represented the most fundamental modification since the establishment of the first public high school in Boston in 1821. The establishment of the Latin Grammar School in 1635 had fixed the pattern for the secondary school as a classical college preparatory institution. That influence persisted in spite of the efforts of the early academies to offer a more liberal and practical curriculum. It is interesting to note that the objectives of the academy were strikingly similar to those accepted for the junior high school one hundred years later. During the intervening years those liberal tendencies were lost in practice, and between 1850 and 1890 the high school became an institution dominated by the colleges, with an offering designed almost entirely for those who were expected to go to college.

The *junior high school* came upon the scene about 1910, the movement having gained momentum for fifteen or twenty years following a report of the Committee of Ten of the National Education Association in 1893. Berkeley, California, and Columbus, Ohio, claim the credit for establishing the first junior high schools, although it is doubtful where the exact idea originated. The new unit was poorly named, because it was destined to become more than a mere miniature, or small-scale imitation, of the high school. Being a new institution it admitted many innovations that markedly changed its character from that of the high school. The wide acceptance of the new program is seen in Table 6, which shows for one state the number of schools and pupils that are operating on a reorganized basis.

Although these figures apply to one state only, they are quite typical of other sections of the country where the effects of the reorganization have been marked. It will be noted that more than

TABLE 6

Statistics from Secondary School Classification Reports in Pennsylvania for School Year, 1945–46 [9]

	Number	Per cent [a]
Pupils in 6–6 and 6–3–3 organizations	377,098	68.8
Pupils in 8–4 organizations	137,777	25.2
Ninth graders in 6–6 and 6–3–3 organizations	81,367	63.2
Ninth graders in 8–4 organizations	47,385	36.8

[a] Includes only pupils enrolled in secondary schools having the indicated organization. The remaining six per cent are in secondary schools having other types of organization.

half of all the pupils and of the ninth graders were in reorganized programs, even though less than half of the schools had been reorganized. It is the larger districts with the heavier enrollments and the greater resources that have attempted such a reorganization.

The extent of the reorganization in the United States as a whole may be seen in Table 7.

The purposes of the junior high school may be studied in some detail to discover the tendencies that have since influenced all secondary school practices:

1. Determination of residue from elementary school. The first responsibility of teachers on this level is to ascertain the kind and amount of work that remains from the elementary school.

---

[9] Prepared by the Division of Child Accounting and Research, Bureau of School Administration, Department of Public Instruction, Harrisburg, Pennsylvania, February 10, 1947.

TABLE 7

Number of Secondary Schools of Different Types in the
United States [10]

	1934	1938
Junior high school	1,948	2,372
Junior-senior high school	3,938	6,203
Senior high school (10, 11, 12)	753	959
Four-year high school	16,574	15,056
Total	23,213	24,590

It is unsafe to assume that all objectives have been attained and that all teaching has been mastered.

2. Exploration. This objective has always received primary emphasis. Its accomplishment is attempted by means of a variety of try-out experiences, which enable a pupil to discover his own interests, aptitudes, and capacities. Exploratory experiences should provide more than mere, sampling of different courses and subjects; each course should be presented so that the leading-on possibilities of such study may be realized by the pupils.

3. Guidance. This has often been called the keynote of the junior high school. It is a sorting period in which a pupil through self-discovery finds his own possibilities and limitations. It is expected that an earlier and more satisfactory adjustment in the world of work will result.

4. Socialization. Instruction procedures have been changed to permit expression of the natural social impulses of adolescents; to afford opportunities to work in groups and situations more like those in life. A program rich in social activities, such as student assemblies, clubs, intramural athletics, and music, contributes much to the all-round development of the pupils.

---

[10] United States Office of Education, *Statistics of Public High Schools,* 1933–34 and 1937–38, Washington, D. C.

5. Individualization.   In contrast to the mass educational techniques of the elementary school, the emphasis is placed upon the individual and his needs and interests.   This objective is undoubtedly the most difficult to reach, but noteworthy efforts in that direction are found in many schools.

The efforts of the State Department of Public Instruction in Pennsylvania were typical of those in many states.   James M. Glass, who had organized the first junior high school in Rochester, New York, a city which made a thorough and systematic study of the new organization, was appointed Director of Junior High Schools for Pennsylvania in 1921.   He was largely responsible for the preparation of a bulletin [11] in which the diagram shown in Figure 6 was used to show the function of the junior high school in relation to the units above and below it.   The junior high school is represented as a period of gradual transition from the uniform curriculum and one-teacher control of the elementary school to the differentiation and specialization of the senior high school.

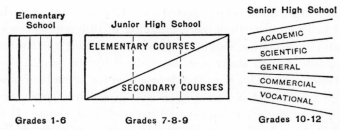

Fig. 6.—The Junior High School in Relation to Elementary and Senior High School.

In the early days of the reorganization movement the *senior high school* retained most of the characteristics of the traditional four-year high school, and it exercised a considerable degree of domination over the junior high school.   In recent years, however, the process has been somewhat reversed.   The procedures and

---

[11] Department of Public Instruction, *Manual for Junior High Schools,* Bulletin 14, 1927, Harrisburg, Pennsylvania.

activities of the junior high school have gradually crept upward until today the philosophy of exploration more or less characterizes all secondary school practices. For example, the literature studied in English classes is chosen with the abilities and interests of the pupils in mind, rather than in terms of some arbitrary standard that prevailed in the past. Science is taught with the emphasis upon developing an attitude of inquiry and an interest in the environment. Less stress is placed upon specific vocational training; more attention is directed toward analyzing the vocational possibilities in many activities.

The number of high schools of different sizes and types is shown in Table 8. Many students will be surprised to learn of the large number of small secondary schools. Forty-six per cent of them enroll less than 100 pupils, and seventy-five per cent less than 200.

The thing that distinguishes public from *private* schools is that the former are tax-supported. Private schools are supported by fees paid by students, supplemented by endowments or grants

TABLE 8

Showing the Number of Public Secondary Schools of Different Types and Sizes in the United States, School Year, 1937–38 [12]

Pupils Enrolled	Number of Schools	Percentage
10 – 24	1,372	5.6
25 – 49	2,243	10.8
50 – 74	3,051	12.4
75 – 99	2,661	10.8
100 – 199	6,407	26.1
200 – 299	2,561	10.4
300 – 499	2,271	9.2
500 – 999	1,940	7.9
1000 – 2499	1,444	5.9
2500 or more	240	1.0
Total	24,590	100

from controlling bodies as in the case of denominational institutions. They are controlled or supervised by State Deparments

[12] United States Office of Education, *Statistics of Public High Schools,* 1937–38, Washington, D. C.

of Education only to a limited extent and then, usually, only in so far as they desire accreditment of their work. Regulations concerning certification of teachers usually do not apply to them, although the standards are frequently as high or higher. The relative number of private secondary schools is seen in Table 3.

The majority of private institutions are church controlled, and are called parochial or parish schools. They are promoted and supported by denominational groups largely as a guarantee that the religious and doctrinal aspects of the training of the children will not be neglected during the training and formative years. On the elementary and secondary level the work is so graded and organized that their pupils may transfer freely to the public schools, or their graduates may be admitted to colleges on the same basis as are the graduates of public secondary schools.

Another influential group of private schools is that comprising the so-called "prep" schools or academies, whose chief function is preparation for college. They are, in a very real sense, the direct descendants of the old Latin Grammar School, many of them being over one hundred years old. Their curricula are almost wholly of a classical nature, and most of their students are preparing for the College Entrance Board Examinations, or are looking forward to entering colleges steeped in academic traditions. Although comparatively few in number, these preparatory schools have long exerted a tremendous influence upon secondary education by reason of the stamp of respectability placed upon the college preparatory curriculum.[13]

Much more recently there has developed a group of schools generally known as "Country Day Schools," and now frequently referred to as "Progressive Schools." This group includes nursery schools, kindergartens, elementary and secondary schools, and occasionally junior colleges, in all sorts of combinations, sometimes all together as one organization but more frequently as

---

[13] *Fortune* magazine published some years ago two fine articles dealing with the private schools in America: "Twelve of the Best American Schools" (Boys), 13:48–53, January, 1936; "Ten Fashionable Boarding Schools for Girls," 13:106–111, April, 1936.

separate institutions. Their students have undergone a highly selective process, in which economic status and social position are important factors. One feature characterizes all of them, in that they are all exponents of the more liberal tendencies in education discussed later in this unit. Great stress is laid on creative activities and leisure time pursuits. For the most part their influence upon public schools has been helpful and wholesome. They have provided healthy competition, or a sort of yardstick by which to measure progressive tendencies in education.

d. *Higher education.* In the academic year 1946–47 there were more than 2,100,000 students enrolled in the institutions of higher learning in this country, an increase of at least 600,000 over the greatest number ever before enrolled in the nation's colleges and universities. Moreover, there can be little doubt but that at least 2,500,000 students would have entered had suitable accommodations been available. Approximately fifty per cent of the college enrollment in 1946–47 consisted of veterans of World War II, who were enabled to enter college, or to return to college, under the educational provisions of the GI Bill of Rights. Enrollment of veterans promises to be an important factor in the college population until well into the 1950's.

Throughout our country's history major wars have always resulted in a large increase in the number of young people seeking higher education. In wartime young men and women in military service learn that education is important. They observe, even more clearly than in peacetime, that those with education, training, and technical skills get ahead faster than those whose education has been neglected. Parents and younger brothers and sisters of the young men and women in military service learn the same lesson. Consequently, it seems safe to predict that college and university enrollments will continue to rise, even after all the veterans enrolling in college under the GI Bill have completed their studies. It is not unlikely that ten years after the end of hostilities in World War II, college and university enrollments in this country will be approximately double the peak enrollment of 1,500,000 attained just before our entry into the war.

At the outset the student should have his attention called to the essential differences between colleges and universities. There is much confusion with regard to terms, although, in general, the differences are clear-cut and are understood by informed persons. Colleges stress undergraduate study in academic or technical fields and grant Bachelor of Arts or Bachelor of Science degrees. For the most part, the work is of a cultural or foundational nature and is nonvocational in character. Universities are composed of several professional or technical schools or colleges and lay greatest stress upon graduate study and research and professional preparation. A liberal arts college is quite the same type of institution whether it is a unit in a university or a separate institution, but if it is the former, its faculty frequently will also have direction of graduate students working toward higher degrees.

The true significance of the university in society is vividly described in a brief quotation from an address by Dr. James Bryant Conant, President of Harvard University:

What is a university? Like any living thing, an academic institution is comprehensible only in terms of its history. For well on a thousand years there have been universities in the western world. During the Middle Ages the air they breathed was permeated with the doctrines of a universal church; since the Reformation in Protestant countries these have undergone a slow and varied metamorphosis. But the essence of the university tradition has remained constant. From the first foundations to the present, four main streams have watered the soil on which the universities have flourished. These ultimate sources of strength are: first, the cultivation of learning for its own sake; second, the general educational stream of the liberal arts; third, the educational stream that makes possible the professions, and last, the never-failing river of student life carrying all the power that comes from the gregarious impulses of human beings. All four streams are easily discerned bringing life to the English universities in the first half of the seventeenth century. If one of the four vital streams I have mentioned either fails or swells to a torrent, thus destroying the proper balance of nourishment, then the true university tradition may perish. The cultivation of learning alone produces not a university but a research institute; the sole concern with the student life produces an academic country club or merely a football team maneuvering under a collegiate banner.[14]

There is some doubt whether the junior college should be discussed here or under secondary education. It first developed as one of the higher education units and still functions in most places as the first two years of a standard college course, in many institutions being designated as the lower division. But when one considers the tendencies shown in column F, Figure 3, he is led to believe that the junior college is more appropriately a part of secondary education. There is abundant evidence that junior college students more nearly resemble those senior high school students with whom they have just recently been associated than they do the upperclassmen with whom they will be associated in college. This statement is particularly true of such characteristics as social maturity, interests, and leisure time activities. Perhaps this unit is best described as the period of transition between the tryout experiences of the secondary school and the responsibilities that come with professional study or with satisfactory adjustment in the occupational world.

Junior colleges fall into four fairly distinct classes: (a) the public or tax-supported; (b) the private or denominational; (c) the branch centers or lower divisions of larger universities; and (d) the adjuncts to established preparatory schools. Junior colleges of all types, and particularly of the tax-supported type, have flourished most in the Middle West and Far West, as shown in Table 9.[15] There are few public junior colleges in the Alantic or New England States, but their number is increasing and may reasonably be expected to continue to do so. An example of the second group is Stephens College, Columbia, Missouri, and of the third group, the Junior College at Martin, Tennessee, a branch of the University of Tennessee. Since 1925 many well-known pre-

14 Adapted from J. B. Conant, "The University Tradition in America— Yesterday and To-morrow," *School and Society,* 44:385–391, September 26, 1936.
15 From the Junior College Directory, 1947, in *Junior College Journal,* XVII: 197–223, January, 1947.

TABLE 9

Junior Colleges in the United States, 1946

	Junior Colleges			Enrollment		
	Total	Public	Private	Total	Public	Private
Alabama	8	1	7	812	47	765
Alaska	1	0	1	31	0	31
Arizona	2	2	0	1,749	1,748	0
Arkansas	9	6	3	2,935	2,225	710
California	76	63	13	119,896	118,044	1,852
Canal Zone	1	1	0	603	603	0
Colorado	7	6	1	2,951	2,527	424
Connecticut	15	2	13	6,375	66	6,309
Delaware	1	0	1	173	0	173
Dist. of Col.	6	0	6	671	0	671
Florida	8	1	7	1,873	178	1,695
Georgia	20	10	10	4,940	3,527	1,413
Idaho	4	3	1	2,553	2,245	308
Illinois	25	13	12	12,602	9,676	2,926
Indiana	4	1	3	617	127	490
Iowa	28	21	7	2,501	1,349	1,152
Kansas	20	13	7	3,131	2,490	641
Kentucky	15	2	13	2,602	571	2,031
Louisiana	2	2	0	982	982	0
Maine	5	0	5	635	0	635
Maryland	6	2	4	824	278	546
Massachusetts	25	3	22	6,424	379	6,045
Michigan	14	10	4	6,905	6,543	362
Minnesota	15	12	3	3,465	3,105	360
Mississippi	22	12	10	5,019	3,707	1,312
Missouri	23	11	12	7,852	4,136	3,716
Montana	4	3	1	476	441	35
Nebraska	7	5	2	2,765	2,558	207
Nevada	0	0	0	0	0	0
New Hampshire ..	1	0	1	377	0	377
New Jersey	10	3	7	3,855	1,102	2,753
New Mexico	1	1	0	118	118	0
New York	25	9	16	10,437	3,013	7,424
North Carolina ...	22	2	20	4,650	446	4,204
North Dakota	5	5	0	1,058	1,058	0
Ohio	10	3	7	3,594	644	2,950
Oklahoma	26	22	4	2,547	2,373	174
Oregon	3	1	2	3,874	1,365	2,509
Pennsylvania	22	5	17	5,071	860	4,211
Rhode Island	2	0	2	480	0	480
South Carolina ...	9	0	9	1,308	0	1,308
South Dakota	5	1	4	994	717	277
Tennessee	13	1	12	2,665	339	2,326
Texas	62	31	31	29,740	21,360	8,380
Utah	6	5	1	3,139	3,009	130
Vermont	3	0	3	553	0	553
Virginia	16	3	13	4,683	2,140	2,543
Washington	9	9	0	3,677	3,677	0
West Virginia	4	1	3	916	223	693
Wisconsin	9	4	5	5,668	5,501	167
Wyoming	2	2	0	471	471	0
United States	648	315	333	294,475	216,325	78,150

paratory schools have extended their offerings to include a junior college department, examples being Kemper Military School, Boonville, Missouri, and Miss Porter's School, Farmington, Connecticut. Table 10 indicates the growth of the junior college movement throughout the nation since 1900.

It is the first group that is of most interest to the student of public education. In California, public junior colleges are supported by a direct state appropriation for each pupil in average daily attendance. In other states, such as Texas, Kansas, and Missouri, they are supported from the general school levies. The junior colleges are frequently housed with the senior high school, whose principal is also dean of the junior college and where many facilities such as gymnasiums, laboratories, and libraries are used by both schools. Occasionally teachers will have classes in both the high school and the junior college, but, as a rule, the faculties are quite distinct. Graduates of approved junior colleges are admitted to full junior standing by the colleges and universities in their respective areas. The curriculum usually parallels that of the first two years of a liberal arts college and is frequently supplemented by vocational or technical training, particularly secretarial and commercial training.

The case for the public junior college may be summarized as follows:

Advantages: (a) Two years of college work are made available to all high school graduates in the community at relatively low cost. (b) Further formal education may be continued by those for whom there are no places in industry. (c) Students may remain at home for a longer period. (d) Transition from high school to college is less abrupt, resulting in fewer maladjustments. (e) Instruction is given by more experienced teachers, when compared with the first year or two in many of the larger universities. (f) In larger institutions more attention may be devoted to professional study and research, if freshmen and sophomores get foundation courses elsewhere.

Disadvantages: (a) Cost of public education is increased. (b) Funds are diverted from elementary or secondary school grades.

TABLE 10

Showing Growth of Junior College Movement, 1900 to 1946

	Public		Private		Total	
Year	Number	Enrollment	Number	Enrollment	Number	Enrollment
1900 [a]	0	......	7 [d]	......	7	......
1905 [a]	1 [c]	......	18	......	19	......
1910 [a]	6	......	47	......	53	......
1915 [a]	22	......	91	......	113	......
1920 [a]	46	......	149	......	195	......
1925 [a]	88	......	221	......	309	......
1930 [b]	163	36,396	266	29,321	429	67,627
1933 [b]	192	69,806	305	36,210	497	106,016
1935 [b]	223	77,111	303	33,007	526	110,118
1939 [b]	258	140,545	317	56,165	575	196,710
1940 [b]	261	168,228	349	67,934	610	236,762
1946 [e]	313	215,959	325	76,268	638	292,237

[a] From Doak S. Campbell, *Critical Study of the Stated Purposes of the Junior College.* Nashville, Tenn.: George Peabody College, 1929.

[b] From "Junior College Directory," published in *Junior College Journal,* 1930 to 1941.

[c] Established 1902 in Joliet, Illinois; from L. V. Koos, *The Junior College.* Minneapolis: University of Minnesota, 1924.

[d] From L. V. Koos, *op. cit.*

[e] Compiled by Winifred R. Long and Shirley Sanders in the *Junior College Journal,* Vol. XVII, No. 5, January, 1947.

(c) It is more difficult for student to find his place in four-year college. (d) Many public junior colleges would bring about elimination of smaller colleges.

Historically, the pattern for higher education in this country is the standard four-year academic college conferring a Bachelor of Arts degree. These colleges, which preceded the universities, have continued to be the most influential undergraduate units and, to a marked degree, have set the academic standards for relationships between the institutions. Table 11 shows the date of establishment of many of our leading institutions.

The typical college in this country was originally a church-controlled institution, founded at first for the purpose of providing clerical, and later lay, leadership for the denomination. In the early days it also maintained the only secondary schools in many communities. It would be difficult to overestimate the influence of many religious groups in the days before tax-supported public school systems, notably the influence of the Moravians, Friends, Presbyterians, Methodists, and Lutherans. Many of the colleges now have only slight connections with the denominational groups that founded them; in numerous instances they have built up large endowments in the custody of boards of trustees and to all intents and purposes are now private or nondenominational institutions. Municipal colleges, supported by taxes, were established in a number of cities, and many of them later became municipal universities.

Higher education for women provides one of the interesting chapters in the development of colleges. Mary Lyon was the real pioneer in this movement, as the founder and first president of Mt. Holyoke College in 1836. Wesleyan Female College, Macon, Georgia, was chartered the same year. Elmira College in New York was founded in 1855. The first coeducational institution was Oberlin, founded in 1833. The *Educational Directory* [16] for 1946–47 indicates that there are 161 colleges and 78 junior colleges for women and 1,225 coeducational institutions. In 1938 there were 550,071 women compared with 811,204 men enrolled in institutions of higher learning.

During the war the civilian college student population was predominantly feminine. In 1943 there were approximately 300,000 women, 147,000 civilian men, and 363,000 trainees in army and navy units under instruction by college and university faculties. In 1944 and in 1945 approximately sixty per cent of the collegiate population were women. By the autumn of 1946 the ratio had swung back to the typical pre-war ratio of approximately two men to one woman student enrolled in American colleges and universities. Women students probably will remain in the minority,

---

[16] *Educational Directory*, Part III, Colleges and Universities, 1946–47. Washington, D. C.: United States Office of Education, Government Printing Office, 1947.

at least until the educational needs of veterans have been met.

Our American universities fall into four groups:

1. The oldest universities in this country are those that developed from some of the early colleges, including such institutions as Harvard, Yale, Columbia, and Princeton. They are richly endowed and enjoy a position of prominence and prestige rivaled only by the great universities in Europe.

2. Second in importance in this country is a long list of state universities that have come rapidly to the front in the last few decades, as a glance at the enrollment figures of a few of them (Table 11) will show. In the first sale of public land, Congress set aside certain tracts to encourage the founding of universities. This act led to the establishment of the universities in the middle western states, which, as a group, are the leading state universities. The first of these, Ohio University, was founded at Athens in 1804, although the real forerunners of the movement were the state universities established in Georgia in 1785 and in North Carolina in 1789. By 1850 fourteen states had established universities. Although the fruitful period for establishing state universities followed 1860, it is since 1900 that they have enjoyed their greatest prosperity and expansion. In 1931–32, twenty-two per cent of the men, seventeen per cent of the women, twenty and six-tenths per cent of all college students were enrolled in state universities. Originally founded to serve the constituents of the state, many of the state universities now occupy a position of national prominence. In 1946 seventeen of the first thirty universities, listed according to enrollment, were state universities. All but eight were publicly supported.

3. A few privately endowed universities have been established since those in the first two groups. Notable among these are the University of Chicago, 1893, Leland Stanford, 1885, and Duke, renamed in 1924 after a rich endowment was bequeathed by the Duke family to Trinity College, Durham, North Carolina.

4. The fourth group is made up of the municipal tax-supported universities of which Cincinnati, Toledo, and Louisville are typical. Many of them were the outgrowth of municipal colleges, or re-

TABLE 11

Date of Establishment of Certain Colleges and Universities
with 1946–47 Enrollments

Institution	Date Established [a]	Enrollment of Full-time Students [b] 1946–47
Colleges		
William and Mary	1693	1,756
Dartmouth	1769	2,806
Dickinson	1783	823
Franklin and Marshall	1787	1,256
Bowdoin	1794	963
Colgate	1819	1,381
Amherst	1821	1,135
Oberlin	1833	2,296
Mt. Holyoke	1836	1,179
Bucknell	1846	2,013
Elmira	1855	393
Vassar	1861	1,344
Smith	1871	2,276
Wellesley	1873	1,683
Bryn Mawr	1880	686
Private Universities		
Harvard	1636	12,076
Yale	1701	8,706
Princeton	1746	3,991
Pennsylvania	1749	9,539
Columbia	1754	21,590
Notre Dame	1842	4,502
Southern California	1879	13,597
Stanford	1885	7,204
Chicago	1890	8,354
State Universities		
Georgia	1785	6,771
North Carolina	1789	6,802
Ohio University (at Athens)	1804	5,795
Missouri	1839	12,281
Wisconsin	1848	18,668
Minnesota	1851	26,055
Iowa	1858	9,783
Illinois	1867	27,276
California	1868	40,800

[a] From *World Almanac*, 1936.
[b] From Raymond Walters, "Statistics of Attendance in American Universities and Colleges," *School and Society*, Vol. 64, No. 1669, December 21, 1946.

sulted from the merging of several independent colleges and professional schools.

In 1862 Congress passed the Morrill Act, which provided for the establishment of institutions in each of the states to furnish instruction and research in agriculture and the mechanic arts. The funds were first obtained from the sale of public lands and later by direct money grants, since which time annual Federal appropriations have been used to supplement the state support. These institutions are commonly known as the land grant colleges. The states took advantage of this Federal grant in three different ways. Some of them added the grant to the endowment of existing state universities and combined the two institutions. Illinois and Wisconsin are examples of this type. Several of the eastern states appropriated the money to existing private institutions, as did New York State at Cornell and New Jersey at Rutgers. The remaining states established separate, new institutions, which are commonly known as A. & M. Colleges or "Aggies." Most of the Southern states established two colleges, one for whites and one

TABLE 12

Showing Total Number of Higher Institutions of the Different Types, 1939 [17]

Type of Institution	Type of Control					
	State	District or City	Private	Protestant	Roman Catholic	Total
College or University	110 [a]	14	184	253	150	711
Professional School ..	20 [b]	1	144	72	23	260
Teachers' College or Normal School ..	162	5	20	4	13	204
Junior College	42 [a]	171	82	98	25	418
Negro Institutions ..	30	8	15	53	1	107
Total	364	199	445	480	212	1,700

[a] Includes 1 under Federal control.
[b] Includes 4 under Federal control

[17] *Educational Directory,* Part III, Colleges and Universities, 1946–47. Washington, D. C.: United States Office of Education, Government Printing Office, 1947, p. 8.

for Negroes, and occasionally a separate college for women.
Many of these land grant colleges have long since outgrown their
"cow college" status and are now rated as first-class universities
with several professional schools. In 1934–35 there were 182,480
students enrolled in the 52 institutions for whites and 8,833 in the
17 Negro colleges.

TABLE 13

Student Bodies in Higher Education [18]

Type of Institution	Institutions for Men	Institutions for Women	Coeducational Institutions	Total
Institutions for Whites:				
College or University	97	158	456	711
Professional School	91	10	159	260
Teachers' College or Normal School	1	26	177	204
Junior College	31	78	309	418
Institutions for Negroes:				
College or University	2	3	67	72
Professional School	1	—	4	5
Teachers' College or Normal School	—	—	12	12
Junior College	—	—	18	18
Total:				
White Institutions	220	272	1,101	1,593
Negro Institutions	3	3	101	107
Grand Total	223	275	1,202	1,700

The study of higher education would not be complete without
reference to teacher education. Beginning with Massachusetts,
which established the first state normal school in 1839, and continuing at a rapidly accelerated pace for forty years, the states
seemed to vie with one another in the establishment of state normal
schools. Every state had one or more, except Wyoming and
Nevada. About 1920 a movement of epidemic proportions to

[18] *Educational Directory*, Part III, Colleges and Universities, 1946–47.
Washington, D. C.: United States Office of Education, Government Printing
Office.

expand these schools into four-year degree-granting teachers' colleges swept the country, until today there are fewer than forty publicly supported normal schools left. Many of the state teachers' colleges grant the master's degree and one has an ambitious program leading to a doctor of philosophy degree. A 1947 directory published by the United States Office of Education lists 167 state and municipal teachers' colleges.

Instruction leading to the professions is given mainly in two types of institutions: (a) the professional schools and colleges in the universities referred to above; and (b) separate private professional and technical schools, such as colleges of pharmacy, medicine, law, dentistry, and the like. There has been a marked tendency for the independent professional schools, other than the teachers' colleges, to disappear or to be merged with or attached to universities. The first professional education on the college level, in medicine, was begun by Pennsylvania in 1765. In other fields we find the beginnings in theology at Princeton in 1812, law at Maryland in 1812, pharmacy at Philadelphia in 1822, and education at Iowa in 1873. Rensselaer, established in 1824, was the first technical school. In the early days there were all manner of variations in professional education, ranging from that offered by racketeering diploma mills to high-grade instruction. In recent years the professional societies have attempted to set standards and weed out the undesirable institutions, until today the vast majority of professional work follows a full college or at least a pre-professional course. For example, the Association of American Medical Colleges publicizes a list of Class A medical schools, and the engineers have a Society for the Promotion of Engineering Education, which concerns itself with policies and programs. The Educational Council of the American Dental Association was organized in 1936 for the purpose of raising the level of training for dentists. All the thirty-eight approved dental schools admit students to the four-year dental course leading to the D.D.S. degree only after two years of approved college work.

The number of higher institutions of different types in this country is shown in Table 12 (page 74).

2.   Administrative Organization for Public Education

a. *Local control.*   Education in the United States is regarded as a local matter.   The American people have always been proud of their public schools and have guarded jealously the local autonomy the latter possess.   The local district is the unit of administration in public education, authority being vested in a board of school directors, usually varying in number from three or five in rural areas to as many as nine to fifteen in the cities.   (In some rural areas this responsibility rests upon one man: in Indiana upon the township trustee and in New York upon the district trustee.) These directors are elected for relatively short terms, necessitating annual, or at least biennial, elections, which means that local school affairs are always before the people, frequently in the form of an old-fashioned school fight.   Few communities escape frequent upheavals caused by a school director (or candidate for the office) who is "gunning" for someone or something.   In such instances one or more of the school employees generally lose their positions. In Unit Five there is a discussion of needed changes in this area.

The local school board has a very great deal of power and authority.   When it is recalled that the members serve without pay, one wonders why men and women seek such positions.   The answer is probably found in the power and responsibility the office carries with it, involving, as it frequently does, the employment of large numbers of people and the expenditure of vast sums of money.   It is a good example of the workings of democratic government at its best—or worst—depending upon the situation. The set-up is at once the strength and weakness of the American school system: strength, because all the people have a direct interest and a voice in school affairs; weakness, because the system is vulnerable to the attacks of scheming politicians and self-seekers. The successful operation of the school district as a unit in a democracy depends upon how this small body of citizens regards this position of trust.

The first duty of a local school board is to employ a superintendent or supervising principal of the schools.   He is the professional leader and educational adviser. The directors really constitute a business and legislative body, which delegates executive and administrative duties to this professional leader. The board receives tax collections and state appropriations and is responsible for the expenditure of school funds. Final authority rests with the members of the school board on such matters as deciding on the tax rate, purchasing building sites, awarding contracts for erection and repair of buildings, approving annual budgets, and electing teachers. They are also responsible for, but usually delegate to the superintendent, the duties of interviewing candidates for teaching positions, selecting more desirable candidates, assigning teachers, purchasing textbooks, equipment, and supplies, preparing budgets, and all matters that are primarily educational in nature. This practice does not mean that the board is a mere "rubber stamp," but it may be safely said that the quality of educational leadership in a community is in direct proportion to the extent to which proper relations between school directors and superintendents are maintained. Figure 7 attempts to show for a typical small city the relationships between the school directors and the superintendent with his staff of assistants and specialists. The chart indicates that all agencies and services are responsible directly to the superintendent and he in turn to the board.

b. *State administration.* The highest educational officer in the state is the State Superintendent of Schools or Commissioner of Education. He is elected by direct vote of the people in thirty-two states, appointed by the governor in seven others, and appointed by the State Board of Education in the remaining nine states.[19] This official is responsible for enforcing the laws relating to education. Through his staff of assistants and directors he provides the necessary supervision over the schools and takes care of such matters as the certification of teachers, allocation and disbursement of school appropriations, minimum courses of study,

---

[19] Ward W. Keesecker, "Selection, Qualifications and Tenure of Principal State School Officials," *Circular* No. 166, August, 1936, United States Office of Education, Washington, D. C.

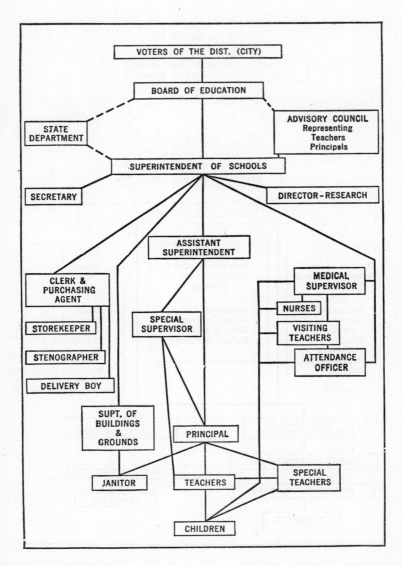

Fig. 7.—Organization Chart for Schools of Binghamton, New York.

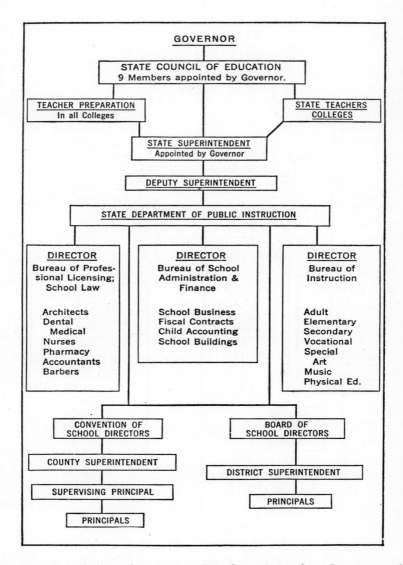

Fig. 8.—Chart Showing Organization of the Pennsylvania State Department of Public Instruction.

and enforcement of compulsory attendance laws.   In a few states,
notably New York, Connecticut, New Jersey, and Pennsylvania,
we find a high degree of centralization of authority, while in many
southern and western states there is very little.   Figure 8 presents
an organization chart showing the functions of a state department
and the relations between the State Superintendent and other
school officials in local districts.

No mention is made of education in the Federal Constitution.
It may have been overlooked, as were many other functions of
government.   The Tenth Amendment leaves to the states those
powers and duties not specifically mentioned in the Constitution.
Thus, the authority for and control of education passed to the
states, and in recent years there has been an increasing tendency
to centralize authority in the state departments and state superintendents.

c. *National organization.*   Federal authority in educational
matters resides in the United States Office of Education, presided
over by the Commissioner of Education.   The office is one of the
divisions in the Federal Security Agency.   The Commissioner has
no direct authority over education in the several states; his relationships are of an advisory nature.   It is the function of his
office to collect, tabulate, and disseminate statistics concerning
schools.   Accurate files are maintained from which any person who
is interested can secure information pertaining to school affairs.

The Federal Government has direct supervision over only three
types of educational institutions.   (1) It maintains the Military
Academy at West Point, the Naval Academy at Annapolis, the
Coast Guard Academy at New London, Connecticut, and the Mer-
chant Marine Academy at King's Point, N. Y.   (2) It organizes
and maintains schools for wards of the government, as, for example,
the Indians.   (3) It controls and supervises the schools in Federal
territories and districts, including Alaska, island possessions, and
the District of Columbia.   In addition, it has made direct appropriations for the support of special types of education, although
exercising only a limited measure of control.   Since 1862 it has
appropriated money for the support of the agricultural and

mechanical instruction in land grant colleges, and since 1917 for high school vocational instruction in agriculture, home economics, and industrial education.   Except for a special emergency allotment for the relief of distressed school districts in the various states during the depression, no other Federal money was granted for general education in the public schools prior to the emergency grants necessitated by World War II.

Since the early twenties there has been intermittent agitation for a Secretary of Education in the President's cabinet, and many bills authorizing such a change have been introduced in Congress, but this agitation has subsided somewhat in late years.   In its place there have come from certain groups urgent demands for direct Federal appropriations to equalize educational opportunities in the several states.   Those who favor such support contend that responsibility for a minimum educational program belongs to the national government and not to the states.   They argue that money should be secured where the wealth is concentrated and used where it is needed.   The opponents point out that if we had Federal support, there would be an increasing measure of Federal control.   Such an argument frightens those who believe strongly in local control, no matter how much they might want the Federal money.   This issue is discussed more fully in Unit Five.

B.   Current Tendencies in American Education

In the foregoing pages, an effort has been made to explain the structure of American schools.   It is a sort of snapshot picture. A better understanding would be gained if one could take a series of snapshots over a period of time, thus showing the changes that are taking place.   Possibly the most marked characteristic of our schools during the last two or three decades is seen in their tendency to modify the traditional practices and procedures. Only to the extent that one understands the nature and scope of these changes can one appreciate the place of education in society and the relative significance of the various educative agencies. These changes involve the curriculum, or what is taught, as well as the methods and procedures used, although less distinction is made between these categories than formerly. Indeed, a prevalent tendency is toward the realization that subject matter and method are interwoven and interrelated and cannot be considered as separate and distinct. Such a trend also necessitates some changes in organization and administration.

1. The Shift from Subject Matter to Pupil Activity

This change is the most noticeable one that has occurred. We are currently seeing more emphasis upon what the pupil does and relatively less upon what he learns. The curriculum is organized in terms of tasks to be performed and goals to be reached, rather than in terms of lessons to be learned. This circumstance does not mean that knowledge and facts have no place at all. Facts are learned, just as well as they ever were, but in situations in which the school is working toward broader objectives. By way of illustration: it is now recognized that learning the multiplication tables is second in importance to deciding when to multiply, and that habituating certain mechanical skills in reading eventually gives place to choosing reading material. Drawing a picture of an impression gained from reading a story requires more appreciation and pupil activity than was formerly demanded by a typical reading or drawing lesson. As the content and expression subjects have assumed more importance, the pupil's activity has become the goal; the subject matter is learned as a means to that end.

This tendency is more noticeable in the elementary school than at other levels. When a parent asked the teacher of one of his children when he could observe a reading lesson, the teacher replied, "Oh, it is all reading; we are always reading." What she meant to imply was that reading is an activity that enters into all study and is not a separate subject. The secondary school still places a good deal of stress upon subject matter and departmental divisions. Comparatively little change of this character has occurred in colleges, where the lecture method and the emphasis upon final examinations continue to place subject matter in the position of dominance.

2. The Shift from Lesson Learning to Child Development

The modern school is more interested in the total growth of the child than it is in what or how much the child learns. This dominant interest does not mean that learning is relegated to a secondary position, nor that the learning of specific subject matter is neglected. It does mean that more emphasis is placed upon the learning experiences provided and the resultant effects of participation in those experiences than upon the subject matter learned. This emphasis is probably the most controversial point with reference to what is ordinarily called "Progressive Education." Possibly some of the more liberal educators have been neglectful of learning in their anxiety to provide activity and furnish experience, and such instances of neglect have laid the schools open to attack by their severe critics. A good school, however, will use all experiences as a means for providing both child development and learning that is worthwhile and important.

3. Integration

Here we have a term—a sort of catchword—used to describe the tendency to bring into a learning situation subject matter from various fields, all contributing to a better understanding and leading to fuller participation in the learning activity. All study centers around this unifying central idea, sometimes called a unit or project, instead of proceeding from one topic to another in logical or chronological order. A study of transportation in fourth grade could be used as the center of interest for most of the reading and arithmetic and spelling, furnish the practice needed in writing, draw largely from historical sources, and provide many opportunities for expression through art or music.

In the elementary grades this organization of subject matter has come to be called the "Activity Curriculum" or "Activity Program" (not to be confused with extracurricular activities in high school). The reader should not get the impression that fundamental skills are neglected. No matter how much integration is attempted, it becomes necessary at intervals to stop and drill in the skill activities. The differences are found in the approach to the practice exercises and in the aims of the drill procedures. No school can be called a good one if fundamental learnings are neglected, regardless of the emphasis upon pupil activity and integration. Logical organization of subject matter from the adult point of view is supplanted by a psychological approach that begins with pupil interests. Indeed, some of the leading advocates of the "Progressive Education" [20] movement insist that reading and arithmetic never should have been called tool subjects—they are pupil activities just as truly as are music and drawing.

Instruction in the social studies furnishes the best illustration of integration in the secondary school. Beginning with Community Civics in the eighth or ninth grade the student gets an early view of local problems, and this unit is supplemented in the senior high school by Problems of Democracy, where national and international issues are considered. The old sequence in history (ancient, medieval, English, and American) has been replaced by world history and American history, and is frequently studied in a course called Social Problems. Professor Harold Rugg of Columbia University strongly advocates a "fusion" of the social studies and has prepared a series of textbooks [21] for junior high school that attempts to merge or fuse history, geography, and civics with a consideration of problems from sociology, economics, and political science. Similarly, the traditional arithmetic of the seventh and eight grades and the algebra of the ninth have been integrated with some intuitive geometry and trigonometry into what is called general mathematics. There are also instances of composite courses in senior high schools that bring together history, English, art, and music.

---

[20] "Progressive Education" is a term quite generally understood to refer to these same integrating and activity tendencies in the elementary schools. When used in this manner, "Progressive" is usually spelled with a capital "P," in reference to the organization formerly called the Progressive Education Association, composed of those who believe strongly in the aforementioned liberal trends in education. In 1944 the Association changed its name to the American Education Fellowship. It continues to publish *Progressive Education* as its official magazine.

[21] Harold Rugg, *Social Science Series* (Boston: Ginn and Co., 1931).

Integration is one of the progressive tendencies that have modified practices on the college level, where it usually takes the form
of orientation or survey courses. Contemporary Civilization, a
one-year course required of all freshmen in many colleges, aims to
furnish a background for the understanding of current social and
technological forces. General courses of a non-laboratory nature
in physical and biological science are frequent replacements for
required courses in chemistry, physics, botany, and zoology. The
University of Chicago has been pioneering for several years in an
effort to secure a more thoroughly integrated study program.
All undergraduate work is done in five main divisions: the college,
corresponding roughly to the junior college, and the four upper
divisions of biological sciences, physical sciences, social sciences,
and the humanities. The course of study at the college is quite
flexible, embracing survey-lecture courses in each of the four
major divisions. Fields, rather than courses, are emphasized.
The student begins in survey courses of a lecture type and continues in seminars and in independent study under the direction of
instructors in the division. The time spent and the credits accumulated are not used as a measure of achievement. General
comprehensive examinations determine a student's competency,
regardless of the number of courses he has taken.

Other colleges and universities are experimenting with general
courses and integrated programs. The general college at the
University of Minnesota and the lower divisions in many institutions are illustrations. Swarthmore College stresses honor courses
for superior students. Bennington College in Vermont attempts
to put its students in closer touch with the problems in the
occupational world by extending the winter vacation to two
months, during which time the students go to art or music studios,
news or editorial rooms, banking establishments, or social service
centers, for work in the fields of their major interests.

4. Socialization

The schoolroom is certainly a happier place than it used to be.
Pupils act more naturally; more as they do in life outside the

school.   One book on the subject expresses the idea very clearly in the title, "Willingly to School." [22]   A former superintendent of schools in Chicago, William McAndrew, led a campaign some years ago against newspapers and periodicals that, through cartoons or editorials, pictured the school as a place to which the pleasure-loving boy went under compulsion, and the teacher as a superannuated, loveless, forlorn creature bent on wreaking vengeance upon the children for her sorry lot in life.   Mr. McAndrew states the case pointedly:

The Saturday Evening Post, founded by Benjamin Franklin, who never showed contempt for the underpaid and lowly, devotes to us its front page, September 14, as the schools open.   A mother, leading an unwilling child, is greeted by a vinegar-faced female holding a hickory whipping stick behind her back.   Norman Rockwell, erstwhile giver of delight by his depiction of lovable and quaint rugged individualists, took the *Evening Post's* money to do this ulcerous thing.   Ten years ago Dr. William H. Allen led a quiet campaign in which thousands of letters before the beginning of the fall term were written to newspaper editors, inviting them on the opening day to come to school to see what teachers look like and to find out whether children hate them and their schools.   The *Educational Review,* for several years, printed the result of this appeal.   By 1928 the clipping bureau that served this magazine reported inability to find any more of the stale-humor libels on our class of public servants.   Milton Potter's committee of the National Education Association offered a resolution, "our women," complimenting and thanking the American press "for abandoning a traditional and stupid practice of ridiculing by cartoons and paragraphs the women of the schools."   No decent allegiance to the American ideals of education, as formulated by Washington, Franklin and other founders of the nation, said the resolution, can be maintained if public prints throw disrespect on education and on women.

I can't find any reason for a renewal of Allen's campaign.   The editorials I see at the beginning of school appreciate the possibilities of a great public service and encourage us to render it.   The cartoonists drawing teachers depict pretty women, now.   The *Saturady Evening Post's* bad break is probably a relapse, a case of atavism, a recollection by some unhappy old man who told Rockwell what to draw.   The proper thing is for you to write the *Post* an invitation to come and

---

22 Claire T. Zyve, *Willingly to School* (New York: Round Table Press, 1934).

see, to set Rockwell to painting opening day as it really is and to offer
to schools at cost both pictures for framing.[23]

Photo from Black Star

Fig. 9.—High School Boys and Girls Work Together in Modern Home Economics Classes.

There is less standing in rows or passing in lines. Pupils are
privileged to go to the dictionary, library table, or pencil sharpener
and to move about the room naturally and quietly without raising
their hands for permission to do so. Children learn from one
another, an unpardonable sin a generation or two ago. The
teacher directs the activity of pupils; the learning takes place
naturally. One veteran teacher [24] expressed this thought aptly:

A school is a place where young people of any age come together
to educate themselves and one another with the help of the faculty.

Pupils are encouraged to work in groups and to accept group
responsibility for the welfare of the school and its program. In

[23] William McAndrew in "Comments on Things Educational," *School and
Society,* 42:473, October 5, 1935.
[24] Ambrose L. Suhrie, School of Education, New York University.

the secondary school much of the socialization is accomplished through the extracurricular activities and this spirit also permeates the classroom. The school today tries to organize the work so that it is similar to life situations, and teachers and pupils work together happily on common problems.

5. Contemporary Problems Studied

Teachers in both elementary and secondary schools are providing opportunities for discussion of contemporary problems. The school of the past was afraid to bring controversial issues of local significance into the classroom or to consider important questions of a social, economic, or political nature. It feared taking sides or bringing politics into the school. This question received much consideration at the meetings of the Department of Superintendence of the NEA [25] and allied organizations in February, 1936. At one session Professor Roy Hatch, of the State Teachers' College in Montclair, New Jersey, taught a class of high school students in the municipal auditorium, demonstrating how controversial subjects may be brought into the classroom. Formerly the school preferred to play safe, to discuss problems from the theoretical or academic point of view, and to refrain from acquainting the students with live current issues.

One instructor, Dr. I. D. Taubeneck,[26] of the Bronxville, New York, high school, has gained considerable fame as a teacher who "teaches history backwards." He admits the charge but insists that the plan is logical and not a backward approach. Copies of every New York daily newspaper are in the classroom for every class meeting. The students begin with a discussion of current news related to some problem they are studying and follow back into history to find similar situations or programs. Another class in Problems of Democracy studied the production and distribution of food and clothing. They collected information about the sources of the daily food supply, discovering, for example, that

---

[25] National Education Association, *Proceedings,* 1936, pp. 175–90.

[26] I. D. Taubeneck, "History Begins with the Present," *Progressive Education,* 11:82–7, January, 1934.

fourteen different bakery trucks from nearby cities delivered bread
to that small town each day, and that this fact partially explains
the wide gap between the cost of bread and the price of wheat. In
another class in social studies the students secured information
from two small local factories and discovered that their products
were distributed over a wide area in the United States, the raw
materials having been collected from many parts of the world.
In such study a firsthand acquaintance with practical problems
of economics, sociology, and political science is encountered.

Little children show great interest in the daily newspapers and
current magazines. The school today does not leave all such problems until the high school years but attempts to capitalize the
budding interests of children. A rich and varied assortment of
collateral reading materials provides the elementary school pupil
with a better foundation for understanding life about him than
the high school was able to offer a generation ago. Such publications as *My Weekly Reader* [27] for elementary grades and *Scholastic* [28] for the secondary school are good illustrations of the type
of current periodicals written for classroom use.

6. Directed Learning Replacing Home Study

The parent who voices the complaint that his children "never
bring books home any more" is describing briefly one of the current
tendencies in American education. Less emphasis is placed upon
home study; more attention is paid to the work done at school under
the supervision of the teacher. Longer school periods and less
clear-cut distinctions between study and recitation combine to
bring into the classroom what is frequently termed "directed
learning." Emphasis is put on starting work at school and continuing it at home, thus reversing the order of studying at home
and reciting at school. Many schools would prefer to have work
expected of all pupils done at school where the teacher can observe
the conditions under which it is done. In a large eastern city
a group of thrifty junior high school pupils built up a profitable

---

27 *My Weekly Reader,* American Education Press, Inc., Columbus, Ohio.
28 *Scholastic,* Chamber of Commerce Building, Pittsburgh, Pennsylvania.

racketeering business in doing homework for different students. As a result the school discontinued all homework of a problem-solving, sentence-writing character that could be forged. A story frequently told at educational conclaves illustrating this point relates that a mother sent the following note to a teacher:

Dear Teacher: I'm tired when I get home from work in the evenings. If it is all the same to you, wouldn't you just as soon teach the lessons at school and let me hear the recitations at home.

7. School Records and Report Cards

The permanent records of the school are becoming more inclusive and descriptive. In addition to the usual scholarship marks, with accompanying notations of "promoted" or "failed," a cumulative folder may contain the health record, mental and achievement test ratings, descriptions of particularly noteworthy achievements, and an account of the participation in extracurricular activities. Likewise, the records in use in many places today would be barely recognizable as such by parents of a former generation. This important link between the school and the home has become less formal and impersonal, describing more accurately and intimately the actual progress of the pupil. As the school has increased the emphasis upon all-round growth and personality development of children, the traditional letter and numerical marks have proved inadequate. Webster, the cartoonist, told this story vividly in one of his "Life's Darkest Moment" cartoons, in which he depicted a little girl with head bowed in shame as her parents looked dole-fully at a kindergarten report card bearing the inscription: "D in blocks and sand piles." Brief informal descriptions of pupils' work, similar to those that follow, are coming rapidly into promi-nence. The State Department of Public Instruction in Pennsyl-vania has published a bulletin, from which these examples were taken, setting forth the merits of a modified form of report card.

Case 1. Jane is making remarkable progress in her school work, especially with her reading. She made a fine record in her vocabulary

test on the first fifty words presented.   Her handwork is not yet satisfactory, but I feel that is a matter of development that cannot be
pushed.

Case 2.   You will be glad to hear that Charles is carrying on the
work of the Fifth Grade in a satisfactory way.   He shows excellent
spirit and ability in all playground activities.   His English is not up
to the quality of the good work he is doing in Arithmetic and Spelling.
Geography and History offer him more difficulty, and he would be in
trouble were it not for his excellent effort.   The help that you have
been giving him at home since our talk last fall has been a real aid in
these subjects.

Courtesy of the "New York Herald Tribune"

Fig. 10.—The Cartoonist Strikes at Some of the Absurdities in Our Marking
System.

Case 3. In passing through the adolescent stage, Carl's physical growth has apparently led to a lack of coördination. This is evidenced by the fact that all his subject teachers have commented upon oversensitiveness, self-consciousness, failure to participate in group activities. Furthermore, he is too easily amused at the faults of others. At times he shows initiative in Science, but in general he is unreliable in carrying out assigned tasks. He shows lack of concentration and serious attitude towards his own success. Only with careful supervision does he approach satisfactory results. You can help by insisting on completion of homework.

Probably the most potent argument for the conventional report card is the traditional hold it has upon the parents of the children now in school. They have always been accustomed to an "A, B, C" or a "70 to 100 per cent" marking system. Most parents do not appreciate the possible ill effects of such a system as they are pointed out to us in the following quotation from an address by Burton Fowler, then Director of the Tower Hill School, a Progressive School in Wilmington, Delaware:

School marks should be abolished along with all other paraphernalia of an antiquated, competitive and artificial educational machine because they make children feel inferior or superior, encourage dishonesty, give a feeling of insecurity, dull the edge of intellectual curiosity, make children course-passers, instead of learners, and provide in general unworthy motives for hard work.[29]

8.   Block Scheduling

A movement that has made much headway recently is referred to as block scheduling of classes. It is frequently accompanied by departmentalized teaching in the upper grades. The daily schedule shown in Figure 11 is typical of those found in the ordinary classroom or rural school. It permits little or no flexibility and is regarded as something to be followed literally, which partly accounts for the distinction between study and recitation. It is difficult to get integration of subject matter when it is presented in such fragmentary bits.

---

[29] Burton Fowler, address quoted in the *New York Herald Tribune.*

9:00 to 9:10...............	Opening exercises
9:10 to 9:25...............	Study arithmetic
9:25 to 9:45...............	Recite arithmetic
9:45 to 10:00...............	Study spelling
10:00 to 10:15...............	Recite spelling
10:15 to 10:30...............	Recess
10:30 to 10:50...............	Study reading
10:50 to 11:10...............	Recite reading
11:10 to 11:25...............	Study language
11:25 to 11:45...............	Recite language
11:45 to 1:00...............	Noon hour

Fig.11.—Daily Schedule of Classes of Traditional Type.

The block scheduling, illustrated in Figure 12, is particularly helpful as an administrative device for integrating subject matter and for combining study and recitation in a period of time of sufficient length to complete a substantial task.   It is also helpful in a one-room rural school where the teacher has several classes of different grade levels.   By alternating and combining classes the work may be organized into larger units.   The schedule permits a maximum of flexibility, enabling the teacher to use the time to better advantage.   For example, in Period III in the fourth grade, spelling might be omitted entirely on a given day to permit more time for writing a composition, or both language and spelling might give way to a period of extensive reading at the library table.

9.   Evolution of Trends in Education

One can get a fairly good background for understanding the current tendencies in American education by tracing elementary education through the several stages in its development.   What has happened to elementary education has also happened in greater or lesser degree at other levels of the school system.   For the purposes of this presentation six stages have been identified.   The first five of these are based upon a statement by Dean John W. Withers,[30] of the School of Education of New York University. The sixth we consider to be the most recent stage.

Period	Fourth Grade	Fifth Grade	Sixth Grade
I 9:00–10:15	Mathematics Science (Health)	Reading Language Spelling	Social Studies
Intermission			
II 10:30–11:45	Social Studies	Mathematics Science	Reading Language Spelling
Noon Hour			
III 1:00–2:15	Reading Language Spelling	Social Studies	Mathematics Science
Intermission			
IV 2:30–3:45	Art Music Writing	Art Music Writing	Art Music Writing

Fig. 12.—Illustrating Block Scheduling of Classes.

a. *Six stages in the development of elementary education.* In considering these six stages the student should bear in mind that we did not abandon the earlier stages as we progressed to the later ones, but rather that we supplemented them with the newer emphases. For example, we have called the first stage the Tool Stage. We are still interested in the tool subjects, but we are interested in many other aspects of education besides.

1. Tool stage. Our first efforts in elementary education were

[30] John W. Withers, *Systematic Supervision* (New York: New York University Press, 1930).

concerned with the tool subjects, reading, writing, and arithmetic, the Three R's. Although we now feel that these are quite inadequate for modern needs, they probably served the social need of their time, which was the time of our grandfathers, better than later elementary school curriculum served the need of its day.

2. Subject-matter stage. The second stage we have called the Subject-Matter Stage, because it marked the introduction of the content subjects into the elementary school curriculum. With the lengthening of school terms, it became possible to go beyond teaching merely the mechanics of reading, and to devote some time to the teaching of useful information. History, geography, and physiology, for example, were introduced into the elementary school curriculum.

3. Adult activities stage. This stage came in part as a result of a realization that the curriculum was becoming overcrowded, and that practically it was impossible to cover all the subject matter that theoretically could be studied. Some basis for selection of the most desirable or most useful subject matter was needed. One of the early applications of the scientific movement in education was the development of techniques for the selection of subject matter. The basis of selection was that of adult use or need. The result of this selective process was a much-needed reform in the elementary school curriculum. For example, it resulted in the elimination of such topics as the following, which were found, upon analysis of adult activities, to have little value: cube root, naming the bones of the body, tracing the circulation of the blood, much of place geography, the memorizing of unimportant dates in history, and many other similarly useless topics. One can appreciate the importance of this reform by comparing any one of the old textbooks in spelling, published before 1900, with any of their modern counterparts, beginning with the Horn-Ashbaugh Speller, one of the first textbooks in this subject to be based upon a scientific analysis of the words the adult actually uses when he writes.

4. Project, or purposeful activities, stage. The newer philosophy pointed to the need for an elementary school program and

curriculum based upon something more than preparation for adult life and activities. It was urged that education must be concerned primarily not with preparation for life, but with life itself. The best preparation for successful, happy living was held to be successful, happy living. No period in the life of the individual should be sacrificed to another period. Consequently, projects and purposeful activities came into our professional vocabulary, and into best school practice. Tools of learning and adult activities were not lost sight of, but activities that were meaningful and interesting to the child were added.

5. Creative, or child-centered, stage. This stage is really quite new, and is not yet adequately understood by a majority of teachers. It is held to be a principal function of the school to aid the child in the fullest possible development of his potentialities. The child and his development occupy the center of the stage. Many teachers misunderstand the use of the word "creative" in this connection. They point out that there is so little creative talent in the world that the school cannot be expected to develop creative ability among the masses of pupils in the overcrowded public school classrooms. According to their interpretation of the meaning of the term they are correct. What is intended, however, in the use of the term, is that any activity is creative for the individual if through it he develops new powers, abilities, or capacities, or if he gains new insights or appreciations. In this sense, creative education is for the masses, for the underprivileged as well as for the gifted.

6. Social reconstruction, or society-centered, stage. We are beginning to realize that society is and must be constantly in a state of reconstruction. It cannot stand still; it must progress or deteriorate. Furthermore, we are also beginning to understand that education has a major responsibility in social reconstruction. The school, through its curriculum, its policies, and its program will either retard or aid in adapting social institutions to changing social need. It may be the deciding factor in whether there shall be violent, cataclysmic, revolutionary upheaval, or orderly, evolutionary, progressive development. Without sacrific-

ing any of its other goals, the school must face this responsibility. It must center its activities in the needs of society. The important role of schools in wartime illustrates this point.

b. *Current emphasis.* The role of the schools and of education in the post-war period is at least as important as was their wartime responsibility. We must look to education for the development of international-mindedness and for help in gaining an understanding of other countries, their people and their problems; in developing a genuine desire for international coöperation; in preparing ourselves for world citizenship; and in replacing the prevalent chauvinism, hatred, and bigotry with the great ideals of human brotherhood and understanding. Truly no greater task ever confronted education, and it is a task that must be solved if we are to be able to live successfully—or even just to live—in this atomic age.

C.   Comparison With Schools of Other Countries

It is difficult to make comparisons between the schools of the United States and those of other lands because of the vast differences in national philosophy and political organization. A hasty glance will be cast at some of the distinguishing characteristics of different school systems, but the student is cautioned against too much reliance upon categorical generalizations, which are likely to be misleading, if not actually erroneous. They are useful chiefly as introductory statements. World War II exerted a profound influence upon education in all countries, including our own. It is too early to determine the long-time influences, but it is safe to assume that fundamental changes will occur.

Two charts are presented showing the organization pattern in the different countries. Figure 13 presents a diagrammatic representation of the organization of the schools of Baltimore, Maryland, typical of the comprehensive educational offering in our large cities. It shows graphically the graded ladder, one-track plan for all normal pupils and the ease with which a pupil may transfer to a program better adapted to his needs and interests.

Two differences between our schools and those of continental

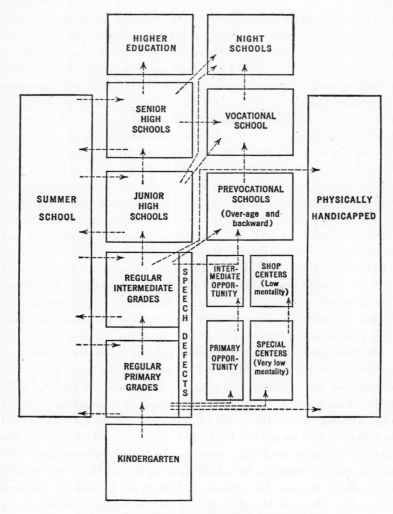

Fig. 13.—Schools of Baltimore, Maryland.

Europe are most noticeable to the casual observer. First, our graded ladder system of schools for all students is to be contrasted with the dual systems providing separate schools for the masses and the classes. Second, most of the European nations, excepting

Great Britain, have highly centralized national systems of education. Other contrasts, not so clear-cut and distinct but quite
apparent, should be noted. Third, a larger percentage of American students of high school age, about seventy per cent, are found
in high school, while the proportions in different European countries range from 1 in 10 to 1 in 50. Fourth, the typical European secondary school pupil gets a more thorough and intensive
knowledge of academic fields, largely because he pursues the subject for six to nine years. Fifth, most teachers in Europe enjoy
considerably more security and tenure; they are also better prepared, doctors' degrees being not at all uncommon among the
secondary school teachers. Sixth, most countries provide part-
time or continuation schools for those who cannot pursue higher
education, and technical and vocational education paralleling our
senior high school and junior college years.

Before the First World War the German system offered one of
the best illustrations of a differentiated program of education
beginning after the first few years of uniform education for all
classes. Figure 14 shows clearly the contrast with our own one-
track plan of organization.

The first great national system of schools in modern times was
established in Prussia. Martin Luther had been an enthusiastic
advocate of an educated laity as the best antidote for the evils
of the church against which he protested so vehemently. Later
political leaders saw the value of universal public schools for all
the children, and we see the *Volkschule* emerging, which most of the
children attended until they were ready for the *Gymnasium*, the
first secondary school to be established, or one of the other schools
indicated in Figure 14. Since World War I, radical changes
have taken place in the direction of better opportunities longer
continued for all children. The *Grundschule* is attended by all
pupils for four years, when they transfer to a *Mittelschule* or another secondary school, or to the *Volkschule*, which completes the
education of the vast majority of the people.

The German schools have long been noted as institutions that
were controlled and dominated by a strong nationalistic policy to

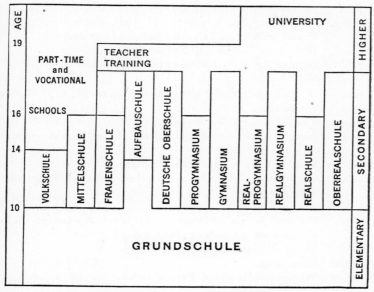

Fig. 14.—The Schools of Germany.

further the interests of the state. Indoctrination characterized all the methods and subject matter, and group study and concert recitations were used to inculcate love of country and intense patriotism, and to glorify the Germans as a superior people, able and willing to sacrifice anything for the good of the *Vaterland*. A brief quotation from Dr. Thomas Alexander's [31] stenographic account of a lesson illustrates how the children were being prepared for the First World War in 1914. Similar preparation preceded World War II.

GEOGRAPHY; III CLASS, FIFTH YEAR, BOYS

Teacher. Where do we live?
Pupil. We live in Europe.
Teacher. What is your Fatherland?
Pupil. Germany is my Fatherland.
Teacher. All together—Germany is our Fatherland.

[31] Thomas Alexander, *The Prussian Elementary Schools* (New York: Macmillan, 1918).

Pupils.   Germany is our Fatherland.

Teacher.   Who is our Landesvater?   (Father of the country.)

Pupil.   Emperor William II is the father of our country.

Teacher.   Why is he called Landesvater?

Pupil.   Because he rules the German Fatherland.

Teacher.   No.

Pupil.   Because he cares for the land and its people as if he were
            the father.

Teacher.   Yes.   He cares for the land as a father cares for his chil-
            dren, whence comes the name.   What is the emperor
            called?   All together.

Pupils.   The emperor is called Landesvater.

Teacher.   Germany is shut in by many other lands.   What country
            is to the west?

Pupil.   France.

Teacher.   We shall hear something about this country today.   What
            country are we to hear about today?

Pupil.   We shall hear about France today.

Teacher.   Once more.

Pupils.   We shall hear about France today.

Teacher.   All together.

Pupils.   We shall hear about France today.

Teacher.   What is the name of this country?
            (Teacher had written the name on the board)

Pupil.   France.

            . . . .

Teacher.   Now let us consider the east boundaries of France more
            closely.   They are the Alps, the Swiss Jura, and the Ar-
            gonnen Wald.   All together; The eastern . . .

Pupils.   The eastern boundaries are the Alps, the Swiss Jura, and
            the Argonnen Wald.

Teacher.   Now one pupil alone give the boundaries on the east.

Pupil.   The eastern boundaries of France are the Alps, the Swiss
            Jura, and the Argonnen Wald.

Teacher.   Now give me all the boundaries of France.

Pupil.   The western boundaries of France are the Atlantic Ocean
            and the Bay of Biscay; the southern are the Pyrenees and
            the Mediterranean Sea; the eastern boundaries are the
            Alps, the Swiss Jura, the Argonnen Wald; and Belgium
            and English Channel on the north.

Teacher.   What you told me of France was not very much.   Can
            anyone give me the name of a ruler of France?

Pupil.   Napoleon I.
Pupil.   Napoleon III.
Teacher.   What wars did Napoleon I wage?
Pupil.   The wars against Prussia one hundred years ago.
Teacher.   What wars did Napoleon III conduct?
Pupil.   The Franco-Prussian War in 1871.
Teacher.   Have the French and Germans gotten along well together?
Pupil.   No, they have had many wars with one another.
Teacher.   Yes. We must now study and find out more about this country, because we may have trouble in the future with them! The chief rivers of France are the Loire, the Rhône, the Garonne, the Maas, the Mosel, and the Seine. Repeat that.

. . . .

(The song "Deutschland, Deutschland, über Alles" was then sung, presumably because the boys were getting a little sleepy.)

Teacher.   What is our Fatherland?
Pupil.   Germany is our Fatherland.
Teacher.   Who is our Kaiser?
Pupil.   William II is our Kaiser.
Teacher.   What can we call him?
Pupil.   We call him the Landesvater.
Teacher.   What country are we studying today?
Pupil.   We are studying France.
Teacher.   What border of Germany is France?
Pupil.   France is the western border of Germany.
Teacher.   What is the capital of France?
Pupil.   Paris is the capital of France.
Teacher.   What is the best train for Paris? (No reply.) The best train for Paris passes through Hannover, Cologne, and Brussels. Repeat that.
Pupil.   The best train for Paris runs from Berlin through Hannover, Cologne, and Brussels. (It was repeated again.)

Following the First World War there was an extensive movement in the direction of promoting liberal tendencies in the schools, as noted in the establishment of the *Grundschule*. The German Youth Movement, which was a spontaneous, unbridled outbreak of youth for freedom of expression and activity, gave promise of becoming an important factor in building the new German Republic. Of course, under Adolf Hitler and the Nazi regime, the schools reverted to the propaganda function and contributed immeasurably toward strengthening the grip of Fascism upon the nation.

D.   Problems and References for Collateral Study

Problems for Students

1. To what extent can we consider an individual the product of the educational system?   (See Preface.)

2. Is there any fallacy in considering the teachers as producers and the pupils as consumers of education?   (See Preface.)

3. As a result of interviews and visits and a study of books and articles on the subject, write a comparison of the elementary school as you knew it with progressive elementary education today.

4. Cite evidences that the junior high school movement has modified practices in your home school.

5. Write an appraisal of your own high school and its program.

6. Make a survey of your own high school graduating class to determine the extent to which the school prepared your classmates for the work they are now doing.

7. Assemble the data that should be considered if a public junior college were to be established in your locality.

8. Make an inventory of curriculum innovations and progressive tendencies on the college level.

9. Prepare a description of the programs of several of the institutions that are pioneering now on the college level.

10. Write an appraisal of the criticisms and comments concerning the schools of a number of citizens in your home community.

11. Make an educational survey of your home community, indicating outstanding achievements, recent developments, and needed changes.

12. Collect data concerning improved records and report cards.

13. What would be the arguments for and against the all-year school in your community?

14. Prepare a detailed analysis of the current tendencies in teaching in the field of your major interest.

15. Make a comparison of a particular educational program in our country with a similar program in one or more foreign countries.   (For example, physical education or vocational education.)

16. Prepare a detailed description of an educational institution or program in some foreign country.   (For example, the Danish Folk High School, or adult education.)

17. What do you think will be the principal long-time effects of World War II upon education in the United States? In England? In Germany? In Japan?

Selected References

Adams, Fay, *Educating America's Children: Elementary School Curriculum and Methods.* New York: Ronald Press, 1946.

Alberty, Harold, *Reorganizing the High School Curriculum.* New York: Macmillan, 1947.

Bowen, Genevieve, *Living and Learning in a Rural School.* New York: Macmillan, 1945.

Butler, F. A., *The Improvement of Teaching in Secondary Schools.* Chicago: University of Chicago Press, 1946.

Cole, Luella, *The Elementary School Subjects.* New York: Farrar, 1946.

Douglass, Harl R., *The High School Curriculum.* New York: Ronald Press, 1947.

———, and Gruhn, William T., *The Modern Junior High School.* New York: Ronald Press, 1947.

Gesell, Arnold, and Ilg, F. L., *The Child from Five to Ten.* New York: Harper, 1946.

Huggett, A. J., and Millard, C. B., *Growth and Learning in the Elementary School.* Boston: Heath, 1946.

Jones, Barbara, *Bennington College: The Development of an Educational Idea.* New York: Harper, 1946.

Koos, Leonard V., *Integrating High School and College.* New York: Harper, 1946.

Lane, Robert Hill, *The Teacher in the Modern Elementary School.* Boston: Houghton Mifflin, 1946.

———, *The Progressive Elementary School.* Boston: Houghton Mifflin, 1946.

Leonard, J. Paul, *Developing the Secondary School Curriculum.* New York: Rinehart, 1945.

Mort, P. R., and Vincent, W. S., *A Look at Our Schools.* Lancaster, Pa.: Cattell, 1946.

NEA Educational Policies Commission, *Education for all American Youth.* Washington, D. C., 1944.

Sexson, John A., and Harbeson, John W., *The New American College.* New York: Harper, 1945.

Stevenson, Elizabeth, *Home and Family Life Education in Elementary School.* New York: Wiley, 1946.

Syrkin, Marie, *Your School and Your Children.* New York: L. B. Fischer, 1946.

Umstattd, J. G., *Secondary School Teaching.* Boston: Ginn, 1946.

Williams, L. A., *Secondary Schools for American Youth.* New York: American Book Company, 1946.

Wolff, Werner, *The Personality of the Preschool Child.* New York: Grune & Stratton, 1947.

Wofford, Kate V., *Teaching in Small Schools.* New York: Macmillan, 1946.

————, *Modern Education in the Small Rural School.* New York: Macmillan, 1945.

Influences Affecting Our Schools

A student would have a better understanding of what the schools are attempting to do today if he could learn something of the influences that have led to the formation of existing programs and policies. A rapid survey of the historical and traditional influences will furnish a background for appreciating those movements that have been most vital to our schools and those that have persisted over the longest period of time. He will thus discover how difficult it is for educational institutions to make progress. By contrasting the philosophical and psychological influences upon educational practices today, an opportunity to evaluate current tendencies will be presented, together with some bases for judging what effects these tendencies are likely to have upon education in the future.

The reader might well inquire where the child—the learner —comes into the picture. It is in this unit that the student is acquainted with the types of research that focus attention upon the nature of child development and the learning problems confronting the teacher. The nonprofessional student will gain valuable insight into the technical nature of the teaching process and will thus become a more appreciative patron of the schools, while the prospective teacher will get a preview and sample of the subject matter that receives chief emphasis in his professional preparation.

A. Historical and Traditional Influences

Any institution or movement can be fully understood and appreciated only if its antecedents or origins are known. The or ganization and activities of the schools today can be understood best if we know the influences leading up to present practices. Enthusiastic young students frequently ask impatiently, "Why don't the schools do something about that?" The best answer is that they never have done anything about it. Social institutions change slowly and gradually and usually lag far behind the social milieu to which they are expected to contribute.

1.   Early Schools a Transplantation from Europe

The early settlers on this continent brought with them their own institutions. It was natural, therefore, that the first schools established should be patterned after those of Europe; it is also natural that since different groups of settlers came here with beliefs in different political theories, we should find three greatly different philosophies dominating the thinking of the people in the original colonies. These three concepts may be characterized briefly as the Aristocratic, the Religious, and the Democratic; and they found expression respectively in the South, in the Middle Atlantic area, and among the New England colonies.

a. *Aristocratic concept in the South.* In contrast with those of the other sections, the early colonists in the South were less strongly motivated by the quest for religious and political freedom. Most of their leaders were adherents to the Church of England. They soon established relationships more nearly like those characterizing the aristocracies of Europe. A moderately wealthy land-owning class developed in Virginia, the Carolinas, and Georgia, and with the coming of slavery we find the re-establishment of a feudal aristocracy further intensified by the race problem. The well-to-do plantation owners provided private tutors for their own children and later sent them to the finishing schools in the North or to Europe. The less favored among the whites had to be content with such educational opportunities as came their way, and it was not until after the Civil War that any serious attention was given to the education of Negroes. All this does not mean that the Southern country gentlemen did not believe in education. They considered it a private affair or left it to the church. Thomas Jefferson strongly believed in a democratic school system. One of our earliest colleges, William and Mary, was established in Virginia in 1693, and the earliest state university was established in Georgia. Still, it is only fair to say that the aristocratic influence dominated the early schools and is the explanation of much that is seen in Southern schools even today.

b. *Religious influence in Middle Atlantic area.* One cannot easily overestimate the influence of religious groups upon educational practices in the Middle Atlantic states, particularly in Maryland, New Jersey, and Pennsylvania. Of course, it is true that the schools were controlled by the church, but their leaders were firm believers in the necessity for the education of all the children. The Catholics, Quakers, Moravians, Presbyterians, and Lutherans set in train the movement that made the transition to free public education, which later became universal, possible. The writings of William Penn contain numerous references to educational problems, and the Friends have long been advocates of adequate educational opportunities. The sectarian influences in education that persisted for so long can be traced to these early beginnings in the colonies settled by religious groups.

c. *Democratic tradition born in New England.* Our school histories place greatest stress upon the fact that the Pilgrims came seeking religious freedom, and that, of course, is true. But the Pilgrims must also have been imbued with a zeal for political freedom, for it was in New England that the democratic ideal gained a foothold. Training of the young for participation, and of the ministers for leadership, in the church was stressed from the beginning. The Latin Grammar School was established in 1635 and Harvard College in 1636. At first it was expected that home instruction of children would be sufficient, but as early as 1674 laws were passed requiring that teachers be provided. This legal provision for education at public expense was the beginning of a state system of schools that was to become the pattern throughout the country.

2. Three Basic Ideals of American Education

The foregoing discussion will give some notion of the crazy-quilt pattern for education that would have developed had not some unifying and coördinating influence soon come to bear upon the situation. It is difficult, if not quite impossible, for a student trained in the free public schools to imagine the conditions that would prevail in this country if his educational opportunities depended entirely upon his economic or social position or the religious group to which his parents belonged. Originally, pauper or charity schools in some communities and subscription (tuition) schools in others furnished the only educational facilities. We are so accustomed to seeing all the children go to school that we may fail to realize the debt we owe to the leaders who worked for the establishment of free public education in the early days of our republic. The following description by Dr. Reisner of the provisions for pauper schools will make us more appreciative of free schools:

Conspicuous among all the state plans for pauper education is that of Pennsylvania. Beginning with a law passed in 1802, but which took final form only in 1809, Pennsylvania attempted to make the education of poor children a public concern and a public charge, while allowing all parents who were able to pay for the schooling of their children to continue doing so. Under the terms of the law of 1809, the township assessors were directed to prepare each year a list of children whose parents were obviously unable to pay for the tuition of their children. These lists were sent to the county commissioners, with whom protests might be lodged looking to the revision of the lists. When the lists were returned to the local communities, any child designated as one entitled to free tuition might apply to any teachers for instruction at the stated rate of two and one-half cents a day and might be provided with the necessary books and materials of instruction. At the close of the school term the teacher would prepare a list of pauper children who had been under his instruction, and a bill for their expenses, have this list approved by two or more of the local managers or patrons of the school, and send this bill to the county commissioners, who were under obligation, according to the terms of the law, to honor this requisition upon the county funds. This system, modified in the larger centers of population as we shall see later, obtained in Pennsylvania from its inception in 1802 until the passage of a free public education law in 1834.[1]

Three basic ideals or principles have guided and molded the thinking of the American people as our educational structure has evolved.

a. *Equality of opportunity.* The first of these ideals, equality of educational opportunity for all the children of all the people, dictated our system of universal, free public schools. This ideal represents one of the first claims of the citizens upon the state governments. Indeed, the exercise of this principle is guaranteed by the constitutions in most states. It brought first the elementary school, later the high school. Today the impetus for the junior college is traceable to an inherent belief that if the young people of one community have access to a publicly supported university or college, then it seems logical to expect college opportunities to be available everywhere. As early as 1642 Massachusetts passed a law requiring that reading be taught and in 1647 also passed the first public school act in this country. This law, which made it mandatory for every community to provide and support schools, is reproduced in part here because it expresses so clearly the philosophy underlying the desire for universal free schools:

THE MASSACHUSETTS SCHOOL LAW OF 1647 [2]

The "Old Deluder" Law

Modernized Form

It being one chief project of that old deluder Satan to keep men from the knowledge of the scriptures, as in former times by keeping them in an unknown tongue, so in these latter times by persuading from the use of tongues, (that so at least the true sense and meaning of the original might be clouded by false glosses of saint-seeming de-

---

[1] Edward H. Reisner, *The Evolution of the Common School* (New York: Macmillan, 1930), pp. 296–8.

[2] Edited and distributed by Committee on Publications, Harvard University.

ceivers,)—(to the end) that learning may not be buried in the grave of our fathers in the church and commonwealth, the Lord assisting our endeavors,

IT IS THEREFORE ORDERED, that every township in this jurisdiction, after the Lord hath increased them to the number of 50 householders, shall forthwith appoint one within their town to teach all such children as shall resort to him, to write and read, (a teacher) whose wages shall be paid either by the parents or masters of such children, or by the inhabitants in general by way of supply (general tax) as the major part of those that order the prudentials (government) of the town shall appoint: provided, (that) those that send their children be not oppressed by paying much more than they can have them taught for in other towns.   AND IT IS FURTHER ORDERED, that where any town shall increase to the number of 100 families or householders, they shall set up a grammar (i.e., Latin) school, the master thereof being able to instruct youth so far as (i.e., that) they may be fitted for the university (Harvard).   Provided that, if any town neglect the performance hereof above one year, that every such town shall pay £5 to the next school till they shall perform this order.

The writings of statesmen and political leaders of colonial days are filled with references to education and the need for common schools. The following statements by Thomas Jefferson and Benjamin Franklin are cited as examples:

I think by far the most important bill in our whole code is that for the diffusion of Knowledge among the people. No other sure foundation can be devised, for the preservation of freedom and happiness.[3]

I think with you, that nothing is of more importance for the public weal, than to form and train up youth in wisdom and virtue. Wise and good men are, in my opinions, the strength of a state.[4]

b. *Compulsory education* is the *second* of these great principles. Its acceptance came later, but is now firmly fixed in the

---

[3] James Truslow Adams, *On Jeffersonian Principles* (Boston: Little, Brown, 1928), p. 122.

[4] From a letter to Samuel Johnson, first president of King's College, (Columbia); John Bigelow, *The Works of Benjamin Franklin* (New York: G. P. Putnam's Sons, 1887), p. 203.

minds of all our people. To be sure, it is necessary to use attendance officers to enforce the laws, but the principle itself is generally accepted. It is, in fact, a necessary accompaniment of the principle of state support. One point that should be noted is that this principle does not imply that children are wards of the state. The press often reports clashes between school authorities and parents who wish to educate their own children. The courts frequently have held that parents have that right. The Oregon legislature at one time passed a law requiring that all the children in the state attend the public schools, but the United States Supreme Court decided that parents have the right to determine where their child shall be educated; the state can only prescribe the minimum program.

c. *Local sovereignty in control* of education, the third principle, is at once the strength and weakness of our educational system. It is a source of strength because the school directors or trustees are the elected representatives of the people. Encroachment upon the democratic ideal is rendered more difficult by the delegation of the control of education to these local school boards. It would be difficult for any individual or group to carry on any widespread program of propaganda in our schools; the teachers, who would necessarily be the propagandizing agents, owe allegiance—and their positions—to local officials who are steeped in the provincial traditions of their respective communities. On the other hand, the local district has frequently been a stumbling block in the path of progress, particularly when efforts have been made to consolidate or enlarge districts or to equalize the burden of financial support.

Inherent weakness also resides in this system of local management when political factions, minority blocs, pressure groups, or vested interests gain control. By overt dictation of policies, by threats and intimidation, or by withholding tax support, a large industrial concern, a mining company, or other intrenched group may easily assume autocratic control over personnel and school practices.

On the whole, however, the net effect of the workings of the principle has been on the side of democracy. The American democratic ideal is inseparably interwoven with the idea of local initiative. American education is truly a product of local origin and community pride.

3. Historical Résumé of Educational Developments

a. *Elementary schools.* Districts and graded schools did not exist from the beginning; they came in due time in the process of the evolution of the educational system. In the early days a mother taught her own children, or perhaps a few of the more ambitious women took on in addition one or two neighboring children. These informal classes came to be called Dame Schools; in them the teaching was confined largely to reading and arithmetic and to religious instruction. As the population increased and the people became more widely scattered, the Dame School disappeared and the district school emerged. In the beginning, the teacher traveled from one locality to another to meet the students, a practice that gave us the term Moving Schools and brought into existence the itinerant schoolmaster, the type immortalized by Washington Irving's Ichabod Crane. The schoolmaster was usually a lowly, humble person who received very meagre pay, and a large share of that was in the form of board and lodging in the homes of his pupils. At first, the compensation was a private transaction between the teacher and the parents, but in due time the community accepted the responsibility and supported the school by means of taxes.

As the number of children increased, the schools were forced to move out of homes into the town hall or into a building built for school purposes. In these one-room structures, housing the children of all ages, we have the beginnings of the district school system. Anyone who has known the old one-teacher district school will enjoy the vividness of this description by Dr. Reisner:

It was a one-teacher school, maintained in a rude building, consistent with resources and standards of the communities which provided it. The number of pupils varied from a mere handful to a hundred or more and their ages from the beginners who were learning their

A-B-C's to the grown boys and girls who attended a short while during the winter season to brighten up their rusty literary accomplishments or to cipher their way once more through the arithmetic.[5]

As the number of children increased, they were usually provided for by organizing another district and using another hall.   Eventually, however, additional teachers were employed and we had the beginnings of the graded divisions of the schools.   City school systems consisted of a number of these district schools, but this set-up was supplanted by a unified organization with a superintendent in charge of all the schools, which were organized into grades as we know them today.   By 1860, there were twenty-four cities with superintendents.[6]   The curriculum at first aimed to teach the children only to read and write and cipher so that they could be admitted to the Latin Grammar Schools; later, geography and history were added.   By 1850 the eight-year graded elementary school was quite generally accepted as the pattern, and this pattern was followed until about 1910, when the junior high school appeared.   A pupil's progress was judged by the reader he studied, and in due time the successive grades came to be regarded as distinct units or compartments rather than as convenient designations for the successive steps in a progressive development.   That circumstance has been one of the hindrances to the development of integrating and unifying programs.

b. *Secondary education.*   The first secondary school in America was the Latin Grammar School, established in Boston in 1635.   This new school, like its predecessor in Europe, emphasized religious training and the study of Latin and Greek.   Other communities organized similar institutions, which soon became the established pattern for secondary education throughout New England.   These schools were public, in the sense of being established by law and in part supported by the people, although the greater part of their revenue was derived from fees.   They were

---

[5] Edward H. Reisner, *op. cit.,* p. 311.

[6] E. G. Dexter, *A History of Education in the United States* (New York: Macmillan, 1904), says the first were in Buffalo, New York, and Louisville, Kentucky, in 1837.

open to all who could qualify for entrance, which meant virtually
all who desired admittance.   They were not confined to any particular social class or denominational group, as were their proto-
types in Europe.   Although they made lasting contributions to
the colonial period, they were destined to be supplanted by another
type of institution more responsive to the needs of the people.

This new school, the academy, was the first departure from the
Old World pattern.   It opened its doors to girls, the first institution to do so, and liberalized its curriculum to include English,
modern history, and the developing sciences.   It continued to
prepare students for the rapidly increasing colleges and introduced
instruction in practical utilitarian subjects.   At that stage our
industries and commerce were developing and a new type of community leader was taking his place alongside the minister and
lawyer; hence, it was inevitable that a new type of school should
develop.   This new school was open to boys and girls, whether
they were preparing for college or not, and was supported in large
part by fees collected from the students.

Benjamin Franklin was a prime mover in securing popular
acceptance of the idea of the academy, publishing in 1749 some
"Proposals Relating to the Education of the Youth in Pennsylvania." [7]   His ideas concerning the curriculum were indeed
revolutionary, placing emphasis upon practical and useful knowledge:

As to their studies, it would be well if they could be taught everything that is useful, and everything that is ornamental.   But art is
long, and their time is short.   It is therefore proposed that they
learn those things that are likely to be most useful and most ornamental, regard being had to the several professions for which they
are intended.

Youth will come out of this school fitted for learning any business,
calling, or profession, except such wherein languages are required;
and, though unacquainted with any ancient or foreign tongue, they
will be masters of their own, which is of more immediate and general

---

[7] David C. Cloyd, *Benjamin Franklin and Education* (Boston: Heath, 1902),
pp. 73–85.

use, and withal will have attained many other valuable accomplishments.[8]

Largely through his efforts money was raised and the Philadelphia Public Academy, later to become the University of Pennsylvania, was established. The idea behind the new program of study
spread rapidly and met with popular approval, but because of the
text materials used and the training background of the teachers,
the academy reverted in time to the classical curriculum. The
vestiges of the academy movement may still be seen in the preparatory schools of the country. It had made its mark, however.
By 1800, according to Dexter,[9] there were 102 academies, and
they continued to increase until about 1850, when there were 6,085
academies with 12,360 teachers and 363,096 pupils. By this
time another new institution had appeared and was rapidly becoming the American secondary school.

The first public high school was the English high school,
established in Boston in 1821. This was followed by a similar
school for girls in 1826. In 1827 the Massachusetts legislature
passed a law making mandatory the public support of high schools
in every district having 500 families. This conception of a state-
supported school system to include the high school spread
throughout the country only after many bitter struggles. In
1872 the Supreme Court of Michigan handed down a decision on
the famous Kalamazoo case, which was followed by many similar
decisions in other states, removing any question of doubt about
the right of the community to tax itself to support public high
schools.

United States Commissioner of Education William T. Harris
quoted the attitude of many taxpayers of that day:

It is doubtful if the constitution permits the education of the people
in free high schools. District schools are all right but our forefathers

---

8 From "Sketch of an English School," in Jared Sparks, *Works of Benjamin
Franklin* (Boston: Whittemore, 1856), Vol. II, pp. 125–32.
9 E. G. Dexter, *op. cit.*

TABLE 14

Chronology of Significant Events in Development
of American Schools

Elementary	Secondary	Higher
1642–Massachusetts law requiring teaching of reading	1635–Boston Latin School	1636–Harvard University
1647–Massachusetts law requiring communities to support schools	1751–Franklin Academy in Philadelphia	1693–William and Mary College, Williamsburg, Virginia
1837–Horace Mann Secretary Mass. State Board of Education	1821–English High School, Boston (boys)	1785–University of Georgia, first state university
1852–Compulsory Education law in Massachusetts	1826–High School for Girls, Boston	1833–Coeducational college at Oberlin
1873–Public Kindergarten in St. Louis.	1856–Coeducational High School in Chicago	1836–Mt. Holyoke College, first women's college
1896–Experimental School at University of Chicago, beginning of Progressive movement	1872–Kalamazoo Decision. Upheld taxation for High School	1839–State normal school, Lexington, Mass.
	1884–Manual Training High School in Baltimore	1862–Land Grant Colleges established
	1896 – Departmentalized 7th and 8th grades, Richmond, Ind.	1868–Hampton Institute, first higher education for Negroes
	1910–Junior High School, Berkeley, Calif.; Columbus, Ohio	1902–Public Junior College, Joliet, Illinois

never intended to furnish a liberal education to all the children at the expense of the taxpayer.[10]

In the same article he indicated the increase in public high schools as shown below:

1860............	40 high schools	
1870............	160 "	"
1880............	800 "	"
1890............2,526	"	"
1900............6,005	"	"

[10] William T. Harris, "Growth of Public High School in the U.S.," *NEA Proceedings*, 1901, p. 174.

After the Civil War the new schools increased rapidly, although until about 1890 they attracted only the same type of student and in about the same proportions as had their predecessors, the academies. The period following 1890 is generally referred to as the period of reorganization, during which we have already seen the development of the junior high school and the rapidly expanding curriculum and enriched program of the extended secondary school. Throughout its history secondary education aimed primarily to prepare for college. That this country did not develop a dual system with separate types of schools for different classes, particularly since such separate schools were really implied in the Massachusetts law of 1827, is undoubtedly explained by the persistence of the first of the three ideals discussed earlier, namely, equality of opportunity.

Historical and traditional influences are frequently reactionary and obstructive, but they may also serve as anchors or conservers of a tradition or ideal, the persistence of which is essential if the goals of a people are to be realized. Study of Table 14 should assist the student to develop a time sense with respect to these matters of historical significance in education.

B.   Philosophical Influences

1.   Conflicting Tendencies in American Education

During the past thirty to forty years American schools and, in greater or less degree, those or other lands, have undergone far-reaching changes. The changes have resulted from two influences that are always more or less in conflict. The first of these might be called the philosophical or theoretical influence; the second is generally referred to as the scientific movement in education. The former is progressive and forward-looking, stressing the growth of the child and the development of personality, with great emphasis upon intangible values; the latter, although not denying these aims, places chief emphasis upon measurable results, which by the very nature of things are dependent upon subject matter of a factual nature. A good illustration of this contrast is found in the social studies, where the aims of instruction are shifting toward the development of attitudes and points of view, but the method of instruction continues to employ objective tests, scientific measures that gauge chiefly factual knowledge. Philosophy speaks in terms of aims; science in terms of results. When studied from this point of view it may be seen that the two influences are not always in conflict. It might be better to say that they are complementary, in that science checks and tests philosophy. In the parallel columns below an attempt is made to show these contrasting points of view, after which each type of influence is studied in detail.

Philosophy	*Science*
1. Emphasizes aims and purposes.	1. Stresses results and achievements.
2. Suggests what to teach.	2. Tells how to teach.
3. Proposes theories and hypotheses.	3. Tests theories and hypotheses.
4. Reaches conclusions by reasoning.	4. States results of experimentation.
5. States claims and arguments.	5. Presents evidence.

2.   John Dewey (1859–   ) and the Progressive Movement

Our foremost educational philosopher for four decades has been John Dewey, now Professor Emeritus of Philosophy at Columbia University. Educated as a psychologist (Ph.D., Johns Hopkins, 1884) he went to the University of Chicago when the Herbartian Movement was at its height and there he established the first experimental school in America. He sensed the dangers and weaknesses in the formalized procedures current in that day and began experimenting with the liberal, socializing tendencies that were the beginnings of the Progressive Education movement in this country. The John Dewey philosophy embodies the teachings of Rousseau, the practices of Pestalozzi, the social emphasis of Froebel, the findings of G. Stanley Hall and others engaged in the child study movement, and the pragmatism of William James. To this social, natural child-development concept he added an exceedingly valuable corollary, namely, that the school is responsible for seeing that the pupil receives his education through participation as a useful contributing member of society. This principle has been called by some writers [11] the social-civic-usefulness concept. It might more appropriately be referred to as the democratic ideal for education. John Dewey has long been the undoubted spokesman for the democratic tradition. Brief quotations from two of the earlier and more detailed treatments of his point of view show clearly his stand on the question of the school's responsibility in civic life:

From the standpoint of the child, the great waste in the school comes from his inability to utilize the experience he gets outside the school in any complete and free way within the school itself; while, on the other hand, he is unable to apply in daily life what he is learning at school. That is the isolation of the school—its isolation from life. When the child gets into the schoolroom he has to put out of his mind a large part of the ideas, interests and activities that predominate in his home and neighborhood. So the school, being unable to utilize this everyday experience, sets painfully to work, on another tack and by a variety of means, to arouse in the child an interest in school studies.[12]

The development within the young of the attitudes and dispositions necessary to the continuous and progressive life of a society cannot take place by direct conveyance of beliefs, emotions, and knowledge. It takes place through the intermediary of the environment. The social environment consists of all the activities of fellow beings that are bound up in the carrying on of the activities of any one of its members. It is truly educative in its effect in the degree in which an individual shares or participates in some conjoint activity.[13]

It is impossible, of course, to reduce so comprehensive a philosophy to a few summarizing statements. A brief statement, however, of a few of the tenets of the Dewey philosophy may be of

11 J. S. Butterweck and J. C. Seegers, *An Orientation Course in Education.* (Boston: Houghton Mifflin, 1933), p. 70.

12 John Dewey, *Democracy and Education* (New York: Macmillan, 1916), p. 26.

13 John Dewey, *The School and Society* (Chicago: University of Chicago Press, 1900), p. 67.

value to the beginning student. One of the best summaries has been prepared by Frazier and Armentrout, extracts from which are presented below:

a. *Education is life.* It is more than a preparation for life; it is a continuous process from the beginning to the end of life, both in and out of school.

b. *Education is growth.* When a child grows from what he is one day into what he is the next day, the great process of education is taking place. As long as growth continues, education is going on. Growth that begins in school and continues throughout life is the great goal of modern education.

c. *Education is a continuous reconstruction of experience.* The activities of each day are based on past experience. Every day of a child's life is conditioned upon previous days. However, if education is growth, some new element is added. When the new experience is added to the old, it is all reorganized in the light of new experiences. This forms a new basis for experiences to come later.

d. *Education is a social process.* Education in America must be education for a democracy. If education is life and growth, then it must be life within a social group. Schools must be democratic communities wherein children live natural, democratic lives with their companions and grow into adulthood with good citizenship a part of their experience.[14]

Another statement of this philosophy in miniature—a masterly educational classic—is *My Pedagogic Creed*, written by John Dewey in 1897. Excerpts from this credo are included here so that the student may obtain in the great philosopher's own words the essence of his hopes and aspirations for the schools:

Article I—*What Education Is*
    I believe that:
        . . . all education proceeds by the participation of the individual in the social consciousness of the race.
        . . . the only true education comes through the stimulation of the child's powers by the demands of the social situations in which he finds himself.
        . . . this educational process has two sides—one psychological and

---

[14] G. W. Frazier and W. D. Armentrout, *An Introduction to Education,* Rev. ed. (New York: Scott, Foresman, 1927), Chapter 2.

one sociological—and that neither can be subordinated to the other, or neglected, without evil results following. Of these two sides, the psychological is the basis. The child's own instincts and powers furnish the material and give the starting-point for all education.

. . . knowledge of social conditions, of the present state of civilization, is necessary in order properly to interpret the child's powers. The child has his own instincts and tendencies, but we do not know what these mean until we can translate them into their social equivalents.

Article II—*What the School Is*
I believe that:

. . . the school is primarily a social institution.

. . . education, therefore, is a process of living and not a preparation for future living.

. . . the school must represent present life—life as real and vital to the child as that which he carries on in the home, in the neighborhood, or on the playground.

. . . under existing conditions far too much of the stimulus and control proceeds from the teacher, because of neglect of the idea of the school as a form of social life.

. . . the discipline of the school should proceed from the life of the school as a whole and not directly from the teacher.

Article III—*The Subject-Matter of Education*
I believe that:

. . . the social life of the child is the basis of concentration, or correlation, in all his training or growth.

. . . we violate the child's nature and render difficult the best ethical results by introducing the child too abruptly to a number of special studies, of reading, writing, geography, etc., out of relation to his social life.

. . . the true center of correlation on the school subjects is not science, nor literature, nor history, nor geography, but the child's own social activities.

. . . the only way to make the child conscious of his social heritage is to enable him to perform those fundamental types of activity which make civilization what it is.

Article IV—*The Nature of the Method*
I believe that:

. . . the question of method is ultimately reducible to the ques-

tion of the order or development of the child's powers and interests.

. . . the active side precedes the passive in the development of
the child-nature; that expression comes before conscious impression.

. . . interests are the signs and symptoms of growing power.

Article V—*The School and Social Progress*
I believe that:

. . . education is the fundamental method of social progress and
reform.

. . . all reforms which rest simply upon the enactment of law,
or the threatening of certain penalties, or upon changes in mechanical or outward arrangements, are transitory and futile.

. . . the teacher is engaged, not simply in the training of individuals, but in the formation of the proper social life.[15]

3. Other Contemporary Educational Philosophers

a. *William H. Kilpatrick* (1871–   ), Professor Emeritus of
Education in Teachers College, Columbia University, is best known
as an interpreter of the Dewey philosophy.   Through his writings
and classroom teaching he has helped countless students to a
better understanding of the liberal tendencies in education.   Few
teachers in America have ever directly influenced so large a number of students.   In summer sessions he has regularly taught
two classes numbering over five hundred students each.   No matter how large the group, he employed only to a limited extent the
overworked lecture method, depending rather upon participation
by the students in the class discussion.   He conducted his classes
so as to require "activity leading to further activity" on the part
of the students.   In one of his books [16] he employed a conversa-
tional style reminiscent of the method for which Socrates was
noted.   Dr. Kilpatrick was one of the early advocates of the
project method, the immediate ancestor of the activity curriculum.
His concise description of this procedure, "a purposeful activity
carried to completion in a natural setting," has served students

---

[15] John Dewey, *My Pedagogic Creed,* reproduced in *NEA Journal,* December, 1929, and January, 1935.

[16] W. H. Kilpatrick, *Foundations of Method* (New York: Macmillan, 1925).

and teachers as a criterion for judging worth-while, lifelike school situations. His *Source Book* [17] is an exceedingly valuable reference for students of philosophy.

In an article in the *NEA Journal*, Dr. Kilpatrick has outlined "The Case for Progressivism In Education":

The title of this article is the editor's. The writer himself questions whether labels as applied to a living and growing outlook may not do more harm than good. Still, for certain purposes, a name is desirable. In what follows the writer tries to state his own position in a way to seem fair and true to that growing number who approve the same general outlook.

1. The center and nub of what is here advocated is that we start with the child as a growing and developing person, and help him live and grow best; live now as a child, live richly, live well; and thus living, to increase his effective participation in surrounding social life so as to grow steadily into an ever more adequate member of the social whole.

2. The second main point has to do with two types of learning, differing so much in degree as to amount to a difference in kind. In one the learner faces a situation of his own, such that he himself feels inwardly called upon to face it; his own interests are inherently at stake. And his response thereto is also his own.

With the other kind of learning, the situation is set by the school in examination or recitation demands. This accordingly seems to the typical learner as more or less artificial and arbitrary; it does not arise out of his own felt needs.

3. Each learner should grow up to be a worthy member of the social whole. Thus to grow up means to enter more fully and responsibly into the society of which one is a member and in so doing to acquire ever more adequately the culture in terms of which the group lives.

4. The world in which we live is changing at so rapid a rate that past-founded knowledge no longer suffices. Intelligent thinking and not mere habit must henceforth rule. Youth must learn better to think for themselves. They must understand the why of our institutions, of our system of legal rights, of moral right and wrong—because only then can they use these essential things adequately or change them intelligently.

---

[17] W. H. Kilpatrick, *Source Book in the Philosophy of Education* (New York: Macmillan, 1934).

5. The curriculum, where pupil and teacher meet, is of necessity the vital focus of all educational theory.

The older curriculum was made in advance and given to the teacher who in turn assigned it as lessons to the pupils. It was a bookish content divided into separate subjects, in result remote from life. The pupils in their turn "learned" the lessons thus assigned and gave them back to the teacher in recitation or examination, the test being (in the main) whether what was given back was the same as what had been given out.

The newer curriculum here advocated is first of all actual living— built jointly by pupils and teacher, the teacher remaining in charge, but the pupils doing as much as they can. For these learn by their thinking and their decisions.[18]

b. *Boyd H. Bode* (1873–   ), until 1945 Professor of Principles and Practice in the School of Education at Ohio State University, is much in demand as a lecturer at educational conventions because of his clear, practical, witty enunciation of fundamental philosophical principles as they apply to current problems. His is an eclectic approach. He is not the originator of a new theory of education, nor is he an adherent of any particular brand or species of social philosophy. His expositions are critical, evaluative, interpretive treatments of contemporary issues, with discussion centered on practical problems. A quotation from one of his books on the limitations of the project method furnishes a good illustration:

This is no objection to the project method, unless we apply it too widely. If we do so, we find that our practicality overreaches itself. Learning that is limited to this method is too discontinuous, too random and haphazard, too immediate in its function, unless we supplement it with something else. Perhaps children may learn a great deal about numbers from running a play store or bank, but this alone does not give them the insight into mathematics that they need to have. They may learn a great mass of historical facts from staging a play, but this is not a substitute for a systematic study of history.[19]

18 W. H. Kilpatrick, "The Case for Progressivism in Education," *NEA Journal,* 30: 231–2, November, 1941.
19 Boyd H. Bode, *Modern Educational Theories* (New York: Macmillan, 1927), p. 150.

c. *Herman Harrell Horne* (1874–1946), until his death Professor of the History and Philosophy of Education at New York University, was another great teacher of philosophy, another interpreter. In 1932 he published a book in which his chief aim was to paraphrase and clarify Dewey's *Democracy and Education.* The background for the treatise and his negotiations to secure Dr. Dewey's permission provide an interesting story in the preface:

> For years we have used Dewey's *Democracy and Education* as a text in the philosophy of education because of its importance and influence. . . . The instructor has had certain views of his own to express that differed notably from those in the text. Consequently a twofold need has arisen for this work: to understand Dr. Dewey more readily, and to estimate his views more discriminately.[20]

The treatment is unique. The typical sequence is identical with Dewey, Professor Horne first stating the Dewey position, as an "exposition," then expressing his own, frequently contrasting, view as "comments." Thus, we see him at his best. If Kilpatrick is called the interpreter of Dewey, then we should designate Horne a critic—albeit a friendly one. Like Bode, he values, judges, and questions, as in the following excerpt from his statement of Interest and Discipline:

> Again concerning subject matter, it is a little difficult to appreciate the objections to separate branches of study in view of the increasing specialization of our day and the impossibility of any encyclopedic mind knowing even the rudiments of all learning, of having knowledge classified. Nor is it clear why the demand for the functional acquisition of knowledge should lead to the elimination of separate branches of knowledge.[21]

4. William C. Bagley (1874–1946) and the Essentialists

William C. Bagley, at the time of his death Professor Emeritus of Education at Teachers College, Columbia University, is included

---

[20] H. Harrell Horne, *The Democratic Philosophy of Education* (New York: Macmillan, 1932), p. viii.

[21] *Ibid.*, p. 173.

in this discussion, not because he was a member of the group of educational philosophers, but because he was not. He was the severest critic of the liberal philosophers. Before his retirement he was head of the department of Teachers College and Normal School Education, having assumed that position after many years as Dean of the School of Education at the University of Illinois. He was the acknowledged leader of the conservatives.

In 1938 a group of educational leaders organized a society called "The Essentialists in Education." It was natural that Dr. Bagley should be acclaimed their leader, inasmuch as they were the avowed spokesmen of the opposition to the liberal preachments and practices of the Progressives. The platform of the Essentialists was quite adequately summarized in an article by Dr. Bagley, "The Case for Essentialism in Education":

a. Effort against Interest. Progressives have given the primary emphasis to interest, and have maintained that interest in solving a problem or in realizing a purpose generates effort. The Essentialists would recognize clearly enough the motivating force of interest, but would maintain that many interests, and practically all the higher and more nearly permanent interests, grow out of efforts to learn that are not at the outset interesting or appealing in themselves.

b. Teacher against Learner Initiative. Progressive theory tends to regard teacher-initiative as at best a necessary evil. The Essentialist holds that adult responsibility for guidance and direction of the immature is inherent in human nature—that it is, indeed, the real meaning of the prolonged period of necessary dependence upon the part of the human offspring for adult care and support.

c. Race against Individual Experience. It is this plastic period of necessary dependence that has furnished the opportunities for inducting each generation into its heritage of culture. The cultures of primitive peoples are relatively simple and can be transmitted by imitation or by coming-of-age ceremonies. More highly organized systems of education, however, become necessary with the development of more complicated cultures.

d. Subjects against Activities. The Essentialists have always emphasized the prime significance of race-experience and especially of organized experience or culture—in common parlance, subject matter. They have recognized, of course, the importance of individual or personal experience as an indispensable basis for interpreting organized race-experience, but the former is a means to an end rather than an educational end in itself.

e. Logical against Psychological Organization. The Essentialists recognize, too, that the organization of experience in the form of subjects involves the use of large-scale concepts and meanings, and that a certain proportion of the members of each generation are unable to master these abstract concepts. The tendency throughout the long history of Progressivism, however, has been to discredit formal, organized, and abstract learnings in toto, thus in effect throwing the baby out with the bath, and in effect discouraging even competent learners from attempting studies that are "exact and exacting." [22]

Virtually all of Dr. Bagley's public utterances were warnings and protests against tendencies that "weaken the fiber of education." He contended that education "needs a tincture of iron," a plea for disciplinary values to be discussed later. His position is clearly stated in an article, quoted in part as follows:

I am not personally concerned with the practicability of our dominant American educational thory, but I do challenge its validity as a theory on the following grounds:

(1) Its tenets regarding child-freedom are inconsistent with the plain biological implications of the greatly extended period of human immaturity which has clearly been a fundamental factor in human evolution and which derives its significance from the inescapable need of the human offspring for responsible support, control, direction, training, discipline and instruction on the part of the adult. To assume that children can grow normally without having this need met is to assume that natural laws can be transcended at the bequest of human doctrinaires. Normal children crave direction and control.

(2) The tenets of the theory imply that freedom is a gift. In the history of the race, true freedom—whether freedom from personal thralldom or freedom from fear, fraud, want, superstition and error— true freedom has never been a gift but always a conquest. In one way or another each generation must make this conquest for itself if it would be truly free.

(3) The tenets of the theory obviously lack virility. I do not mean that they are feminine; I mean rather that they are effeminate. They are weak in their very nature and enfeebling in their influence.

---

[22] Bagley, W. C., "The Case for Essentialism in Education," *NEA Journal*, 30:201–2, October, 1941.

Today the progressives are shocked to look out on American society well-nigh wrecked on the rocks of individualism. But do they look back on their own teachings over the past two decades? Twenty years ago it was I who was declaiming against the evils of an excessive individualism. Just twenty years ago in addressing this department at the Philadelphia meeting I warned you of the dangers in an educational theory that even then threatened to compound rather than correct these evils—a theory that even then, as I have proved by duly documented evidence, was softening the fiber of American education. I have repeated the warning at intervals ever since. I have been both pitied by my friends and condemned by my enemies for persisting in this attitude, and whatever professional reputation I may once have had dwindled with every reference that I made to this problem. But even though my profession may persist in the pleasant pastime of chasing butterflies, I still maintain that I would rather be right than Progressive.[23]

This is not to say that Dr. Bagley was out of date, nor that the procession passed him by. He insisted that educators test the new theories before applying them, and that they look ahead to the consequences. He contended, and rightly so, that there is a place for the conservative in education. On the constructive side, he was consistent and steadfast in insisting that education must be used to perpetuate democracy. Many years ago he formulated a clear-cut exposition [24] of education, its aims and functions. More recently he directed his energies toward problems of teacher preparation and some of the social problems facing the schools. He is generally credited with the term "professionalized subject matter," which expresses the idea that methods and subject matter should be integrated in the preparation of teachers, not isolated as they have been in the past. Subjects should be studied in situations where effective teaching will be emphasized. His interest in social questions found expression in *Education, Crime and Social Progress*, which we quote briefly:

As I see it, public education today is between two fires. On one side, it is tempted by the soft sentimentalism of the extreme Freedom

---

[23] W. C. Bagley, "Modern Educational Theories and Practical Considerations," *School and Society*, 37:409–14, April 1, 1933.

[24] W. C. Bagley, *The Educative Process* (New York: Macmillan, 1905).

theory; on the other side, it is assailed by the hard materialism which stigmatizes the budgets for public education as "sanctified squander."

From between these opposing pressures of soft sentimentalism and hard materialism, we can climb to a new plane—the plane of a virile, practical, and dynamic idealism. Sixteen years ago I warned the Department of Superintendence that we could not build our democratic structure on the shifting sands of soft pedagogy. That statement still holds. There must be iron in the blood of education and lime in the bone. The only freedom that is thinkable today is disciplined freedom. In the individual as in the race, true freedom is always a conquest, never a gift.[25]

5. Contrasts Between Progressives and Conservatives

In beginning this discussion we pointed out the conflict between philosophy and science. It should also be profitable to summarize the contrasting positions of the Progressives and the Conservatives. With a warning against the dangers of oversimplification and the risks of broad generalizations, the student's attention is directed to the following contrasting pairs in parallel columns. No one school embodies all the characteristics of either type; these are extreme positions. The Conservatives are fearful of the effects of those tendencies in the left column; the Progressives are convinced that those on the right are a hindrance to progress.

Progressive or Liberal Point of View	Conservative or Traditional Point of View
1. Education is life.	1. Education is preparation for life.
2. Pupils' present need.	2. Adult goals.
3. Immediate pupil interests.	3. Ultimate needs.
4. Freedom.	4. Discipline.
5. Pupil initiative.	5. Teacher domination.
6. Individual emphasis.	6. Mass instruction.
7. Results.	7. The process.
8. Freedom is a gift.	8. Freedom is a conquest.
9. Interest leads to effort.	9. Effort produces interest.
10. Expression.	10. Repression.
11. Pupil growth.	

---

[25] W. C. Bagley, *Education, Crime and Social Progress* (New York: Macmillan, 1931), pp. 38–39.

Progressive or Liberal *Point of View*	*Conservative or Traditional* *Point of View*

(*Continued*)

12. Experience.	11. Subject matter.
13. Psychological.	12. Knowledge.
14. Active and alert.	13. Logical.
15. Pupil activity.	14. Quiet and orderly.
16. Extensive reading.	15. Acquiring knowledge.
17. Moveable furniture; more flexible arrangement.	16. Intensive study.
	17. Fixed desks; more orderly arrangement.
18. Pupil participation.	18. Teacher control.
19. Integration of subject matter.	19. Departmentalized subject matter.
20. Intrinsic values.	
21. Group activities.	20. Extrinsic values.
22. Play while you work.	21. Individual recitation.
23. Creative activities.	22. Work; then play.
	23. Formal drill.

6.   Other Educational Theories, Now Generally Discredited

We have seen, thus far, that the issue is pretty clearly drawn between the Progressives, who are strong believers in the social-civic-usefulness concept of John Dewey, and the traditionalists, who adhere to one or more of the theories that have held sway in former times.   We shall examine some of these theories.

a. *"Knowledge is power" concept.*   With the revival of learning during the Renaissance the liberating power of knowledge was felt. As man acquired knowledge through the invention of printing, he also gained freedom and independence.   This development led to the erroneous belief that acquiring knowledge was sufficient as an aim.   It is, indeed, a necessary intermediate step forward, but it is not adequate as an ultimate goal.   James Madison expressed this belief thus: "Knowledge will forever govern ignorance; and a people who mean to be their own governors must arm themselves with the power which knowledge gives." [26]

---

[26] James Madison, in J. C. Butterweck and J. C. Seegers, *An Orientation Course in Education* (Boston: Houghton Mifflin, 1933), p. 83.   Quoted by permission.

b. *Education is "preparation."* Our early Latin Grammar
Schools were established to prepare boys for Harvard, and soon
elementary schools were organized to prepare for the secondary
schools. Each school thought of its task as one of preparation
for the next and all of them were preparations for something to
come later. The chief weakness of this concept lies in its emphasis
upon remote values and ultimate goals. Children live in the
present and need to see immediate values. Dr. Horne expresses
it this way:

Education does prepare for the future but it is not preparation for
the future. Being a child does prepare for being a man, but the purpose of childhood is a rich childhood and not a preparation for manhood.[27]

c. *Formal discipline.* The disciplinary conception of education has been the dominant philosophy for many generations, and
many of the practices still found in the schools are traceable to
this influence. As a theory it was closely linked with a belief in
what was called a "faculty psychology," which taught that the
mind consisted of many separate faculties, such as reasoning, judgment, imagination, memory, and the like, which could be trained
by exercise. Latin and mathematics were stressed so much because they afforded such fine opportunities for training the mind.
Mental discipline was the chief argument for requiring many subjects, "mental arithmetic," for example. (What other kind of
arithmetic could there be?) This concept was gradually replaced
as the findings of psychological research became known among
school people. John Locke, an English philosopher, gave classic
expression to this belief that persisted for so long, until experi-
mentalists like Herbart and Thorndike tested its validity scientifically. The disciplinarians held that the more difficult and distasteful a task, the better the learning situation that is created.
Learning could come only as a result of great effort and through
a painful process. It was John Dewey's participation in this

---

[27] H. Harrell Horne, *op. cit.,* p. 57.

"Interest versus Effort"[28] controversy that brought him into prominence as an educational leader and laid the foundation for the "interest" approach to learning of the Progressives.

d. *Education as recapitulation.* An interesting and speculative theory that drew many adherents for a time was formulated by G. Stanley Hall. It was known as the culture-epoch or recapitulation theory, and held that a child lives over the history of the race, developing gradually as man is thought to have evolved from lower forms and as the race has progressed from one level to another. The education of a child was supposed to consist of activities that matched the successive stages of man's development. There is some plausibility in the theory, but it is mentioned here in passing chiefly because it calls attention to the child-study movement, which marked an important change in the attitude toward children and their place in society.

e. *Herbartian concept.* The earlier theories were based on the assumption that education was a pouring-in process; that it was a matter of acquisition of knowledge. The "back to nature" emphasis of Rousseau directed attention to child nature. The experimental attitude and object teaching of Pestalozzi pointed in the direction of first-hand learning through pupil activity. Herbart integrated these ideas into a systematized organization of the teaching process, and thus provided us with a highly formalized—almost ritualized—classroom procedure. This concept prevailed for two or three generations and provided an important transition step from the humanistic and disciplinary theories to the interest concepts of the Dewey era, on one hand, and the scientific study, on the other. It was the basis for the scientific movement that has made such valuable contributions since 1900. This theory conceived the learning process as dependent upon the nature of the learner and as taking place in accordance with natural laws. Like many other good ideas it was overworked at first, resulting in formalized and stereotyped routine activities in schools. The five formal steps of recitation—Preparation, Pre-

---

28 John Dewey, *Interest and Effort in Education* (Boston: Houghton Mifflin, 1913).

sentation, Comparison, Generalization, and Application—served as the basis for all pedagogical instruction for a generation or more. The concept came to the front at a time when it was sorely needed, only to be replaced in time by the liberalism of Dewey and the scientific approach of Thorndike.

7. Earlier Exponents of Educational Philosophies

Our current educational theories, if traced back to their sources, will bring the student into contact with several national and international figures, known for their contribution to educational thought. A glance at their records will assist the student in experiencing a better orientation in philosophy.

a. *Jean Jacques Rousseau* (1712–1778) heads the list, not only because his views form the basis of modern education, but also because he was one of the foremost political thinkers of his time. His educational classic, *Emile* (1762), stated so clearly and forcibly his conception of the education of youth that all educational practices, particularly in France and the United States, have felt his influence. Likewise, his *Social Contract* helped to crystallize these hopes and aspirations of the rising proletariat that culminated eventually in the French Revolution. The principal tenets in his philosophy were expression and freedom, and his teachings did much to shift the emphasis in education from subject matter to the child. He was an impractical man, constantly in revolt against the social evils of his day and frequently in difficulties with political or religous leaders because of his revolutionary ideas.

b. *Johann Heinrich Pestalozzi* (1746–1827). If Pestalozzi's influence was less widespread than Rousseau's in the social struggle of his day, it was more specific and immediate in the realm of education. Unlike Rousseau, he was a great teacher. Visitors came from afar to observe his classes. His *Leonard and Gertrude* is an accurate description of his own teaching practices. Coming to manhood about the time Rousseau passed from the scene, he carried on in the same tradition, making a distinct contribution in the introduction of elementary science and home geography, and in the development of a systematized technique of teaching. He advocated letting children discover by doing, and insisted that discipline proceeds from within and is not imposed from without. In a sense, he is the father of our teacher-training program, inasmuch as he was one of the first to advocate specific training for teachers. His ideas on this question gained a foothold in this country through the efforts of Edward A. Sheldon at the Normal School in Oswego, New York. The "Oswego Movement" became a far-reaching influence throughout the United States, as normal schools were established with training schools in which young teachers were to become stamped with the formal Pestalozzian pattern. In this system the teacher, through questioning and control of pupil discussion, completely dominated the classroom, and as this became the pattern for elementary teachers to follow, it is easy to see how formalism and routine practices became so deeply rooted in our educational procedures.

    c. *Johann Friedrich Herbart* (1776–1841). One of the many visitors to Pestalozzi's classes was Johann Friedrich Herbart, a young German scholar and teacher of philosophy. He is frequently referred to as the father of educational psychology because of his analysis of the learning process, the psychological concept, which was discussed in a previous topic. He was a gifted and original thinker who influenced many people of his day. Many American educators came under the spell of his influence through European study and returned to this country to popularize his ideas. Among them were Charles De Garmo and Charles and Frank McMurry, who were instrumental in organizing, in 1895, the Herbartian Society, since renamed the National Society for the Study of Education, which annually publishes a yearbook [29] bringing up to date the literature on some current educational topic.

    d. *Friedrich Wilhelm Froebel* (1782–1852). One of the most stimulating and invigorating influences to come into our schools

---

[29] National Society for the Study of Education, *Forty-fourth Yearbook,* "American Education in the Post-War Period" (Chicago: University of Chicago Press, 1945).

was the kindergarten movement, the brain child of Froebel, another
young German teacher who got his inspiration from an extended
visit with Herbart.   The success of the movement did much to
lessen the emphasis upon book learning and formal drill, inasmuch
as the movement stressed the play activities of children, with much
attention to their social development.   Music and drawing and
other creative activities have a large part in the program.   Froebel's ideals were none too favorably received by the Prussian government, the opportunities for free development of children being
thought inimical to the national program of child training, which
was based on the belief that children existed for the welfare of the
state.   The kindergarten was accordingly banned for a period of
ten years.   German emigrants, fleeing the reactionary political
tendencies in Prussia following the revolution in 1848, introduced
the kindergarten idea into America.   Uncounted millions of children owe a debt of gratitude to Froebel for the happy, healthy
wholesome surroundings in present day elementary school classrooms.   The spirit of the kindergarten is gradually, but all too
slowly, creeping upward into the other grades of the school.

And now we come to the names of four men whose lives were
devoted to the cause of education in this country; men who stand
out as mountain peaks among their contemporaries:

e. *Horace Mann* (1796–1859).   No figure in American history
contributed more to the cause of state-supported public schools
than did Horace Mann.   Although educated as a lawyer and
admitted to the bar, he early saw the necessity of furthering the
interests of democracy by means of a thoroughgoing educational
system.   His contributions took two forms.   First, he stressed
the extreme importance of adequate preparation for teachers.   He
became impressed with the system of normal schools in France, and
it was through his efforts that the first state normal school in the
United States was established at Lexington, Massachusetts, in
1839.   It was his idea that the elementary schools were the guar-
dians of the democratic ideal and that the training of the teachers
should be provided at state expense.   The teachers were to be recruited from all classes, economic or social status not being per-

mitted to operate as selective factors. This idea spread rapidly
to virtually every state in the Union. When it is recalled that the
public high school did not appear in most communities for several
decades, and that when it did it was largely dominated by the college, it is easy to understand how the tradition of preparing elementary teachers in normal schools and secondary school teachers
in colleges developed. As the normal schools changed to teachers'
colleges in recent years, this distinction has become less and less
significant.

Horace Mann's second, but not less important, contribution was
to provide a healthful environment for the growth of the seed that
was planted in New England a hundred years earlier, namely, a
free, compulsory public school system. He saw ahead with clear
vision and organized and built accordingly. We have not yet
caught up in practice with many of his progressive theories. As a
member of the Massachusetts Legislature, he worked diligently for
the passage of a law providing for a State Board of Education.
He later became its first secretary, continuing in this office for
twelve years, during which time he became so much interested in the
cause of education that he never returned to the practice of law.
In 1853 he established and became the first president of Antioch
College, Yellow Springs, Ohio, an institution unique today for its
coöperative integration of cultural and vocational training.

f. *Henry Barnard* (1811–1900). A contemporary of Horace
Mann who served first as secretary of the State Board of Education in Connecticut and later as State Commissioner of Education
in Rhode Island was Henry Barnard, another monumental figure
of the nineteenth century. Like Horace Mann, he prepared for
a career in law, assisted in the establishment of a normal school—
the one at New Britain, Connecticut—, and sought to raise the
level of effectiveness of the state school systems in the two states
that employed his leadership. In 1867 he became the first United
States Commissioner of Education, establishing the policy that still
persists of collecting and disseminating information about schools
and educational problems. He traveled widely, early became a
believer in the ideas of Pestalozzi and Froebel, and was a scholar of

marked ability and a prolific writer.   He established in 1855, and continued to publish for thirty-eight years, the *American Journal of Education,* an encyclopedic account of educational progress during that period.   He was without question the outstanding educational authority of his time.

g. *Francis W. Parker* (1837–1902).   One of the early converts to the Herbartian psychology was Francis W. Parker, one of our greatest leaders in the field of educational method.   He studied in Berlin in 1872, where he encountered the Herbartian conception of the educational process.   He returned to take a prominent part in the work of the Cook County Normal School and, later, of the University of Chicago, where as a colleague of John Dewey he assisted in the organization of the famous laboratory school that served as an incubator for germs of Progressive Education.   Educators from all parts of the United States went to Chicago to study with Parker, and his institution assumed a position of great leadership and influence in teacher preparation.

h. *William T. Harris* (1835–1918).   A towering figure in education in the latter half of the nineteenth century was William T. Harris.   He is frequently called America's first educational philosopher.   He was that and considerably more.   He became associated in 1857 with the schools of St. Louis, where he came in contact with the influence of the German philosophers, Kant and Hegel.   Had he chosen to devote himself to scholarly pursuits, he might easily have become our foremost American philosopher. Instead he turned to the practical business of school administration, serving as the superintendent of schools in St. Louis from 1867 to 1880.   He was in the front rank in progressive movements, establishing the first kindergarten in a public school system in 1873.   From 1889 to 1906 he served with distinction as United States Commissioner of Education.   The Department of Superintendence of the NEA paid tribute to his life and career at the annual meeting in St. Louis in 1936.   One of the speakers appraised his career thus:

For more than thirty-five years he was universally recognized both here and in Europe as the most distinguished philosopher and educator in America.[30]

8. Conclusion

Philosophy gives order and direction to educational movements. We have traced our current theories back to earlier beginnings and found explanations of present practices.   A few brief quotations will serve to make a transition from the influence of philosophy to the place of science in education.   From W. T. Harris we have:

Philosophy needs to discover the bearing of all the conditioning circumstances on a situation.[31]
and from Bagley:

Thus, though philosophy "bakes no cakes," as the ancient proverb reminds us, its influence may still operate to render even the baking of the cakes more efficient.[32]

Kilpatrick sees philosophy improving itself through criticism, which seems to imply that science is needed to test the hypotheses of the philosophers:

It is thus not a question of philosophy or no philosophy.   Each one does have a philosophy.   The only question is whether one shall be content with a philosophy that he just happens to have or whether he will become conscious of his philosophy, take it in hand, and try to improve it.[33]

And finally, Will Durant helps us to see the need for both approaches to a problem:

Philosophy is a hypothetical interpretation of the unknown (as in metaphysics), or of the exactly known (as in ethics or political phi-

---

[30] John W. Withers, "Tribute to William Torrey Harris," *School and Society*, 43:356–60, March 14, 1936.

[31] W. T. Harris, *Psychologic Foundation of Education* (New York: Appleton, 1898), p. 387.

[32] W. C. Bagley, *The Educative Process* (New York: Macmillan, 1905), p. 163.

[33] W. H. Kilpatrick, "The Relation of Philosophy to Scientific Research," *Journal of Educational Research*, 24:110, September, 1931.

losophy) ; it is the front trench in the siege of truth.   Science is the captured territory; and behind it are those secure regions in which knowledge and art build our imperfect and marvelous world.   Philosophy seems to stand still, perplexed; but only because she leaves the fruits of victory to her daughters, the sciences, and herself passes on, divinely discontent, to the uncertain and unexplored. . . .

Science gives us knowledge, but only philosophy can give us wisdom.[34]

C.   Scientific or Psychological Influences

The scientific movement in education, like the philosophical influences, may also be traced to Rousseau and Pestalozzi, although their efforts merely laid the foundations for the experimentation that later proved significant.   The former made much of the natural responses of the child and advocated the "back to nature" movement.   Pestalozzi interpreted this expression to mean that we should study the child as the basic factor in the learning process. He also introduced the experimental procedure and object lesson into the classroom.   These activities, coupled with the emphasis upon specific training for teachers, paved the way for what later became a scientific study of education.   Herbart added to the emphasis in this direction and laid the foundation for combining the study of education and psychology.   Thus we see the beginnings of educational psychology, the first phase of the scientific influence.   The second we shall call the measurement movement. The third will be presented under the caption, The Scientific Study of Education.

1.   Educational Psychology Systematized by E. L. Thorndike (1874–   )

Standing out as John Dewey does among the educational philosophers, we find Edward L. Thorndike of Teachers College, Columbia University, topping the list today of those who approach the study of educational questions from the scientific or psychological point of view.   He was not the first to study educational

---

[34] Will Durant, *The Story of Philosophy* (New York: Simon and Schuster, 1927), p. 2.

problems experimentally, nor did he originate all the theories and hypotheses dealing with mental processes and learnings. He did, however, organize and systematize into a coherent treatment, the vast body of information that was being assembled. He fashioned a pattern for study and research that came to be called the scientific method, a method that has influenced classroom procedures and the preparation of teachers and textbooks ever since the late nineties. From then until 1913, when he published his three-volume treatise on educational psychology, he was carrying on research and investigation in the areas noted in this quotation from the preface to that monumental work:

This *first* volume, which describes man's original mental equipment —the inherited foundations of intellect, morals and skill—is the first of three, which, together, give the main facts of educational psychology. The *second* volume, on "The Psychology of Learning," treats of the laws of learning in general, the improvement of mental functions by practice and their deterioration by fatigue. The *third* volume, on "Individual Differences and Their Causes," treats the variations of individual men around the general type characteristic of man as a species, and of the influence of sex, race, immediate ancestry, maturity and training in producing these variations.[35]

These topics, together with a few others we shall mention, furnish the core for the study of educational psychology. While studying at Columbia with J. McKeen Cattell, who may be regarded as a pioneer in mental testing, Thorndike shifted his attention from puzzle boxes for animals to experiments with children. That shift marked the beginning of far-reaching studies that made Thorndike the foremost exponent of mental testing in this country. Other investigators adapted these techniques in the construction of test materials to the measurement of achievement, and so inaugurated the measurement movement, a story which we shall study in greater detail presently. These studies were closely linked with those involving individual differences, the findings of which have resulted in revolutionary changes in school practices.

---

[35] E. L. Thorndike, *Educational Psychology*, 3 vols. (New York: Teachers College, Columbia University, 1913).

Another action that produced a lasting effect upon educational practices was his attack upon the then generally accepted belief in transfer of training, one of the components in the disciplinary theory of education. His investigations furnished little support for those who believed that an individual possesses certain faculties such as reasoning, discrimination, or memory, the training of which results in automatic and inevitable transfer of those abilities to other situations. When Thorndike studied 8,564 high school students to determine the disciplinary value of school subjects, his findings also proved disturbing to those who believed in formal discipline. The results were contrary to the traditional views. Bookkeeping and science were found superior to Latin and mathematics in developing thinking power, but in all cases the transfer effect was small. Peter Sandiford has summarized these investigations admirably and quotes Thorndike as follows:

The expectation of any large difference in general improvement of the mind from one study rather than from another seems doomed to disappointment. The chief reason why good thinkers seem superficially to have been made such by having taken certain school studies, is that good thinkers have taken such studies, becoming better by the inherent tendency of the good to gain more than the poor from any study. . . . Disciplinary values may be real and deserve weight in the curriculum, but the weights should be reasonable.[36]

Thorndike's contribution brought clearly into focus the need for studying education objectively. His efforts were so rewarding that numerous other scholars were encouraged to make similar studies. As a result, the study of mental processes and learning problems was taken into the laboratory, where objective evidence supporting the theories could be secured. The contribution of Thorndike and his contemporaries might be summarized as follows: First, an analysis of the learning process and the resulting formulation of laws or principles of learning; second, the development of techniques or methods that have been adapted to all types of

---

[36] Peter Sandiford, *Educational Psychology* (New York: Longmans, Green, 1928), p. 296.

educational situations. In short, these investigations signaled
the arrival of a science of education.

2.   Earlier Contributions to a Science of Education

It would be misleading to leave the student with the notion that
this development came all at once, as though a great discovery or
invention had been made. The movement had been gaining momentum gradually. There are three other Americans whose work
should be noted:

a. *J. McKeen Cattell* (1860–1944). For a generation the dean
of American psychologists was J. McKeen Cattell. He was important not so much for his individual scientific output as for
his influence, exerted through vast and varied editorial enterprises and through the work of his students, among them Thorndike, Woodworth, Hollingworth, Kelly, and many others. Cattell, developing an interest in Darwin's theory of evolution and
in the question of individual differences, became the first person to
attempt to measure intelligence. After graduation from Lafa-
yette in 1880 he went to Leipzig to study with Wundt, the real
pioneer in experimental psychology. In 1888 he established a
laboratory at the University of Pennsylvania, leaving there for
Columbia in 1891. Here for twenty-six years he had charge of
the new laboratory he established, where many of our leading psychologists studied and received doctoral degrees under his direction. For a year Cattell was associated with Galton, from whom
he caught his enthusiasm for the study of individual differences.
Soon after this visit Cattell wrote an article on "mental tests,"
thus introducing the term. He also presented a series of physical
and mental measurements in his classes at Columbia University,
thus making the first use of psychological tests with large groups
of persons.[37]

From the time he was dismissed in 1917 for pronounced pacifist
leanings, he became a free lance, devoting himself to many editorial
enterprises related in one way or another to psychological and ed-

---

[37] Wilbur S. Hulin, *A Short History of Psychology* (New York: Henry Holt,
1934), p. 118.

ucational interests. His work on the measurement of individual differences characterizes the essential difference in point of view between American and German psychology.

b. *G. Stanley Hall* (1844–1924). Going backwards chronologically we next consider G. Stanley Hall, another one of the pioneers and the one generally credited with establishing the first psychological laboratory in America. This he did at the new Johns Hopkins University in 1881. Hall, too, had studied at Leipzig, having been the first American student to study with Wundt. While at Johns Hopkins he attracted many able students—among them John Dewey and, for a brief time, Cattell— many of whom soon made important contributions to the new science. In 1888 he accepted the presidency of the new Clark University, whose policies he established and directed. Here again he founded a laboratory and carried on research of far-reaching significance. He was a pioneer in the real sense, leaving one area for another; he was possessed of a restless mind and great intellectual curiosity. His interests moved from philosophy and religion through genetics, child study, and adolescence. He is probably best known for his *Adolescence* (1904), and, more than any other one person, he focused attention on this period in life, the interest thus aroused culminating in the junior high school movement. His dynamic nature is seen in the following quotation:

His mind was of the kind that is characterized by a succession of enthusiasms for fresh objects rather than a steady devotion to a single cause; evolution, however, remained for him a master key throughout his intellectual wanderings. He took over Galton's questionnaire method and made extensive use of it, while at another time he became much concerned with Pavlov's conditioned reflex and the psychology of food. During his thirty-six years at Clark, he gave no less than eighty-one doctorates.[38]

c. *William James* (1842–1910). The real pioneer in American psychology was William James, but his place in this connection is

---

[38] J. C. Flugel, *A Hundred Years of Psychology* (New York: Macmillan, 1933), p. 208.

probably best appreciated after one has seen what Cattell and Hall did to establish the new science. He combined with the philosophical approach the new experimentalism of Wundt. Although he had constantly to battle against ill health, and disliked work in a laboratory, his philosophical bent led him to become an important influence in the development of the new psychology. His *Talks to Teachers* (1899) has been studied by countless prospective teachers and his *Principles of Psychology* (1890) contains expositions that have withstood many verbal and experimental attacks. His contributions were made possible by his engaging personality, his lucid literary style, and his clear vision. He saw "implicitly the possibilities of the new American psychology, which has since come into being; that is to say, functional psychology, with its cousin, the mental tests, and its child, behaviorism." [39]

We have just seen that educational procedures in America have been greatly modified by psychology, as it rapidly developed as a new science in Europe. First, we imported the beliefs of Herbart. Later, the experimental influence of Wundt came in, and from it we developed a distinctly American point of view. To James at Harvard, Hall at Johns Hopkins, and Clark and Cattell at Pennsylvania and Columbia, we can trace the development of our educational psychology.

3. Contemporary Schools of Psychology

It will be in order at this point to introduce the student to the somewhat conflicting points of view held by the various so-called schools of psychology. From the comparison the student will be able to set up guideposts that will help him to get his bearings in this ever-changing flow of educational and psychological theory. We shall merely mention a few of the most pronounced and distinct groups.

a. *Structuralism.* This school is important for our study because it is the source from which American psychology evolved.

---

[39] Edwin G. Boring, *A History of Experimental Psychology* (New York: Century, 1929), p. 498.

It was concerned with knowing, feeling, and willing. Its method was introspection: analysis and classification of mental states. Knowing was analyzed into concepts, percepts, and sensations, the elementary and structural elements of thinking. Hence the name, *structuralism*. It is best understood when contrasted with the next group. Among its adherents were to be found Wundt and Titchener.

   b. *Functionalism*. James described mental life as a biological function, not as mere existence. Titchener characterized the difference in point of view thus: The basis of structuralism is an "IS," while of *functionalism*, it is an "IS FOR." Or it might be expressed as the difference between "to be" and "being." It is the functional relationship between consciousness and the environment of the individual. This was the point of view of Thorndike, Dewey, Judd, and others of the new American school. Angell expressed the conflict as a psychology of "mental operations in contrast to mental elements." To this school we can trace most of the fundamentals in educational psychology, such as the stimulus-response concept or S-R bond theory. This theory holds that learning occurs when connections are established or bonds are formed in the nervous system. A given stimulus in the environment produces a specific response.

   c. *Behaviorism*. A direct outgrowth of the functional emphasis is *behaviorism*, initiated by Max Meyer and developed and popularized by John B. Watson. It is also an outgrowth of animal psychology. It lays stress upon behavior, not the mind, as the fundamental thing. The basis of the belief is the conditioned reflex theory of Pavlov, the Russian. Behaviorism attaches greatest importance to factors in the environment, protests against the method of introspection, and minimizes the importance of instincts. Chief emphasis is placed upon mathematical and instrumental measurements. The system is attacked by its critics as being too mechanistic and materialistic. Some wag once expressed the trend toward behaviorism in facetious fashion: "Psychology first lost its soul, then its mind, then its consciousness; it has left behavior of a sort." The contribution of this group has been the emphasis upon objective study of behavior, particularly that of infants, and upon the environmental influences.

d. *Gestalt.* The newest body of beliefs to appear is the *Gestalt* psychology. *Gestalt* is a German word for which there is no exact English equivalent, but its meaning is adequately expressed by the term "configuration," the total picture or pattern. *Gestalt* psychology arose in Germany as a protest against the analytic tendency of structuralism. Its adherents oppose the S-R bond theory and the mechanistic explanations. They believe that learning comes by insight, through the integrating action of the mind. They insist that learning is more than a mere aggregation of isolated responses, of unrelated elements. Expressed paradoxically, their view is, "the whole is greater than the sum of the parts." It substitutes a unitary concept for the atomistic analysis. Most of the experimentation has been carried on with apes. Its advocates include Wertheimer, Koffka, and Köhler. This school offers a very plausible justification for the integrated programs of Progressive schools and the Activity Curricula, and it really gives promise of bringing fundamental changes into educational practices.

e. *Purposivism.* It is worthwhile, in passing, to mention another viewpoint, another protest against the mechanistic explanation of human behavior. It is called the *purposivistic* or *hormic* school, and McDougall, of Duke, was its most enthusiastic spokesman. He believes that all the other theories fail to explain sociological problems, that all human activities are motivated and controlled by inner drives or forces, and that there is something besides mere mechanism and functioning. This theory attempts to account for those impulses, for the creative urges, that drive men on to great achievements. The arguments it advances are not clear nor convincing, but they do have an appeal for those who think there is room for some spiritual, nonmaterial explanation of human behavior.

f. *Psychoanalysis.* This last school is included here chiefly because of the attention that was directed toward the importance of emotional responses and the later emphasis upon mental hy-

giene. The first to formulate the theory of psychoanalysis was
Freud; later adherents include Jung and Adler. Modern psychia-
try, an outgrowth of psychoanalysis, attempts to study personality by discovering what sort of conflicts are going on within the
individual, resulting in his possession of a divided personality.
Freud, a physician, believed that all behavior abnormalities can be
explained in terms of the thwarting of the sex impulses, which leads
to conflicts and "complexes." When first formulated, these views
were considered shocking, and the many attempts at popular treatment of the theory have greatly distorted its real implications.

4. The Measurement Movement

The second phase of the scientific influences to be presented is
generally referred to as the measurement movement. We have
already seen the beginnings of this movement in the work of Cattell
and Thorndike. We shall now trace it in more detail.

a. *Measurement of intelligence.* Cattell tested the students
entering Columbia in 1896. Thorndike continued the experimentation, publishing important findings during the following decade.
Binet, meanwhile, had been experimenting with the idea for a number of years in France. In collaboration with Simon he published
in 1905, and revised in 1908, a series of tests arranged in order of
difficulty. From the use of these tests the two were able to establish norms for each year of growth, as a result of which they
coined the expression "mental age." These tests proved to be a
great success and were translated and used in many countries.
In this country H. H. Goddard translated them and, because they
were used largely to study below-grade children, adopted them
(1911) for use in the Vineland (N. J.) institution for feeble-
minded. Lewis M. Terman,[40] of Stanford University, gave the
movement a great boost when he revised the Binet scale (Stanford
Revision, 1914) for use with normal children in the public schools.

All these were efforts to measure children as individuals, a process requiring from one to two hours. It was obvious that little

---

[40] Lewis M. Terman, *Measuring Intelligence* (Boston: Houghton Mifflin,
1937).

progress could be made in measuring the intelligence of numerous school children on that basis. Steps were taken to develop tests that could be applied to groups. This effort came to a head during World War I, when Thorndike, assisted by Terman, A. S. Otis, and many others, was assigned the task of developing techniques for finding superior men who would make good officers for the army. The Army Alpha Test was the result, the first group intelligence test. Following the War many adaptations of this work were prepared especially for school and group use. Among these the tests bearing the names of Otis [41] and Terman [42] have probably been most widely used.

In the early days the group tests were used principally with upper elementary and high school students. Later, reliable tests were devised to measure the mental abilities of primary and preschool children; among these were the Haggerty,[43] Detroit,[44] and Pintner-Cunningham [45] tests. Progress was likewise made in the construction and use of psychological tests on the college level. One test [46] attempted to provide a measure that might be used for all levels from first grade to maturity, the user choosing the appropriate combination from a battery of thirty-nine separate tests. Another interesting innovation was a so-called self-marking test,[47] which reduces the amount of clerical work necessary in handling it.

There have been many criticisms of mental tests, the chief one

[41] Arthur S. Otis, *Self-administering Test of Mental Ability* (Yonkers, N. Y.: World Book Company, 1922).

[42] Lewis M. Terman, *Group Test of Mental Ability* (Yonkers, N. Y.: World Book Company, 1920).

[43] M. E. Haggerty, *Intelligence Examination* (Yonkers, N. Y.: World Book Company, 1920).

[44] Anna M. Engel, *Detroit First Grade Intelligence Test* (Yonkers, N. Y.: World Book Company, 1921).

[45] R. Pintner and Bess V. Cunningham, *Primary Mental Test* (Yonkers, N. Y.: World Book Company, 1923).

[46] F. Kuhlman and Rose Anderson, *Intelligence Tests* (Minneapolis, Minn.: Educational Test Bureau, 1927).

[47] V. A. C. Henmon and M. J. Nelson, *Test of Mental Ability* (Boston: Houghton Mifflin, 1932).

being that they do not measure all the aspects of mental ability. That limitation is at once admitted by the test makers. Extravagant claims for the tests are made only by persons with too limited knowledge and experience. One is on safest ground in describing mental tests as instruments that measure capacity to do schoolwork, because the test items are essentially samples of learning activities employed in school. It was Thorndike's idea in the beginning that if we could measure the amount of an individual's learning, we should thus secure an indirect measure of his capacity to learn. If a given group of pupils have had approximately equal opportunities for learning (that is, in the same school for the same length of time), those who are able to perform the largest number of increasingly difficult intellectual tasks must possess the most capacity. The tests might more appropriately have been called scholastic aptitude tests. There are admitted weaknesses and errors in the testing procedure, but explaining the process in this manner goes far toward answering the critics. The net result of our attempts to measure intelligence has been clear gain, for much of the guesswork in education has been eliminated.

b. *Measurement of achievement.* The attempts to measure the results of learning parallel the mental-testing movement. One of the earliest studies in this field was made by J. M. Rice, when he applied scientific method to the measurement of results in spelling. That effort was the real beginning of the movement to supplant the traditional essay examinations by objective measures. Thorndike made valuable contributions in this field, publishing a handwriting scale in 1910. C. W. Stone developed an arithmetic test in 1908, and S. A. Courtis a series of survey tests in arithmetic for all grades in 1911.

It is becoming more and more apparent that the evaluation of essay examinations depended too largely upon the point of view, the bias, and the subjective judgment of the teacher. The new tests were so constructed that only one answer was considered correct, no matter who did the marking. The idea spread rapidly, being at first applied to the so-called common branches of the elementary school only, but later extended to all the high school sub-

jects.   In the early twenties there was a deluge of educational
tests, some of them good, but many of them poor or actually bad.
Since 1925, the tendencies have been toward the improvement of
the better tests and the elimination from the market of most of the
poorer ones, until today there is a variety of good tests available
for virtually all subjects at all levels of the school.

Attempts to measure achievement have taken two forms: first,
the construction and marketing of the standardized tests, and
second, the improvement of the informal classroom tests given by
teachers.   Good standard tests are scientifically constructed by
subject-matter specialists and tried out with large numbers of students for the purpose of establishing norms.   They are then ready
for publication and may be used for making comparisons between
individuals and among schools.   The grade classification of a new
pupil in a school may be more accurately determined by the use
of this method.   The improved classroom tests are frequently referred to as "new-type" tests, although there are many instructors,
especially those in colleges, who doubt whether they are improvements.   These new forms include completion exercises, short answer, true-false, multiple choice, and matching tests.

It should be pointed out that the prevalent use of objective tests
places greatest emphasis upon factual knowledge presented to the
student in fragmentary, unrelated bits.   Critics contend that organization of knowledge and expression of ideas are neglected by
the exclusive use of objective tests.   That charge must be admitted.   If a teacher does nothing to offset this tendency, the
emphasis will become one-sided.   Proponents of the tests, however,
insist that we should reduce to objective measurement the measurable aspects of learning; that facts are basic to knowledge and
ideas.   This view seems reasonable.   There is no denying the importance of accurate knowledge.   Best practice would undoubtedly
dictate that we use a combination of objective tests for examination
purposes and written work that provides opportunities for organization and expression.

Space does not permit the listing of several representative tests.
The reader is directed to those publications dealing specifically

with educational measurements, which furnish detailed descriptions
of the tests in different subject-matter fields.

c. *Measurement of specific aptitudes.*   One of the promising
fields of research in recent years has been the measurement of aptitudes.   Dean Carl E. Seashore, of the University of Iowa, has
developed a "Measurement of Musical Talent" [48] consisting of six
phonograph records, each of which attempts to secure a measure
of an individual's ability to discriminate pitch, rhythm, tempo,
tonal sequence, and the like.   Stenquist [49] and others [50] have developed tests of mechanical aptitude.   Similar measures have been
devised for mathematics,[51] science,[52] and other school subjects.
To this list should be added a large variety of performance tests
now in use, which may be found in the catalogues of the publishers
of test materials.   An Art Judgment Test [53] attempts to discover
the extent to which individuals can discriminate between good and
poor pictures.   Thurstone's [54] Clerical Test assists in selecting
those persons most adapted to jobs of a clerical nature.

d. *Measurement of personality traits.*   So much attention has
been given lately to personnel and guidance problems, it is only
natural that attempts should be made to measure personality
traits, vocational interest, and other factors.   The Bernreuter
Personality Inventory,[55] one of the most successful of these tests,
provides a measure of an individual's neurotic tendencies, self-
sufficiency, introversion-extroversion, and dominance-submission,
depending upon how the test is scored.   The vocational interests

---

[48] May be secured from C. H. Stoelting & Company, Chicago.

[49] J. L. Stenquist, *Mechanical Aptitude Test* (Yonkers, N. Y.: World Book
Company, 1933).

[50] Harry J. Baker and A. C. Crockett, *Detroit Mechanical Aptitude Examination* (Bloomington, Ill.: Public School Publishing Company, 1928).

[51] H. A. Greene and H. W. Bruce, *Iowa Plane Geometry Aptitude Test*
(Iowa City, Iowa: Bureau of Educational Research, 1933).

[52] D. L. Zyve, *Stanford Scientific Aptitude Test* (Stanford University, Calif.:
Stanford University Press, 1930).

[53] N. C. Meier and C. E. Seashore, *Art Judgment Test* (Iowa City, Iowa:
Bureau of Educational Research, 1929).

[54] L. L. Thurstone, *Examination in Clerical Work* (Yonkers, N. Y.: World
Book Company, 1919).

[55] R. G. Bernreuter, *The Personality Inventory* (Stanford University, Calif.:
Stanford University Press, 1931).

of either men or women may be analyzed by means of a series of
tests developed by Dr. Strong.[56] Allport and Allport [57] have
prepared a test that attempts to measure dominance and sub-
missiveness as personality traits. The Downey [58] Will-Temperament Test gives an examiner a clue to the self-confidence and
adaptability of the subject. These and many other tests of a
similar nature are being developed and used in psychological clinics
and by personnel workers to assist students in making a better adjustment to their social and occupational environment.

e. *Measurement of attitudes.* With so much emphasis being
placed upon the development of attitudes, particularly in such
subjects as the social studies, it is natural that considerable
thought should be given to the measurement of attitudes. It seems
logical that if we expect to develop attitudes, we should include
that aim in our stated objective of a course. Furthermore, the
measuring of the results should be in terms of those objectives.
Some of the most noteworthy research in this area has been conducted by Professor Thurstone,[59] of the University of Chicago.
He has developed a number of attitude scales to determine students'
attitudes on patriotism, war and peace, and many other contemporary social questions. This field of investigation holds great
promise for research workers and for teachers of subjects in which
attitudes are important outcomes. A few of the fields in which
investigations have been conducted may be enumerated to acquaint
the student with the possibilities in this area. The work of Bogardus [60] on social distance, Droba [61] on militarism, Glen [62] on

[56] E. K. Strong, *Vocational Interest Blank* (Stanford University, Calif.:
Stanford University Press, 1930).
[57] G. W. Allport and F. H. Allport, *The A-S Reaction Study* (Boston:
Houghton Mifflin, 1928).
[58] June E. Downey, *Will-Temperament Test* (Yonkers, N. Y.: World Book
Company, 1922).
[59] L. L. Thurstone and E. J. Chave, *The Measurement of Attitude* (Chicago:
University of Chicago Press, 1929).
[60] E. S. Bogardus, "Leadership and Attitudes," *Bibliography of Sociology
and Social Research,* XIII (March, 1929), 377–81.
[61] D. Droba, *Measurement of Attitude Toward Militarism, Pacifism.* Un-
pub., University of Florida.
[62] M. Glen, "Attitudes Toward Music," *Music Supervisors Journal,* XV
(March, 1929), 75–84.

music, Lasker [63] on racial issues, Neumann [64] on internationalism, and Vetter [65] on politics are good illustrations.

f. *Measurement of interests.*   Closely related to personality and attitude as factors in vocational success is the question of interest.   There is no doubt that an individual makes better progress and is more successful in the performance of any task when he possesses a high degree of interest in that task.   What interest consists of is not clearly known, but it is definitely a complex combination of factors not easily measured directly.   The earliest efforts to measure interests were made by E. K. Strong,[66] and probably the most rewarding work in this area of measurement has employed his techniques.   The tests developed in these studies reveal the degree of similarity between interests expressed by people taking the test and those of "successful" people in a limited number of occupations.   (The tests were standardized by administering them to workers known to be successful.)   For example, if an individual's responses tend to be similar to those of salesmen, then the deduction is made that his interest in the activities and methods of salesmen is probably high.   These tests have been improved through the years, until today the Strong Vocational Interest Blank has been standardized for use in thirty-five occupations, there being six groups for men and sixteen for women.   Other recent experimenters in this area of measurement are G. F. Kuder [67] and Glen U. Cleeton.[68]

g. *Interpreting and using test results.*   Tests as used in school must be regarded as instruments, as tools.   They serve as means,

---

[63] Bruno Lasker, *Race Attitudes in Children* (New York: Holt, 1927, 1929).

[64] G. B. Neumann, *A Study of International Attitudes of High School Students* (New York: Bureau of Publications, Teachers College, 1926, 1931).

[65] G. B. Vetter, "Measurement of Social and Political Attitudes and the Related Personal Factors," *Journal of Abnormal Psychology*, XXV (July, 1930), 149–81, Bibliog.

[66] Edward K. Strong, *Vocational Interest Blank for Men* (Stanford University, Calif.: Stanford University Press, 1938).

[67] G. F. Kuder, *Kuder Preference Record* (Chicago: Science Research Associates, 1942).

[68] Glen U. Cleeton, *Vocational Interest Inventory, Grades 9–16* (Chicago: McKnight and McKnight, 1939).

never as ends in themselves.   They furnish the measuring instruments that enable us to judge the results of various educational
procedures.   We shall discuss these uses briefly under the three
headings noted below.

1. Standardized tests used for comparisons.   Standard tests
of mental ability and achievement are used now to measure the
extent to which the schools are attaining the results expected.
When survey tests are used, comparisons may be made between
an individual and his class, between two or more classes in a
school, between two or more schools in a district, or between districts.   That is, teachers or parents may determine how well a
pupil or a class is doing compared with other pupils of the same
age or grade.   Diagnostic tests help a teacher to determine the
exact nature of the learning difficulties of an individual pupil.   It
is not enough to know that a student makes low marks; the teacher
must ascertain the causes.   For example, one particular test
breaks up long division units into seven distinct operations.   A
survey test in long division would merely indicate how many answers each pupil had correct; this diagnostic test reveals where
and why the errors are made.   There need be little guesswork today about the proper grade placement of a pupil.   By means of a
good battery of achievement tests, the level that will provide the
best challenge to the abilities of the student may be determined.
Using tests thus for classification is made easier as a result of the
interpretative measures that have been employed.

2. Interpretative measures provide a technical vocabulary by
means of which teachers may record or transmit from one school
to another what is known about the achievement of pupils.

(a) Norms of standard tests.   Norms are determined by finding the average scores made by all pupils who have taken a particular test.   Three types of norms are in common use today—
age norms, grade norms, and percentile norms.   The first two are
more applicable to the elementary school and junior high school
subjects; the latter may be used for any level, and for that reason
are coming into more frequent use.

TABLE 15

Age and Grade Norms for Otis Self-Administering Test of Mental Ability [69]

Score	Age Norm.	Grade Norm.	Score	Age Norm.	Grade Norm.
31..........	11-0	5.4	39..........	12-2	6.4
32..........	11-2	5.5	40..........	12-4	6.6
33..........	11-3	5.6	41..........	12-6	6.8
34..........	11-5	5.8	42..........	12-8	7.0
35..........	11-7	5.9	43..........	12-10	7.2
36..........	11-9	6.0	44..........	13-1	7.4
37..........	11-11	6.2	45..........	13-3	7.6
38..........	12-0	6.3			

In Table 15 we find an illustration of a table of norms. The Otis test has been administered to many thousands of school children of all ages. Those who treat the test results statistically have computed the averages for children of various ages and grades. For example, the pupils who are just twelve years old (12–0) have made an average score of 38; those who have just entered the sixth grade (6.0) have averaged 36. The score of any pupil who may subsequently take the test can be referred to the table to find his age or grade equivalent. Thus, a pupil making a score of 33 is possessed of mental ability equivalent to that of pupils who were eleven years, 3 months old (11–3), and to that of pupils who were in the sixth month of the fifth grade (5.6), at the time they took the test.

Percentile norms are more useful when age or grade status is not so significant as it is in the elementary school. It is readily seen that, for college students, to express the score equivalents in terms of age or grade would be relatively useless because of the extreme variation in their curricular and age adjustment. For

[69] Adapted from A. S. Otis, *Manual of Directions for Self-Administering Test of Mental Ability,* Intermediate Exam. (Yonkers, N. Y.: World Book Company, 1928), pp. 6–7.

example, Table 16 presents percentile norms for 2,516 students in 21 colleges who took the Otis Higher Examination. The average score (50th percentile) made by all the students was 53; so that a student who makes a score of 62 is better than seventy-five per cent of those taking the test.

TABLE 16

Percentile Norms for 9,050 High School Students Taking Otis Higher Examination [70]

Score	Percentile Rank
75	100
71	97
67	90
62	75
53	50
40	25
39	10
32	3
20	0

The use of percentile norms is also illustrated in Table 17, which shows percentile norms for the Sones-Harry High School Achievement Test.[71]

TABLE 17

Percentile Norms for 9,050 High School Students Taking Sones-Harry Achievement Test

Score	Percentile	Score	Percentile
300	99	120	40
255	95	105	30
230	90	97	25
195	80	90	20
182	75	72	10
170	70	60	5
152	60	40	1
135	50		

[70] *Ibid.,* p. 6.
[71] W. W. D. Sones and D. P. Harry, *High School Achievement Test* (Yonkers, N. Y.: World Book Company, 1929), Manual of Directions, Table 1, p. 9.

(b) Ages and quotients furnish very effective means of recording and reporting the standing of pupils. This effectiveness may be best seen in the case of mental tests. In the development of these, the average scores made by a large number of pupils of different ages were recorded. For example, the 11-year-olds averaged 136 and the 12-year-olds, 152. Consequently, a pupil taking the test later and making a score of 136 is said to have a Mental Age of 11–0, eleven years and no months. Likewise a pupil with a score of 144 is said to have a Mental Age of 11–6. If this latter pupil were 10 years, four months old, that is, if his chronological age were 10–4, then by means of the formula

$$IQ = \frac{\text{Mental Age}}{\text{Chronological Age}} \times 100$$

we could compute his Intelligence Quotient thus:

$$IQ = \frac{MA}{CA} = \frac{11-6}{10-4} = \frac{138 \text{ (months)}}{124 \text{ (months)}} \times 100 = 111$$

These two measures, Mental Age (MA) and Intelligence Quotient (IQ), have come to be standard terminology for describing the mental ability of pupils. But even though the terms are in common use, there is much mystery surrounding them and much misunderstanding and misinterpretation of them. The term, Mental Age, is an indication of the level of mental maturity that has been reached or attained. The term, Intelligence Quotient, expresses the ratio between mental and physical development; it reveals the rate of mental growth and may be used as an indication of the rate of learning. Many unwarranted and unjust generalizations have been made concerning the IQ. An IQ of 100 is considered normal; that is, it is interpreted to mean that mental growth has kept pace with physical growth; but due allowance needs to be made for errors inherent in the testing process. It is better to consider any IQ between 90 and 110 as within the normal range. Table 18 indicates the commonly accepted interpretations of mental levels.

TABLE 18

*Interpretations of Intelligence Quotient
In Terms of Mental Level*

Above 140 — Gifted
130 — Very superior
120 — Superior
90–110 — Normal range
80 — Dull
70 — Border line
Below 70 — Feeble-minded

Ages and quotients may also be derived from achievement tests, but, in practice, the latter are not so frequently used. For example, a score of 65 in the New Stanford [72] arithmetic test is the equivalent of an arithmetic age of eleven years, one month (11–1). Likewise a total score of 70 on the New Stanford Test produces an Educational Age (EA) of 11–6. When the chronological age is known, the formula

$$EQ = \frac{EA}{CA} \times 100$$

may be used to compute the educational quotient. If the student's chronological age were 12–8, then the EQ would be derived as follows:

$$EQ = \frac{11\text{--}6}{12\text{--}8} = \frac{138 \text{ (months)}}{152 \text{ (months)}} \times 100 = 91$$

(c) *Mean* and *median* are two measures, called measures of central tendency, that are used to represent an entire group. *Average* is a generic term that includes both of them; that is, they are used as averages. The mean is the same as the arithmetical average, and is found by adding all the scores together and then dividing by the number of scores. The median is the mid-score or

---

[72] *New Stanford Achievement Test* (Yonkers, N. Y.: World Book Company, 1929).

mid-point in the distribution of scores. It is found by arranging all the scores in order from highest to lowest, and then counting to find the middle or median score. Both these measures are in such common use today that the student needs to be familiar with them, particularly if he is to understand the discussion that follows concerning marking systems. Table 19 illustrates the use of these measures.

(d) Quartiles are points that divide a distribution of scores into quarters or fourths. The upper or third quartile is midway between the median and the highest score and separates the first quarter of the class from the second. Likewise the lower or first quartile divides the lower half of the distribution into third and fourth quarters or fourths. Table 19 shows these quartiles in relation to the mean and median.

(e) Percentiles are points in a distribution that show the standing of a given score in relation to the entire group. Centiles divide a distribution into one hundred divisions, deciles into tenths, and quartiles into fourths. That is, a score at the tenth percentile (a percentile rank of 10) is better than 10 per cent, but is exceeded by 90 per cent, of the scores. A percentile rank of 70 indicates that a given pupil is excelled by 30 per cent, but is better than 70 per cent, of the pupils. It is when percentile ranks are published, rather than age or grade equivalents, that percentiles are used as norms. Table 17 illustrates the use of percentile scores, showing particularly that the 25th, 50th, and 75th percentiles represent respectively the first quartile, median, and third quartile.

TABLE 19

Frequency Distribution of 172 Scores in 10th Grade English Test

Scores	Frequency
110–114	1
105–109	2
100–104	0
95–99	2
90–94	4
85–89	11 — 90th Percentile, 86.27

TABLE 19 (*Continued*)

Scores	Frequency
80–84	15
75–79	16 — Third Quartile, 75.5
70–74	22
65–69	26 — Median, 67.5; Mean, 65.15
60–64	24
55–59	10 — First Quartile, 57
50–54	14
45–49	11 — 10th Percentile, 46.45
40–44	4
35–39	7
30–34	2
25–29	1

N = 172

3. Objective tests necessitate a relative marking system. The use of objective tests, composed of a large number of test responses, 135 for example, necessitates a different approach to the marking system from that employed when five or ten essay questions have been used. The traditional method of marking is done on the basis of 100 per cent, with 70 or 75 as a passing mark. The instructor determines before reading the papers what the passing mark will be and marks the papers accordingly. Two changes in point of view and in practice are necessary if a teacher is to secure the most benefit from the objective examination. First, the teacher must realize that the passing mark cannot be determined in advance; he must wait until he learns what scores all the pupils have made. The larger number of test items employed by the objective test is used to get a better distribution—more spread —among the students taking the test. It would, therefore, be out of order to say in advance that 70 per cent is the passing mark. Possibly only five per cent of the class will exceed that score. This fact suggests the second change to be made; namely, that the teacher begin in the middle of the distribution instead of at the top, or at the failing mark, to assign the marks. There is danger, of course, in using this procedure, of a lowering of standards, but the teacher must employ effective checks to offset this danger and must reteach some of the material if the whole class makes low

scores. The point of this discussion is that many of the benefits of comprehensive objective tests are lost if the teacher adheres to the traditional percentage marking system, which was based upon two false assumptions: first, that a mythical perfection exists, represented by a mark of 100; and second, that an arbitrarily determined passing mark can be justified. When objective tests are used, the marks obtained are based upon the achievement of the class as a whole; consequently, the marks have only relative, not absolute, value.

This principle may be illustrated by Table 20, in which 31 scores

TABLE 20

Illustrating How Objective Test Scores Are
Changed Into Marks

Letter Making System	Scores	Percentage Marking System
A	88	95–100
	84	
	78	
	76	
B	74	90–94
	72	
	70	
	63	
	63	
	61	85–89
	60	
	58	
	53	
	51	
C	50	80–84
	44	
	43	
	39	
	36	
	34	75–79
	33	
	32	
	25	
	23	
D	22	70–74
	21	
	18	

Table 20 (*Continued*)

Letter Making System	Scores	Percentage Marking System
	17	
	12	
F	11	Below 70 (failure)
	8	

in a chemistry test are shown first in an order distribution and then translated into marks. The column on the left indicates how marks would be distributed if letters are used; on the right we see the principle applied to a percentage marking scale. The test contained 109 items. The highest score was 88, the lowest 8, the median 44. We begin by assigning to the middle 50 per cent of the class a mark of C, or marks between 75 and 89, and scale the remaining marks up or down from that central point. If the instructor had designated 70 as the passing mark, only seven, or 22.6 per cent, of the class would have passed. When a relative marking system is used, only three students, or slightly less than 10 per cent, are considered failures; even so, the reader should be cautioned against thinking that a certain percentage of students is obliged to fail.

5. Meaning of the Scientific Study of Education

There is considerable support for the belief that education is a science; that the work of a teacher is that of an applied scientist, one trained to use a body of technical information and to apply specialized skills and techniques in the complex situations of the classroom. The extreme statement of this position is to be contrasted with the view that teaching is an art; that the work of a teacher cannot be reduced to the cold, analytical procedures of the scientist. Actually, the teacher must be both artist and scientist, and so the wise position maintains that much progress will come through a scientific attack upon educational problems, rendering more effective the artistry of the teacher. It will be our purpose in the next few paragraphs to set forth the possibilities and the limitations of a scientific study of education.

a. *Possibilities.*   A most extreme statement is that of John B. Watson, an experimenter who did much to show the possibilities of scientific investigation, particularly in the study of infant behavior:

> With the Behavioristic point of view now becoming dominant it is hard to find a place for what is called philosophy.   Philosophy is passing—has already all but passed.[73]

One of our foremost exponents of a science of education was Dr. Charles H. Judd, director of the Department of Education in the University of Chicago until his retirement in 1939.   Like Cattell, Hall, and James, he studied in Europe in the early days of the Wundt laboratory and made valuable contributions to the new psychology in America.   He directed many students in scientific studies of education, and, until his death in 1946, was much in demand as a platform lecturer because of his clarity of expression and forcefulness of presentation.   He was in the front ranks of those urging that more scientific inquiries be used in education, as evidenced by two quotations:

> We must guide education by applying to this field of human endeavor the same forms of scientific analysis that have been successful in the mastery of the physical world.[74]

> The science of education aims to collect by all available methods full information with regard to the origin, development, and present form of school practices and also full information with regard to social needs. It aims to subject present practices to rigid tests and comparisons and to analyze all procedure in the schools by experimental methods and by observation.   It aims to secure complete and definite records of all that the school attempts and accomplishes.[75]

---

[73] John B. Watson, *The Ways of Behaviorism* (New York: Harper, 1928), p. 14.

[74] Charles H. Judd, *Conference on Examinations, Eastbourne, England* (New York: Teachers College, Columbia University, 1931), p. 57.

[75] Charles H. Judd, *Introduction to the Scientific Study of Education* (Boston: Ginn, 1918), p. 305.

Dr. Leonard P. Ayres gives a clear exposition of the method of science in a symposium on "Measurement of the Educational Product":

The scientific method is at base analytic scrutiny, exact measuring, careful recording, and judgment on the basis of observed fact. Science in education is not a body of information, but a method, and its object is to find out and to learn how.[76]

In the same volume Dr. Thorndike restates his own conception of measurement as a phase of scientific method:

Whatever exists at all exists in some amount. To know it thoroughly involves knowing its quantity as well as its quality. Education is concerned with changes in human beings; a change is a difference between two conditions; each of these conditions is known to us only by the products produced by it—things made, words spoken, acts performed, and the like. To measure any of these products means to define its amount in some way so that competent persons will know how large it is, better than they would without measurement.[77]

Another group would apply the methods of science in determining educational objectives, among them W. W. Charters, Franklin Bobbitt, and C. C. Peters. The last mentioned made a good case for determining scientifically what should be taught, in his chapter on "Scientific Method and the Curriculum":

We need to replace these empirical conclusions regarding the values of the several subjects with scientific investigations that will be impersonal, systematic, observational.
1. Fundamentally, we need to know, on a scientific basis, what are the abilities that are needed in society.
2. What subject matter can make the largest contributions toward these desired ends. . . .

---

[76] Leonard P. Ayres, in *Seventeenth Yearbook of the National Society for the Study of Education* (Bloomington, Ill.: Public School Publishing Co., 1918), p. 14.
[77] E. L. Thorndike, in *Seventeenth Yearbook of the National Society for the Study of Education,* p. 16.

3. What are the methods of handling the subject matter that will be most economical of time and energy. . . .[78]

Dr. Judd was hopeful also that science could contribute to clearer statements of objectives. In his chapter on "A Forward Look" in the *Yearbook* dealing with "Measurement of the Educational Product," he said:

The answer to the objection that measurement is limited to a few trivial aspects of teaching is steadily becoming more cogent. This hopeful conclusion is fully supported by one fact which serves at the same time to reveal one of the most important advantages of measurements, namely, the fact that with the development of measurement there is coming into education a greater general clearness and definiteness of purpose.[79]

A sort of antidote for the tendencies toward activity for its own sake is found in a clear-cut statement from Symonds:

Activity is essential in learning, but one must be able to measure success or failure and improvement. This is what measurement in education aims to accomplish.[80]

b. *Limitations*. It will be in order now to present the contrary point of view. The adherents of philosophy are doubtful, if not skeptical, about the possibilities of borrowing the techniques and procedures of the physical and natural sciences and applying them to education. They sound a warning that science can measure only certain limited aspects of educational outcomes; that it places undue emphasis upon these and neglects others.

All things that can be measured, and all things, just as far as they can be measured, come within the purview of science. The realm of

---

[78] Charles C. Peters, *Foundations of Educational Sociology*, rev. ed. (New York: Macmillan, 1930), p. 81.
[79] Charles H. Judd, *Seventeenth Yearbook of the National Society for the Study of Education*, p. 158.
[80] Percival M. Symonds, *Measurement in Secondary Education* (New York: Macmillan, 1930), p. 9.

science is quantity.   Quality can be appraised, but it cannot be measured.[81]

John Dewey [82] thinks that "educational science cannot be constructed simply by borrowing the techniques of experiment and measurement found in physical science."   Likewise, Professor Beard [83] says: "I think we should be slow to assume that the analyzing and adding method of natural science is equally appropriate to human affairs and will prove equally fruitful in results."

Professor Bode pays his respects to one of the favored research techniques of the scientists (the questionnaire) in discussing the futility of appeal to consensus of opinion:

> The net result of such procedure is either to cover up real differences in point of view, or else to make the consensus a means of perpetuating the prejudices of the past.   The irony in the present enthusiasm for scientific method lies in the fact that tradition is placed in the saddle and acclaimed in the name of scientific method.   This technique is adapted only to fact-finding, to a determination of what is, not of what ought to be.[84]

The limitations of science in studying education were clearly seen by Counts, and pointedly stated in his *American Road to Culture:*

> Many prominent educators seem to believe that there is no educational problem which is incapable of objective solution. . . . This complete absorpton in educational science, however, is beginning to relax. Many able students of the question are contending that the solution of educational problems does not follow automatically from investigation and that provision must be made for a process of synthesis and evaluation which lies somewhat beyond the confines of science.[85]

---

81 B. H. Streeter, *Reality* (New York: Macmillan, 1926), p. 26.

82 John Dewey, *The Sources of a Science of Education* (New York: Liveright, 1929), p. 26.

83 Charles A. Beard, *Research in the Social Sciences* (New York: Macmillan, 1929), p. 281.

84 B. H. Bode, *Modern Educational Theories* (New York: Macmillan, 1927), p. 134.

85 George S. Counts, *The American Road to Culture* (New York: John Day, 1930), p. 169.

Henry G. Hullfish says that scientific development in the field of measurement has "glorified both the administrator and the teacher" but that we are "beginning to realize what we should always have known, that it is deadening and fruitless for both the student and the teacher." [86]

The issue may be brought more clearly into focus by allowing Dr. Thorndike a word of rebuttal, so to speak:

These tests will not replace skill, they will not replace tact, they will not replace kindness, they will not replace enthusiasm nor nobility. On the other hand, they will not in any sense harm us, and they will be useful as helps, no matter how ideal our aims. Our ideals may be as lofty and subtle as you please, but if they are real ideals, they are ideals for achieving something; and if anything real is ever achieved, it can be measured. Not perhaps now, and not perhaps in fifty years; but if a thing exists, it exists in some amount; and if it exists in some amount it can be measured. I am suspicious of educational achievements which are so subtle and refined and spiritual that they cannot be measured. I fear that they do not exist.[87]

The foregoing citations may leave the student in a state of bewilderment about the place of science. The differences in point of view expressed here represent the old conflict between science and philosophy. Now, let us examine the methods of science and mention a few problems or questions for which the educators are seeking answers. This will doubtless bring into clearer outline the truth of the situation, namely, that both science and philosophy can contribute to the solution of most of our problems. Philosophy points the way; science tests the results.

c. *The method of science* is experimentation, systematic observation. Science proceeds on the assumption that "nothing is uncaused"; it tries to find the cause. It is this point of view, called the scientific attitude, that is needed in education to offset the effects of blind following of traditional practices and empirical, impressionistic decisions.

---

[86] Henry G. Hullfish, *The Educational Frontier* (New York: Appleton-Century, 1933), p. 171.

[87] E. L. Thorndike, quoted by Kilpatrick in *Source Book in the Philosophy of Education*, rev. ed. (New York: Macmillan, 1934), pp. 38–39.

Dr. Peters summarized the essential elements in scientific procedure very clearly:

But what is involved in making a scientific survey of social needs and of educational values? How will a scientific study differ from the empirical ones that have from time to time been attempted? In exactly the same way in which all science differs from common sense —namely, merely in being more systematic.

1. Repeatability is the basic demand of scientific research.
2. Scientific procedure involves suppressing the personal equation of the investigator.
3. The scientific method is analytical.
4. Scientific procedures are largely quantitative.
5. Scientific method demands that one generalize only on the basis of representative cases.
6. Scientific method forbids generalization on too few cases.[88]

A complete scientific solution usually involves five rather distinct steps, which will be outlined here and illustrated with well-known examples of scientific study. First step, recognition of a problem. Second step, formulation of a *hypothesis*, that is, venturing a guess (theory) as to its solution. Third step, *testing*, trying out the hypothesis. This last involves modification of the hypothesis as a result of the testing. The re-guessing and re-testing go on until the investigator becomes convinced he is working on the right theory. Fourth step, stating the results in the form of a *conclusion*. Fifth step, *applying* the results to other similar problems, that is, generalizing the conclusion so that the theory becomes a law or principle.

These five steps may be illustrated by referring to the study of yellow fever by Dr. Walter Reed and others.

First: The problem was clear. Yellow fever was causing the death of thousands of people annually.

Second: One theory was that the mosquito was a carrier of the disease; that the ravages of the disease could be checked if the mosquito were eliminated.

88 Charles C. Peters, *Foundations of Educational Sociology*, rev. ed. (New York: Macmillan, 1930), pp. 83–85.

Third: Dr. Reed tested the theory by studying the symptoms of persons who were bitten by mosquitoes that were known to have bitten victims of the disease.   He even allowed himself to be bitten, contracted the disease and died.

Fourth: The conclusion of Dr. Reed's investigations, and of others studying the same problem, was that the mosquito was the cause of the spread of yellow fever.

Fifth: With the cause known, a solution was possible.   Accordingly the breeding places of mosquitoes were eliminated, and today every precaution is taken to prevent the disease.   Only in very limited sections of the world is yellow fever known today.

There are many good reasons why educational problems are difficult to solve by such methods.   First, the problems are frequently complex and lacking in clear definition.   Second, it is always difficult, often impossible, to isolate one factor or set of factors and study it alone.   A physicist or chemist eliminates all the variable factors except the one he is studying.   Third, educational problems always involve human beings, and it is not practicable to set up laboratory conditions for the control of the experiment.   Fourth, education is a gradual process, requiring long periods of time for the study of problems.   We have had comparatively little long-term study of educational outcomes.   To shorten the process leads to hasty conclusions.

Coupled with these plausible explanations are some excuses, not reasons, for refraining from attacking our problems scientifically. The first of these, human inertia, is a powerful deterrent to action. It is so easy to let well enough alone.   Second, there is the ever-present fear that conditions might become worse.   Third, school people generally have not welcomed measurement of the results of their efforts.   Too many have been motivated by the belief that "What they don't know won't hurt them."

d. *Some benefits of scientific study.*   Citation of a few educational practices that have been modified as a result of scientific study will assist the student in evaluating this influence.

1. Reading.   There is little excuse today for a teacher who does a poor job of teaching reading, a subject that has been studied

probably more than any other. The shift of emphasis from oral
to silent reading, and from word-calling to getting thought, is the
result of this investigation. By use of motion pictures and other
optical instruments, much has been learned about motions of the
eye and mechanics of reading. The eye must come to rest before
it "sees"; it moves across the line on a page by a series of stops
and starts, which are called fixations. If these are regular, few
to the line, and if there is no zig-zagging back and forth, the
chances for error are reduced and the amount of comprehension is
relatively greater.

2. Spelling. The investigations of Thorndike, Horn, Ashbaugh,
and others have caused the elimination of much of the wasted motion in the teaching of spelling, the first subject to be studied
objectively. Instead of using words of the demon, jaw-breaker
type, we now teach those words in most common use.

3. Writing. Instruction in penmanship has produced uniformly better results since we have ceased to work toward copybook
perfection and have set up legibility as a standard. By means of
handwriting scales a teacher may show a pupil his need for improvement and the successive stages of his progress.

4. Classification of pupils. We are now able, with a reasonable
degree of success, to place pupils in classes or sections best suited
to their individual learning rate, as a result of the measuring instruments in use.

5. Behavior problems. We no longer hold to the old belief that
all boys are bad; that their wills must be broken and their natural
impulses thwarted. Instead we try to provide wholesome, healthy
surroundings and furnish activities that call for the best responses
of the individual. The few cases of maladjustment are studied
with the desire of finding their cause.

e. *Problems that need to be studied scientifically.* We need
objective data about the Activity Curriculum. It is easy to see
that children are happier in such a school, but do they learn as
much, and do they retain what they do learn? Is the "fiber of education" being weakened?

At what levels should various subjects be studied most in-
tensively? One superintendent proposes postponing serious study

of arithmetic until the seventh grade. Possibly foreign languages could be learned more painlessly if introduced earlier.

What are the measurable benefits of unit instruction and contract plans? Are pupils more able to think for themselves and to work independently? What are the effects of integration of subject matter? Which produces the better results, intensive or extensive reading?

Do extracurricular activities make positive contributions to better citizenship? What are the effects of more freedom in cooperative student management?

The radio and the movies present challenges to the schools. What is the most effective use of radio broadcasts? Very little research has been done in this area. Such investigations as the Payne Fund Studies [89] of the effects of movies are revealing and suggest the need for other scientific inquiries.

One superintendent proposes that boys, in particular, be admitted to the junior high school on height. We need evidence as to the ultimate effects of assigning pupils to grades where they are socially and physically better adjusted, regardless of their scholastic attainments.

Most of these suggestions would involve long-term investigations carried on in actual classroom situations. We have undoubtedly reached the stage requiring a good share of our research to be of that character. Much of it in the past has been of the snapshot variety, collecting a sample of what is being done, a method criticized by Bode in one of the citations quoted. Wider dissemination of the benefits of scientific study will cause teachers to be less afraid of inquiries and will make parents more willing to have experiments tried out in their schools.

6. A Socio-scientific Approach

In this unit we have discussed the historical and traditional influences affecting American education, the philosophical influences, and the psychological and scientific influences. The attempt, in the entire volume, has been to consider education as a social force,

---

[89] W. W. Charters, "Motion Pictures and Youth," *Payne Fund Studies,* **13** vols. (New York: Macmillan, 1933).

and the study of education as a social study. Although this view-point is emphasized throughout, it may be well in this discussion of influences affecting our schools to mention specifically the influence of the modern sociological approach to education. We have chosen to call it the *socio-scientific* approach.

Sociology is attempting to utilize the contributions of philosophy and of psychology in the building of an educational practice that will square with the needs of a modern society. Thus it becomes an integrating force, recognizing and utilizing the contributions of science and of theory, but insisting upon the necessity for judging and interpreting the resultant practices in the light of their usefulness to society.

The weakness of the limited application of science to the determination of educational practices has been demonstrated frequently. The sociological approach demands that scientific techniques be used, but also that the whole life of the pupil be taken into account. It demands that the teacher take account of all the factors that influence child behavior, and not merely certain limited classroom factors. The sociological approach demands that all these influences be coördinated and utilized in the development of a unified personality appropriate to the needs of modern life.

D.   Problems and References for Collateral Study

Problems for Students

1. Trace the development of education in your community from the earliest settlers to the present time.

2. Trace the development of secondary education in your home community, stressing the agencies and persons that were influential.

3. Make a list of traditional practices that persist in your community.

4. Make a detailed study of the educational activities of one religious group or denomination in your state.

5. Evaluate a number of current practices in education in the light of the conflicting theories of education.

6. Compare the points of view of John Dewey and W. C. Bagley, as expressed in their books and magazine articles.

7. Prepare a critical analysis of the views and writings of one of the educational leaders mentioned in this unit.

8. Write a detailed analysis of one or more of the contemporary schools of psychology.

9. List the practices in your home schools that are traceable to the influences discussed in this unit.

10. What are some of the benefits of the scientific study of education in the schools as you know them?

11. Write a critique of the tests and measures that would be useful in some educational situation with which you are familiar.

Selected References

Arlitt, A. H., *Psychology of Infancy and Early Childhood.* New York: McGraw-Hill, 1946.

Brubacher, J. S., *A History of the Problems of Education.* New York: McGraw-Hill, 1947.

Butts, R. Freeman, *A Cultural History of Education.* New York: McGraw-Hill, 1947.

Fenner, Mildred S., and Fishburn, Eleanor C., *Pioneer American Educators.* Washington, D. C.: National Education Association, 1945.

Fenton, Norman, *Mental Hygiene in School Practice.* Stanford University, Calif.: Stanford University Press, 1945.

Garrison, K. C., *The Psychology of Adolescence,* 3rd ed. New York: Prentice-Hall, 1946.

Good, Harry G., *A History of Western Education.* New York: Macmillan, 1947.

John Dewey Society, *The American High School: Its Responsibility and Opportunity.* New York: Harper, 1946.

Lodge, Rupert C., *Philosophy of Education.* New York: Harper, 1945.

Melvin, A. G., *Education: A History.* New York: John Day, 1946.

Mulhern, J., *A History of Education.* New York: Ronald Press, 1946.

Pressey, S. L., and Robinson, Francis P., *Psychology and the New Education.* New York: Harper, 1945.

Ulich, Robert, *History of Educational Thought.* New York: American Book Company, 1945.

Van Ormer, E. B., and Williams, C. O., *Elementary Statistics for Students of Education and Psychology.* New York: Longmans, Green, 1945.

Wahlquist, John T., *The Philosophy of American Education.* New York: Ronald Press, 1945.

The Significance of Education in Society

What is the relation of the schools to the other educative agencies? What is the function of education in society? Should the schools lead or follow social progress? Those are the questions discussed in this unit. Education is broadly interpreted as seeking to "help young persons fulfill the unique, particular functions in life which it is in them to fulfill, and fit them so far as it can for those common spheres which, as citizens and heirs of a joint culture, they will share with others." [1] Education is presented as a social science, not merely as a professional subject for prospective teachers. A hasty exploration of the field of comparative education will enable us to discover how political leaders and statesmen in other countries employ educational techniques and work through the schools to accomplish their nationalistic aims and purposes.

A. Various Educative Agencies in Society

Too often we think of education as being synonymous with schooling. When it is said that an individual is well educated, such a statement is usually interpreted to mean that he has had the benefit of a great deal of formal schooling. A moment's reflection will reveal how erroneous such an interpretation is. Many able leaders in former generations attended school only a few months in their entire lifetime. Much of our work in school is done as though we were overlooking all other educative agencies entirely. We shall find it profitable to list some of these non-school agencies, to study their methods, and to see what relation they bear to the school system.

---

[1] *General Education In a Free Society,* Report of the Harvard Committee, Harvard University Press, Cambridge, Mass., 1945, p. 4.

1. Non-school Educative Agencies

a. *The home.* In spite of statements and warnings that the influence of the home is declining, it probably continues to be, for good or ill, the most effective educational agency in society. Its decline is a relative matter, inasmuch as it now has so many competitors. From the point of view of society, the influence of the home may be positive or negative, but in either case it is effective to a marked degree. Children from homes where the family relationships are wholesome and where the parents participate in the cultural and civic life of the community usually enter into the life of the school coöperatively and wholeheartedly and experience little difficulty finding their places as participating citizens. On the contrary, the children from homes that are lacking in cultural advantages and where antisocial attitudes prevail have difficulty entering into coöperative relationships and frequently run afoul of the law. If their home life provides stimulating, constructive activities, children do not need to find outlets for all their energies and interests in the neighborhood gangs. Case studies of inmates of penal institutions reveal an alarming proportion of children from broken homes.

It is in the home that the child learns the language. He develops certain attitudes toward society and its institutions. Whatever ideals he possesses have their roots in those of the home. The pattern his personality ultimately assumes is stamped in during the early years. He accepts the religion of his parents so completely that he seldom departs from it. All these influences make up what is called the social inheritance, a force probably just as potent in shaping the child as his biological heritage. The behaviorists' extravagant claim that they could make anything they wished out of a child if they could control the environment contains a large element of truth.

The school has made two somewhat contradictory mistakes in relation to the home and its influence. On the one hand, it has been a bit too ready to accept the popular notion that the home is declining. That is, there is a tacit acceptance of that notion, with a resulting negligence in preparing pupils for future home responsibilities. The organized school probably has no more important function than to prepare its products for future family relationships. This it can do only half-heartedly if it has doubts concerning the place of the home in society. On the other hand, school officials have erred in "passing the buck" to the home. They have not tried sufficiently to understand the contributions of the home to the individual pupil's development and to build a school program that would supplement those influences. One frequent error of the school consists in its assumption that all pupils from a given locality are alike in needs and interests, and, consequently, in offering them a uniform curriculum. There has been a good deal of determinism in the school's attitude. We have been too ready to assume that nothing could be done for those folks living "across the tracks" or "on the south side." Such activities as those of visiting teachers and community and school nurses are of great benefit in bringing the school and home into better functional relationship.

The term *Visiting Teacher* [2] is a comparatively new one in educational parlance. It is used to describe the activities of a school official whose chief duty it is to establish coöperative relations between the school and the home. Such persons are usually part-time teachers who spend part of each day in the classroom and the remainder visiting pupils' homes, or former teachers who devote all their time to making home contacts. Among their other duties are those usually assigned to attendance or truant officers. The latter officials have always been at a distinct disadvantage from an educational point of view because they are generally regarded as police officers. As a rule, they are none too tactful in approaching the home, and they are more interested in enforcing the compulsory attendance laws than in securing a satisfactory adjustment of the child's difficulties. The visiting teacher, on the other hand, is a sympathetic, mature person who understands the school's point of view and knows how to help the parent to under-

---

[2] The American Association of Social Workers, 130 East 22nd Street, New York 10, N. Y., will furnish information concerning this movement.

stand it.   Parent-Teacher organizations have contributed much to bringing the home and school closer together, but too often they have reached only those homes already in sympathy and coöperation with the school.   The visiting teacher movement offers much of promise.

b. *The church.*   The religious impulses are among the most universal characteristics of man, and probably spring from his desire to understand the factors of his environment.   In the early days when he could find no satisfactory explanations, he developed fears and superstitions and beliefs, which were handed down from one generation to another and eventually became formalized and ritualized as elaborate ceremonials.   In due time a priest class arose to provide instruction in the mysteries of the church.   For many centuries the only formal instruction was carried on by the church.   So, through the ages, the church has been one of the most effective educational agencies.

In modern times the church is faced with a number of handicaps when it attempts to operate as an educational institution.   First, its chief problem grows out of its difficulty in distinguishing between instruction and worship.   Man has a natural desire to worship a supreme being, and it is in the worship services of the church that opportunities are provided for the expression of that impulse.   Worship suffers when instruction in theological doctrines and denominational creeds is introduced.   Many churches try to provide for the instructional phases of their program in the Sunday School and leave the worship to the church services.   Because this distinction is not made clear, the instruction is frequently shrouded in doctrines and creeds, and its objectives are not clearly defined.

A second handicap is found in dependence upon voluntary leadership that is subject to frequent turnover and great irregularity in attendance.   Many city churches engage educational directors who are able to organize a program around definite educational objectives and to train partially those volunteer workers who will do the instructing.

A third handicap is that the church is definitely and naturally

conservative.   Of course, it is the church's function to be so; it
is the conserver of the moral and ethical traditions.   But this
conservatism may be the rock over which the whole program
stumbles when attention needs to be given to the ills of society.
One devout, sincere church member said, "The thing I like about
our pastor is that he doesn't monkey with the social order."   Who
should be concerned about the social order if the church is not?

In spite of these handicaps, the church exerts a tremendous influence as an educational agency.   It keeps before its constituents
moral ideals and ethical standards.   It serves as a spiritual res-
ervoir, rendering a much needed service in a society constantly being
drained by materialistic and mechanistic influences.   In these days,
when so much emphasis is placed upon adult education, the church
finds a great opportunity in that field.

c. *The press.*   The late Will Rogers may have been speaking for
all of us when he said, "All I know is what I read in the papers."
There is no way of determining to what extent our ideas and our
attitudes depend upon the press.   We do know that the press is
a tremendously powerful educative agency.   We need only to remind ourselves that there are newspapers and magazines for people
of all ages and classes and nationalities, and that within each group
there is a wide range of appeal to interests and tastes.   Probably
in no other area of contemporary life do we find the offering so
varied; from the cheap "pulps," which play up the mystery,
thriller, or love theme, to the cultural and literary periodical; from
the ten cent weekly with mass appeal to the one dollar monthly,
from the popular science magazine to the highly technical journal.
There are newspapers in all languages, trade and professional and
fraternal house organs, magazines for children, women, men; no
group at any level is overlooked.

Educators simply cannot ignore the influence of the press.   On
the contrary, they should use it, try to help students to be more
critical in appraising its content, and endeavor to supplement or
offset its effects, as the need arises.   The school will not go far in
preserving the traditions we now possess, in creating a more desirable social order, or in preventing the encroachment of political

theories we do not desire, unless it has the help of the press in its efforts or is able to aid its students to understand and interpret what the press is trying to do, who controls it, and what motives are back of its activities.

In America we take great pride in the freedom of the press. We are convinced that our democratic liberties would be jeopardized by a press under government control. Our theory is that the newspaper reader should have access to the pros and the cons of every question. He should be able to ascertain the point of view of the administration in power, and equally free to determine that of the opposition. This belief is good democratic doctrine. Increasingly, however, a serious limitation is being imposed in actual practice upon the extent to which the citizen really is free to get both sides of a question through reading the newspapers. The truth is that although our population is increasing and becoming more literate, the number of daily newspapers is decreasing. This development is having the serious effect of giving us more and more one-newspaper cities. It is difficult to obtain all points of view on any matter if there is only one newspaper available.

In 1909, wth a population of 92 million, the United States possessed 2,600 daily newspapers; in 1920, with 106 million population, 2,324 daily papers; in 1930, with 123 million population, 2,219 daily papers; in 1940, with 132 million population, only 1,988 daily papers. The result of this trend is that in more than 1,200 cities there is now only one newspaper. In only 117 of our cities is there more than one newspaper ownership. All too often the one newspaper also owns the one local radio station. The grave dangers in this situation are pointed out by Morris Ernst:

One of the ugliest impacts of the decimation of our daily press is found in the number of towns formerly with several dailies which now have been reduced to only one. These one-paper towns are now the overwhelming majority of communities which have any daily papers. This is very important in terms of daily living. How easy is it, for example, to press for local reforms in a town where the only paper supports the local administration? How do you elect a mayor, a new school board, or debate the problem of parks and playgrounds? What price democracy in such an area?[3]

d. *The radio.* There can be no doubt as to the great educational potentialities of radio. This statement is true in spite of the fact that the radio networks and commercial stations must depend for revenue upon advertisers who are willing to pay enormous prices to become sponsors of 15 to 60 minutes of entertainment so that they may have the privilege of using from 15 seconds to 15 minutes to tell an unseen audience about their products. Radio advertisers spent 397 million dollars in 1944 to make their products known to the American public. Inasmuch as there are 55 million radio receivers in the United States, this amounted to an expenditure by the radio advertisers of two cents per radio receiver per day. The cost to listeners per receiver per day was estimated to be three cents.[4]

The radio has high potentialities for developing world-mindedness, and unquestionably it is making in some degree a substantial contribution toward this end. The amount of such contribution, however, would seem to be small in relation to the need, according to the findings of the Federal Communications Commission, which has made some effort to determine the extent to which radio is serving this need. In the five-month period from January 1, 1941, to May 31, 1941, five major questions of foreign policy were before the American people: lend-lease, the convoying of ships to Britain, the obtaining of foreign bases, the acquisition of foreign ships, and the maintenance of the British blockade. The Commission found that, on the average, each of the four major radio networks broadcast one program dealing with one or more of these issues every third day for the five-month period. But although the networks made these programs available, considerably less than one-half of the affiliated stations carried them.

---

[3] Morris L. Ernst, *The First Freedom* (New York: Macmillan, 1946), p. 68.
[4] *Public Service Responsibility of Broadcast Licensees,* Report by Federal Communications Commission, Washington, D. C., March 7, 1946.

Even more significant in the Commission's study is the fact that of 842 stations reporting, only 288 claimed to have originated even one program on any subject relevant to the study. The remaining 454 stations did not report having carried a single non-network program on foreign policy during the entire five-month period. It is little wonder that the Federal Communications Commission has raised serious questions relating to the extent to which radio is meeting its public responsibilities.

A number of systematic attempts have been made to make radio programs available to schools. One of the most successful is the Ohio School of the Air, promoted by Ohio State University. Teachers' bulletins and study outlines are prepared and distributed to the public schools a week in advance, thus enabling the teachers to prepare to use programs designed especially for the schools. Similar state-wide radio programs for schools are provided by the University of Wisconsin, the University of Illinois, the University of Iowa, the University of Texas, and others. Cleveland, Ohio, and Chicago, Illinois, are examples of city school systems that provide excellent regular radio programs for the public schools. Formerly the Walter Damrosch concerts of the National Broadcasting Company and the American School of the Air of the Columbia Broadcasting System provided radio programs intended for use by the schools during school hours. The Walter Damrosch concerts are no longer on the air, and the American School of the Air has ceased to broadcast during school hours. It is probable that the small number of radio receivers available in classrooms was largely responsible for this change in policy. Perhaps something needs to be done to get more radio receivers in our classrooms.

The main point at issue in this section is not how to use the radio during school hours, because only a comparatively small number of schools are equipped to use the radio in the classroom. A more important problem is concerned with taking cognizance of the influences of the radio during the out-of-school hours of the pupil. What enrichment of their study of school subjects do we find? Is the public more interested in other parts of the world?

Possibly the school should organize a sales resistance program to offset the ballyhoo and palaver of the sponsored program. Perhaps the radio news flashes take the edge off the news of the day so that the population at large awaits the arrival of newspapers with less eagerness. The commercial radio interests, like the newspapers, give the public what they think is wanted. This fact suggests that efforts should be made to develop discriminating tastes and judgments and to encourage people to become more articulate in expressing their wishes. So far the radio industry has developed commercially, unaided and unhindered except for some nominal regulation by the Federal Radio Commission. If radio seems destined to become a powerful educative factor in society, then society as a whole should be taking steps now to control and direct its activity into educative avenues and channels beneficial to all, rather than allow it to continue as an agency of commercial advertising and selling.

The Cleveland public schools provide an excellent example of the use of radio as a regular part of the educational program of the school. In 1925 they began using radio time made available by local commercial stations. In 1938 a school-owned station was acquired, which in 1941 was changed to FM (frequency modulation). This station, WBOE, broadcasts eight hours every school day, scheduling both enrichment programs and demonstration lessons. Its programs are designed for all the educational levels represented in the school system, from elementary through senior high school. WBOE has arrangements with the local commercial stations whereby it can utilize sustaining educational programs from the major networks. If the particular program cannot be relayed at the time of the broadcast, because of conflicting schedules or other difficulties, WBOE makes a transcription. By this experience of more than twenty years in the utilization of radio, the Cleveland public schools provide convincing evidence that radio has a vital contribution to make in enriching, vitalizing, and improving teaching and learning situations in the schools.

Perhaps the most important question relating to the future of radio in the schools is this: Will school systems, colleges and universities, and state education departments claim the FM reserve frequencies that are available to them?   If they do, it will be possible to bring radio into American classrooms.   If they do not, radio will continue to be of only incidental value to organized education.

e. *The motion picture.*   In the development of the motion picture, we have a good illustration of a promising industry with great educative possibilities that has been allowed to grow up under the control of a few people interested in it only as a commercial enterprise.   For years the schools took little cognizance of the film industry except to condemn it as an evil influence.   The churches were even more outspoken in their condemnation.   It is only since about 1930 that any serious efforts have been made to develop the tastes of school pupils for better motion pictures.   Dr. Edgar Dale [5] and others of Ohio State University have conducted some of the most important research in the direction of improved movie appreciation.

It is not an overstatement to say that school people were slow to recognize the movies as an educational medium, as something more than mere entertainment.   But, as in the case of the radio, it is the movies as a supplementary educational agency that should concern us here.   A good case can be made for the geography that children learn from newsreels and many short subjects, and history and literature are richly supplemented by such films as "The Tale of Two Cities," "Little Women," and "Henry V."

The school should take full advantage of the opportunities afforded now to help its students to become more discriminating in their judgments of the motion picture, with, possibly, the result of creating a demand for better films.   After all, the producers, commercially minded though they are, try to meet the demand as they see it.   Valuable in this connection is the comprehensive study [6] financed by a grant from the Payne Fund that attempted to dis-

---

[5] Edgar Dale, *How to Appreciate Motion Pictures* (New York: Macmillan, 1933).

[6] W. W. Charters, ed., *Motion Pictures and Youth,* Payne Fund Studies, 13 vols. (New York: Macmillan, 1933).

cover the social values of the cinema. Moreover, the efforts of the National Council of Teachers of English [7] are aiding high school students in making a better evaluation of the movies, and the work of Edgar Dale [8] is tremendously valuable in helping teachers to make better use of the motion picture, as well as of other audio-visual aids.

The seriousness of the responsibility of the schools is well stated in the following quotation:

Home and church and community have abdicated not to the schools, but to the forms of cheap, mechanical, mass entertainment and mass information—to the movies, the radio, the press, and the advertisements. These may seldom have an educational purpose but they have a pronounced educational effect. They tend to present as desiderata the trappings of material success, of false comfort, of egotistic adventure; they appeal to personal avarice and personal vanity; they play up and down on the child's nerves, and furnish him mechanical emotional outlets at the same time that they apply to him that most insidious of regimentations, mass anesthesia. Against this deadly passivity, our schools are the only bulwark. If they are not strengthened and if they do not teach the student to discriminate and to evaluate, not they but commercial indoctrination, or still worse, political mobstering will form the minds of our children, and in so doing destroy whatever capacity is within them for democratic thinking.[9]

As an agency for the development of better international understanding, the motion picture leaves much to be desired:

It was not until the war broke out that we came to appreciate that the impressions of America registered abroad by films produced in Hollywood were not always of a kind to enhance our prestige or to register a true impression of our way of life. The foreign missions of the State Department then began to bring home to us some of the problems involved in the export of films conceived for our domestic audience. Thus, from Australia it was reported in 1944, "A country boy or girl could not be blamed for thinking that the majority of

---

[7] W. Lewin, *Photoplay Appreciation in American High Schools* (New York: Appleton-Century, 1934).

[8] Edgar Dale, *Audio-Visual Methods in Teaching* (New York: Dryden Press, 1946).

[9] *Fortune* magazine, July, 1943.

Americans are engaged in crime or frivolity." From Morocco came a similar report. "To any American who lived abroad before the present war it will be only too obvious that American pictures were of such a character as to convince foreigners that we were largely a nation of morons and gangsters." [10]

Training aids in the form of films, film strips, and other devices that were developed for use in the training programs of the armed forces during the war proved remarkably successful. Public schools are only now beginning to capitalize on the results of this experience. As they do, there will be a greatly increased use of films and film strips for direct teaching purposes. *Movies That Teach* [11] is an important contribution toward this end.

f. *The theatre.* When we recall that "Uncle Tom's Cabin" was said to have been an important factor in precipitating the Civil War, we get a suggestion of the force of the drama in society. The theatre is an important educational agency. Possibly its influence has declined during the last decade or two; like the family, it is a matter of decline by comparison. The movies have "stolen the show" from the theatre. The "road," as theatre people refer to the one-night stands of a generation ago, is almost non-existent. Only the larger cities get a chance to see the Broadway plays. But virtually every community in the land sees the films produced from them. They are often distorted and "movie-ized," of course, but the message is there, and it is carried to an audience far surpassing anything the spoken stage ever knew. As a matter of fact, instead of being antagonistic forces and warring factions, both the motion picture and the theatre producers are beginning to realize that they represent complementary angles of the same problem. The stage play has enjoyed a remarkable revival recently, the movies are doing a better job of filming the plays, and all in all, there is more demand for the products of our dramatists, and consequently greater rewards for their efforts.

---

[10] Charles A. Siepmann, "Propaganda and Information in International Affairs," *Yale Law Journal*, August, 1946, p. 1269.

[11] Charles F. Hoban, Jr., *Movies That Teach* (New York: Dryden Press, 1946).

The theatre will continue to be an educative force of a high order. It may not touch directly as large a proportion of the population as do many other agencies, but because of its place in the entertainment world, it will exert an influence out of proportion to the number of people it reaches. The dramatist has a story to tell, a message to convey. He is the severest critic of his times. He can use satire, humor, tragedy, ridicule, comedy, or other appeals as his vehicle. His message is compelling because dramatization is a most effective educational method. One of the most serious limitations on the playwright's influence, however, is the fact that a play must be supported through paid admissions at the box office. Patrons must continue to pay to see a production, else the actors cannot continue to present it. If the message it contains is not a particularly appealing one and does not draw crowds, the producer will have to close the show, no matter how urgent is the need for its message.

One solution of this difficulty is a subsidized national theatre, a solution that Eva Le Gallienne and others have long advocated. A hopeful beginning was made in this direction during the depression years with the allotment of relief funds for a theatre project, but this project proved to be merely temporary. Perhaps in another generation or two we shall use government subsidies for supplementary educational activities such as the drama. In the meantime the theatre shows great vitality and excellent promise for the future. One of the most promising auguries is the establishment of the American National Theatre and Academy, which is in the process of organizing itself to support dramatic production throughout the country, and which has been devoting most of its energies to establishing the Experimental Theatre as a token of its function.

At present, the school can make more effective use of the drama as a form of art and as the voice of the critics of our civilization. Too large a proportion of emphasis has hitherto been placed upon dramatizing as a method, and as a vehicle for the histrionic abilities of a few students, and not enough upon the drama and its influence in contemporary life. Keeping in touch with the theatre and its offering is an exceptionally rewarding way to follow current tendencies in social, economic, and political life, and with the assistance we get from the radio and the movies is much easier to do today than ever before.

   g. *Group associations, organizations, and societies.* We are truly a nation of "joiners." It would be difficult, indeed, to calculate the effect of our association with other more or less like-minded people in the multitude of organizations and societies in which we hold voluntary membership. People are drawn together because of similar tastes and temperaments, and they become more alike because of being together. Group contacts are undoubtedly educative. Beginning with the gangs of small boys in cities and running through the intimate primary groups of early adolescence and the college fraternity and sorority to the fraternal and civic organizations of adult life, we find associations that are challenging to the vast majority of the members of society at all age levels. Some of them are quite intimate, loose-knit, informal organizations, such as the gangs; others, like the Boy Scouts, are quite formal in program and dignified in purpose, being organized on a national or international scale. In all cases the groupings tend to produce like-mindedness that results in similar patterns of thinking and uniformity of action. These groupings may be very useful in society, setting standards of conduct, preserving and handing down traditions, as in the case of the person who says, of a rowdy action, "Our set doesn't go in for those things"; or, they may produce undesirable results, as in the case of an individual who does something he is not proud of because he feels he must "go along with the crowd." On the whole, however, their influence is on the side of conservatism.

   The school has been none too alert in taking into account the influence of these societal groups upon the lives and characters of the boys and girls and upon the homes from which they come. We have made some progress in late years through our community contacts, and particularly as a result of the guidance program of the school. Cumulative records enable the teacher to collect a vast amount of pertinent information, which, when supplemented by occasional visits to the homes, makes possible a much more thorough individual diagnosis. Then, too, school practices are being modified to take advantage of the gregarious tendencies of boys and girls, and to give expression to those impulses. These socialized procedures of the classroom are not so much at variance with life as the pupils would like to live it outside the school. A comprehensive program of extracurricular activities furnishes outlets for virtually every type of interest that growing boys and girls have. The school is probably in a better position to take advantage of the educative values of association as a supplementary agency than is true of any of the other agencies we have discussed. To take that advantage pays big dividends in terms of a more vitally functioning school program; to fail to do so means lessened effectiveness.

h. *Advertising.* It would be difficult to overestimate the influence of advertising in our daily lives. If we say that education produces changes in the responses and reactions of an individual, we are certainly justified in referring to advertising as an educational medium. "We are living today under the subtle tyranny of the advertising man," Professor Park [12] reminds us. "He tells us what to wear, and makes us wear it . . . what to eat and makes us eat it. We do not resent his tyranny." That is where the danger of advertising lies. The "subtlety and effectiveness of the means" make it a powerful agency of social control.

Writing about advertising, Morris Ernst tells us:

There is no area of our economy that needs an airing more than advertising—its impacts on our daily lives and its indirect control over our mores. The large advertising agencies, realizing the power of boiler plating, have proposed to continue after the war their present practices of inserting as paid ads virtually identical copy to deal with peacetime trends and problems instead of bond drives and the like. As one leading advertising agent said, 'You can't expect 1,000 editors to comply with your request to write editorials on the same day with the same slant on a single selected national problem. Advertising

---

12 R. E. Park and D. W. Burgess, *Introduction to the Study of Sociology* (Chicago: University of Chicago Press, 1924), p. 830.

can, however, carry on with an identic imprint to influence the thinking of the nation." [13]

Not only do we need to have our attention called to the fact that advertising is a powerful agency; we should also be encouraged to study its objectives and its methods. We are told that some consumer items have to be sold at five times their cost of production, owing to the fact that so much money is spent for advertising them. The producers of these items work diligently to get us to buy a product that is no better and that does not differ fundamentally from a dozen other articles manufactured for the same purpose. What is worse, we allow ourselves to be persuaded to use commodities that are actually harmful, as, for example, hair tonics containing dangerous proportions of arsenic and dentifrices that damage the enamel of the teeth. Consequently, the schools should help their pupils develop sales resistance. At least, it would be in order for them to encourage pupils to seize upon every opportunity to be critical and inquiring concerning the relative merits of products and the techniques of advertisers. Advertising is too powerful an agency to be merely tolerated.

i. *Propaganda.* Here we have a medium that is even more subtle than advertising and consequently more dangerous. Its perpetrators and purveyors are exceedingly anxious to find teachers willing to receive their material and use it in the classroom. Propaganda is usually prepared for an appropriate emotional setting, which renders its effects more penetrating into the attitudes of those on the receiving end. In wartime, propaganda drives reach their peak in intensity. An example is the Axis-inspired propaganda during World War II to the effect that the United States was prepared to fight to the last Englishman, a charge designed to destroy England's confidence in the United States as an ally. Propaganda is usually a one-sided program, working in secret places, aiming to bias, not to liberate.

One duty of the school is to help its students to become more alert and sensitive to the influences and effects of propaganda in

---

[13] Morris L. Ernst, *op. cit.,* p. 102.

society, whether it comes from high places in government at home or abroad or from commercial or pressure groups.   It would not be realistic to expect to eliminate propaganda entirely.   But if we must put up with it, we can at least try to educate people to recognize it when they see it; moreover, we must insist that the avenues of communication be kept open and that there be freedom for the expression of the variety of points of view that may be held on a given subject or problem.   Morris L. Ernst has stated this position ably:

> The American objection to governmental operation of press, radio and movies is that under such direction there is no diversity or clash of opinion.   It is the diversity factor that carries significance with us. Hence, it is argued that it makes little difference to the receiving public whether the absence of competition stems from government or from economic concentration of power.   Philosophically we are still profoundly sound in our adherence to the gospel of free enterprise, particularly in thought.   We must now restore our own market places of the mind not only for the sake of our own freedom, but also so that we can maintain leadership in the world-wide struggle against dictatorship of the mind.[14]

B.   The Function of the School in Society

All of the agencies considered as supplementary educational agencies in the foregoing pages have other functions and render other services.   Education with most of them is at least a secondary objective, or, in some instances, only a by-product.   They were not established primarily as educational agencies.   The school, on the contrary, is society's agent, its one purpose being education.

1.   Primary Function of the School.

Society delegates to the school the formal instruction of its younger members.   There is universal agreement concerning neither the details of what should be taught nor the methods that should be used.   These differences of opinion frequently loom large

---

[14] Morris L. Ernst, *op. cit.,* pp. 270–271.

and are the cause of bitter controversies in many communities. But, in spite of these differences, there is widespread belief in the value of formal education and trustful confidence in the school and its purpose. Society as a whole assigns to the organized educational forces the responsibility for inducting its children into full fellowship in adult society, ready to accept the duties and responsibilities of citizenship.

When it was discovered that one-third of the men drafted for the army in 1917–18 were physically unfit for military service, it was charged that the school program was at fault. Our present-day health and physical education programs in the schools were the result. When President Roosevelt announced in 1942 that close to half a million men were rejected for military service because they failed to pass the literacy tests, the country again became aware of a serious problem that education would have to meet. Moreover, the grave increase in juvenile delinquency that accompanied World War II resulted in demands for greater utilization of the school plant in out-of-school hours and for greater attention by the school to the leisure-time activities of youth. It may fairly be said that every period of crisis in our society results in disclosures of weaknesses in our educational establishment and in insistent demands that these weaknesses be corrected. Five important considerations enter into a clear understanding of the function of the school:

a. There is almost universal acceptance of the notion that whatever society needs to have done, it is the business of the school to help do it. This conviction frequently leads to difficulties and problems for the schools. In America it is traditional for all people to have an abiding faith in the school. Sometimes this interest and devotion become a jealous guardianship, almost a feeling of ownership. Conscientious, sincere, well-meaning patrons get in the way of progress, so zealous are they in their efforts to take a hand in shaping the school's policies.

Another type of problem for school administrators grows out of frequent requests that the school be used to further some worthwhile community enterprise, or that school children be permitted to participate in an educational program conducted by an organization or association that is promoting some particular activity. The widespread use of the schools in wartime for such activities as the sale of war bonds and stamps, and of schools and teachers in connection with the rationing program, undoubtedly has disclosed to many organizations the tremendous possibilities in the use of the schools in connection with their own programs and campaigns.

Many of the demands made upon the schools are for worthy causes, and it might be in order to use the schools to distribute printed material, or to have the students write essays on a given subject, were it not that such drives and campaigns often become a nuisance.   Then, too, some of them are so carefully camouflaged that it is difficult for school officials to distinguish between meritorious educational programs and pure propaganda for commercial interests.   Such difficulties have led many school districts to bar all contests and campaigns and to permit neither speeches nor the distribution of material sponsored by any group or agency.

b. The second consideration in understanding the function of the school is closely related to the first.   It is the business of the school to do what other agencies have left undone.   This duty necessitates on the part of the school a careful study of society and its needs, as well as an appraisal of the extent to which these needs are being served by other agencies.   It is clear that these needs will change from time to time, with the resultant necessity for changes in the program and curriculum of the school.

This fact explains why so many activities have been added to the school's program in recent years.   If, for example, other agencies have not developed an effective health program, it is the duty of the school to do so.   There is little doubt that the mortality from communicable diseases has been lessened by reason of the health inspection in the schools and the subsequent check-up in the home.   Again, when our attention is called to the fact that the majority of crimes are committed by young people and that the average age of inmates of penal institutions is in the early twenties, it is easy to see why the crime problem is laid on the doorstep of the school.

The emphasis in recent years on character education is explained by this consideration. Someone once said that "Wall Street is Main street," meaning to imply that if the brokers and bankers in Wall Street were unscrupulous and untrustworthy, the causes could be traced to the towns and communities all over the land. That is where the Wall Street barons came from. The speculators and the investors live in the same places and are the products of the same educational system. The school must take its share of the blame for unsatisfactory conditions and accept responsibility for a constructive program in the future. The teachers cannot very well say, "We have more than we can do now; let some other agency take that responsibility." If a task within the scope of education needs to be done, and no other agency is doing it, then the school must take the responsibility for it.

It is from this philosophy that those who would have the school create a new social order take their cue. They argue that we cannot solve our present economic problems within the framework of the existing social structure, and that educational efforts in the past have been directed toward perpetuating a system that is doomed to collapse. They contend, therefore, that the school must be used to create a demand and prepare future citizens for a changed social structure. The difficulty arises from the fact that there is little agreement as to the form this new social order should take. A dictator would decide what changes were needed and would direct the school's program accordingly. In a democracy, these changes must come slowly and gradually, by evolutionary processes, and the school has its part to play.

c. It should be noted that the school's program provides a short cut to goals that would ultimately be reached by most individuals. There are very few things the school does that the family or home could not do for the children, or that the individual could not do for himself. The school shortens and systematizes the process. Language is learned in the home, and most youngsters could acquire there enough proficiency in reading and writing and number manipulation to carry on all the business transactions and other relationships in society.   The curriculum of the school, however, consists of those skills and understandings that adult members of society have found useful in compact form.   In its absence children would eventually learn the most essential items from their parents, through practical experiences, if and when they needed to know them.   This system worked fairly well among primitive peoples, whose civilization involved few complex communal relationships.   As civilization advanced, we found increasing emphasis upon systematic organization and instruction, and it was in that manner that our educational institutions have evolved.   The school shortens the time needed to teach these essential skills and understandings.   It would be wasteful and ineffective to continue to allow each family to provide all the instruction needed by its children.   This fact suggests two other very important considerations in trying to evaluate the place of the school.

d. The school's program is more economical.   It actually costs less in the aggregate to organize the situation and provide a minimum education for all the children than for each family to provide tutors and materials of instruction.   Furthermore, and this is of even greater significance, it represents economy to educate all the children and not leave to chance the acquisition of the tools of learning and of the basic understandings of one's duties and privileges as a member of the group.   We cannot afford to leave it to chance.   As Dr. Briggs expressed it, education is a "long-term investment by the state that it may perpetuate itself and promote its own interests." [15]   In a democracy it is essential that all the people be intelligent, participating citizens.   In the long run, it will be an economy to provide more education for all the people. It costs much less to support schools than jails and almshouses. Not only does more and better education result in fewer crimes and criminals, but it also results in higher national and per capita income.   For example, the per capita farm income of farmers in the

---

15 T. H. Briggs, *The Great Investment* (Cambridge, Mass.: Harvard University Press, 1930), p. 48.

ten states ranking highest in education facilities averaged $632 in 1940, whereas the average for the farm population of the ten states ranking lowest in education facilities was only $161.

e. The school's program is more effective. A final argument in favor of delegating society's educational problems to the schools is that the schools can do the educating more effectively. The program will be more effective because there is more or less uniformity of practice throughout the country. All schools are working toward common objectives, at least as far as the minimum program is concerned, a statement that would not be true of the instruction of the young if it were left to the family. The trained teaching personnel is more efficient, inadequate as they are sometimes, than the adult members of society at large would be. Furthermore, the social environment of the school makes for a more effective program. The momentum of the group carries many individuals along, stimulating and motivating their actions. The individual gains much from association, and through the group-mindedness that develops, the goals of society are more easily attained. Parents soon realize this fact when they try to help their children, forced to remain in quarantine or during convalescence at home, to keep up with the class at school. Drill work that would be entered into heartily at school is accomplished only with great difficulty while working alone at home, and as the result of much prodding or bribing or scolding.

We have tried here to show that society entrusts to the schools the chief responsibility for inducting the young members of society into the group. Society delegates; the schools execute. Society wants certain things done; it leaves to public education the formulation of the detailed plans for getting them done. We have seen how completely this conception of the function of the school is accepted. It is possible, though, that we take the school and its program too much for granted. If the school has so large a share in shaping the destinies of a democratic society, its program undoubtedly calls for much more intelligent and sympathetic understanding and more adequate support than it has received in many places. Controversies and difficulties related to financial support of the program usually result from lack of harmony and understanding as to the program to be pursued.

This circumstance brings us to the most perplexing problem of all, namely, the lack of agreement concerning what the school should do. All are agreed that the school should do what society wants done, but it is difficult to determine what society actually wants. It is a very complicated situation. Society is not sure what it wants, but many of its members feel called upon to press their demands upon school officials and in many cases to dictate the methods to be used. The school, on the other hand, feels capable of organizing and administering the details of the program without assistance if it can ascertain what it is expected to do. A very large proportion of local school fights have their origin in this confusion and misunderstanding.

2. Shall the Schools Indoctrinate?

Is it the function of the school to stand and wait for orders, or should it take the initiative and set up its own program? Should it wait for society to make up its collective mind, or should it step out boldly and attempt to fashion the group mind? Will public education render the greater service by conserving and perpetuating the existing institutions and group relationships, or by trying to improve them and trying to create a new social order? Shall the school take a defensive position and resist fundamental changes in the social structure, or shall it assume the offensive and attempt to reconstruct society in the light of new demands and conditions? These are important and pressing questions.

The duty of the school probably lies somewhere between the affirmative answers to the paired questions asked above. The school cannot safely devote all its energies to maintaining the *status quo*. By doing so, it would assume that society is static and unchanging, and such a position would be denying the realities of life. Neither would it be wise to attempt to re-fashion society, to create a new social order, because school leaders cannot be certain what organizations and institutions are needed, and society itself does not see clearly what should be done. Public education has an obligation to prepare students to accept the changes that are inevitable, to share the responsibility for directing the institutions and agencies into more socially useful channels.   It cannot get its students ready for society as it is; society does not remain as it is.   It cannot get them ready for the society of the future; no one knows what it will be like.   The only safe program lies in the direction of making them sensitive to the constant need for change, alert to the possibilities of being of service, conscious of their responsibilities, and informed on the proposals that are being made for the improvement of the social order.   This position certainly argues for the John Dewey thesis that "education is life," rather than the traditional "preparation for life."

The Golden Rule of Education proposed by Dr. Briggs [16] has often been quoted in this connection.   It states, first, that "the first duty of the school is to teach pupils to do better the desirable things that they are likely to do anyway."   What are they likely to do?   We would get one cue if we could find out what people are doing now, but that is not an entirely safe basis for prediction. A glance backward would reveal that many things that large numbers of adults did a generation ago are not being done now. Teaching them "to do better the desirable things" involves much choice and evaluation.   The values are not absolute, and the standards for judging are not fixed.   This statement represents anything but a static condition.   The second statement, "Another duty of the school is to reveal higher activities and to make them both desired and to a maximum extent possible," is even more suggestive of progress and growth.   A philosophy of change seems the only reliable guide for public education.

This point of view might be criticized because it is a middle position, because it represents compromise, because it lacks aggressiveness.   In truth, this position indicates clear gain and progress.   If it were adopted, education would at least keep pace with social changes.   It has not done so in the past, but has always lagged behind.

---

[16] T. H. Briggs, *Secondary Education* (New York: Macmillan, 1933), p. 258.

It is now widely recognized, for example, that we face the absolute necessity for developing international coöperation and international machinery for reducing armament and outlawing war.
The alternative is a third world war infinitely more destructive
than the last.   Howard Mumford Jones presents this challenge to
education:

> Face to face with the spectre of war, with technology controlled by
> war, and with an intense and irrational nationalism which, as in the
> case of the atom bomb, dreams of going to war before some other
> nation shall invent an even more terrible weapon—and this, in a world
> in which the nations have solemnly pledged themselves to unite for
> peace—what have American schoolmen to offer for the guiding of
> mankind?   There is no more tremendous question before the United
> States.[17]

Confronted with this question, what shall be our policy toward
teaching for better international understanding and coöperation,
toward reducing the emphasis on nationalism, toward giving the
fullest possible support to UNESCO?   The answer should not be
difficult.   It is difficult, in fact, because isolationists and other
minority groups in our society would make it most uncomfortable
for any school or teacher attempting to do anything to reduce
nationalism in this country, beyond paying mere lip service to the
ideal.

If our country were controlled by a dictator or autocratic mon-
arch, the function of education would be much simpler.   The ruler
would have full authority to determine the social or economic or
political goals, and he would organize and control education to
those ends.   If his motives were honorable and his goals socially
desirable, the educational system would be useful and constructive
and would contribute to the betterment of his subjects.   If, on the
contrary, the despot were selfish and unmindful of the consequences
of his acts and unconcerned about the welfare of his people, the
schools would be prostituted to serve his purposes.   The signifi-

---

[17] Howard Mumford Jones, *Education and World Tragedy* (Cambridge,
Mass.: Harvard University Press, 1946), p. 45.

cance of education as an agency for directing the nation is clearly in evidence in either case.

In a democracy, it is presumed that education is controlled and administered by representatives of and in the interests of society at large. When there is fairly general agreement in a community, the schools have little difficulty in determining their goals and in planning a program. If all were agreed on the goals, the school's task would be relatively simple. When society not only is not sure of what it wants to do, but does not sense fully the direction in which it is moving, it becomes increasingly difficult for the school to determine its objectives. If minority groups or blocs can control society, they can also control the schools and can easily do so in the interests of the few rather than of the majority. When there is a clash of interests, the school is tempted to withdraw into a position of safety, assume a defensive position, and hope the struggle will end soon. That is what "keeping the schools out of politics" has meant in too many cases and for too long a time. An attitude of aloofness will not suffice. Public education can make positive, constructive contributions to the democracy that supports it only in terms of its understanding of and participation in contemporary affairs. This position does not require taking sides on controversial issues, but it certainly does insist that the school give the pupils a chance to learn the truth, by presenting all sides of such issues, so that eventually they can take sides intelligently.

Indoctrination, it should be pointed out, could be directed toward maintaining the *status quo*, just as it could be employed in advocating some new principles. Indoctrination would be an appropriate description of one's efforts whether one were trying to make the pupils conservatives and stand-patters or liberals and radicals. Many people err in thinking that indoctrination applies only when one is preaching some new doctrine or urging the adoption of untried plans. A teacher of social studies might be criticized for trying to develop in the pupils favorable attitudes toward the social objectives of the "New Deal" of the Democrats. Such teaching would be called indoctrination by the critics, many of whom would not object if a return to the "rugged individualism" of the Republicans were advocated, which would also be indoctrination. Both courses would be objectionable. It is the desire on the part of the teacher to force his views on the pupil, without giving him any choice in the matter, that constitutes indoctrination. Some people say that all teaching is indoctrination; that trying to make pupils alert and sensitive to social changes would be indoctrination. Superintendent Washburne clears up this point very well:

Indoctrination has only to do with controversial issues. It is not indoctrination if we teach a child that flies carry disease, and try to influence him in favor of having his house screened. It is not indoctrination to give a child a recognition of the value of truthfulness. It is indoctrination to try to convince a child that when he grows up he should refuse to fight in any war, even against armed aggression and invasion, or, conversely, to teach him that no matter whether or not his country is justified in participating in a war, he should immediately enlist his service. It is indoctrination to teach a child that the way out of our present difficulties is through a reversion to rugged individualism, or through fascism, or through socialism, or communism, or any other specified means. It is not indoctrination to show existing evils which are commonly recognized as evils or to show ideals which are commonly accepted as desirable.[18]

The best defense against the encroachments of any unwanted social or political structure would be to learn all we can about it. It is the best debate technique to know one's opponent's arguments even better than he does, if possible. Why not go out to meet the enemy rather than wait for an attack? A good offense is the best defense. We can be more successful in meeting the arguments of communism or fascism if we understand them and try to improve our own conditions accordingly than if we assume a blind, unreasoning, defensive position and resist any and all modifications. If our Constitution had never been changed it would not be as satisfactory as it now is. Honest, intelligent inquiry should lead to

---

[18] Carleton Washburne, "Indoctrination Versus Education," *Social Frontier,* II:212, April, 1936.

confidence and assurance.   Chicago's Chancellor (then President)
Hutchins struck at the heart of the question in discussing the aims
of a university during a radio address in April, 1935, under the
auspices of the National Congress of Parents and Teachers:

> The greatest historian of the South has shown that the War between
> the States arose largely because the Southern colleges and universities
> did not dare to say that there were any arguments against slavery and
> secession.   Those who would suppress freedom of inquiry, discussion,
> and teaching are compelled to say that they know all the answers.
> Such a position is egregiously conceited.   It is also a menace to our
> form of government.

In *No Friendly Voice* Dr. Hutchins states that "democratic
government rests on the belief that the citizens will think for themselves" and that the "greatest danger to education in America is
the attempt, under the guise of patriotism, to suppress freedom
of teaching, inquiry and discussion." [19]   That is where the danger
lies in newspaper headlines announcing that a certain patriotic
organization has passed resolutions opposing any changes in the
Constitution.   Many patrons and teachers of the school are likely
to interpret such utterances to mean that they should adopt a
hands-off policy.

Professor Lumley reminds us when discussing social controls
that "the instruments of control are employed by the enemies of
any given group as well as by its members.   They have nothing
to fight with that the patriots do not have." [20]   That is another
way of saying that we should fight fire with fire.   We need have
little fear of an invader who is no better armed than we are.   If
we make free use of the bright light of inquiry and the renovating
influence of free discussion, we shall go far toward disarming the
foe.   Let him talk; let everyone speak freely.   Unfortunately,
the post-World War II period gives every indication of following

---

[19] Robert M. Hutchins, *No Friendly Voice* (Chicago: University of Chicago
Press, 1936); quoted in *New York Times Book Review*, May 3, 1936, p. 24.

[20] F. E. Lumley, *Means of Social Control* (New York: D. Appleton-Century,
1925), p. 400.

the pattern of that of post-World War I in regard to witch-hunting and restrictions on speech and academic freedom.

Thomas Jefferson, arguing for free common schools, took a firm stand for "general education to enable every man to judge for himself what will secure or endanger his freedom." [21] Education has the responsibility for "training individuals to share in social control" and "for participation in projecting ideas of social change." [22] The school cannot escape this duty. As Professor Moore expresses it, "the school perpetuates and promotes the interests of the society which establishes it . . . if it is the product of social democracy." [23] Educators have long recognized this principle, but one suspects that there has been too much emphasis, or the wrong interpretation, or both, on "perpetuates," and too little stress on "promotes." We have been too insistent upon perpetuation of institutions or practices that have not kept pace with social changes. It is improvement of the social order that is needed, not perpetuation.

All this is not an argument for a propaganda type of education. On the contrary, it is expected to provide the best antidote for propaganda, which cannot thrive where fact and truth are revealed. To attempt to mold the reactions of school children into one common pattern would be unwise. Democracy implies freedom: freedom to think, to choose, to act. We shall not attain freedom as an outcome of a doctrinaire education, whether the indoctrination be to maintain the existing order or to fashion a new one. Even though Dr. Tugwell is an avowed advocate of social planning, he makes himself clear on this point:

Education as an instrument ought never to be used in such a way as to prejudice progress in the coming generations. This is a principle which derives from Dewey's double dictum, that society ought to be self-repairing and that it ought to be a function of education. A

---

[21] Quoted by James Truslow Adams, in *On Jeffersonian Principles* (Boston: Little, Brown, 1928), p. 122.

[22] John Dewey and J. L. Childs, *Educational Frontier*, W. H. Kilpatrick, editor (New York: D. Appleton-Century, 1933), p. 318.

[23] Clyde B. Moore, *Citizenship Through Education* (New York: American Book Company, 1929), p. 148.

frankly propagandist education would be an attempt to make the rising generation accept our present purposes and solve the problems which seem to us important.   But it would endanger the possibility of change by fixing ideas.[24]

Dr. Bagley sounded a needed warning in this connection:

The theory that educational policies and programs must necessarily shift and change with every change in the conditions of social life is very far from a sound theory.   It all depends upon the nature and causes of the social change and upon the relation of these both to the educational program that has preceded and to the program that is proposed to meet the new demands which the social change is alleged to have brought about.[25]

It is not the educational policies and programs that should change. That is just what they should not do.   Rather they should be guided by a philosophy that will lead to establishing policies and organizing an instruction program that will render pupils alert and sensitive to changes in society.   This it cannot do by dodging or evading fundamental issues and contemporary problems.   The educational program must be constant and consistent, unswerving in adherence to the ideals of freedom and liberty.   If the job has been well done, democracy in its broadest scope will become more of a reality.   As Dr. Briggs expresses it, the citizens will be "better able and better disposed" to contribute to the welfare of the state.   They will not be "better able" if they do not understand and they will not be "better disposed" if they have not found satisfaction in learning about the important issues of the day and in participating in them.   One more quotation from Tugwell:

If present problems are to be solved, there must be the concentration upon them which can only be achieved through educational process;

---

[24] Reprinted from R. G. Tugwell and L. H. Keyserling, *Redirecting Education* (New York: Columbia University Press, 1934), Vol. I, p. 81, by permission of Columbia University Press.

[25] W. C. Bagley, *Education, Crime and Social Progress* (New York: Macmillan, 1931), p. 6.

that is, youth must be made aware of them and of the suggestions we are able to make toward solution.[26]

The school is an agency created by society for the purpose of furthering its own interests. It accomplishes this purpose by accepting the major responsibility for inducting the young members of society into full participating membership. This it does by providing systematic instruction aimed to furnish the skills and understandings and appreciations needed by intelligent, coöperating citizens. The school supplements and coördinates and integrates the efforts of all the educative agencies in society. It will contribute most if it attempts to sensitize its products to the needs of society, to changes that occur because of population trends, technological improvements, and more intimate international relations. It cannot be a propaganda agent. It cannot blindly defend existing conditions as though they were unchanging, because change is inevitable. Its only safe course lies in facing contemporary issues squarely, gradually introducing students to the problems of society and furnishing them with experiences that will lead to a better understanding of solutions.

When we entered World War II, the schools knew the nature of their task. Furthermore, they knew that for the period of the war there would be a united public opinion on which they could base their policies. Consequently, the Educational Policies Commission was able to state:

When the schools closed on Friday, December 5, they had many purposes and they followed many roads to achieve those purposes. When the schools opened on Monday, December 8, they had one dominant purpose—complete, intelligent, and enthusiastic coöperation in the war effort. The very existence of free schools anywhere in the world depends upon the achievement of that purpose.[27]

With the end of the war that singleness of purpose disappeared. The schools were as eager as before to serve the society of which

---

[26] R. G. Tugwell and L. H. Keyserling, *op. cit.*, p. 82.

[27] *A War Policy for American Schools,* Educational Policies Commission, National Education Association, Washington, D. C., 1942.

they were a part.   But the issues and the purposes of that society suddenly again became complex, and even apparently contradictory.   Some aspects of the complexity of the problem that education faces in the post-war period are presented in the following statement by Howard Mumford Jones:

We have seen in the fascist states the disastrous results of indoctrinating a younger generation with a fallacious absolute and of training them uncritically to accept whatever the state tells them to believe. Democratic critics of contemporary Russia are certainly right in saying that, however excellently the Soviet system may solve the problem of economic democracy, in that state intellectual democracy (in the sense of intellectual freedom) is severely curtailed.   Moreover, the teaching of "democracy" in the United States, a nation which as time goes on grows more and more rigid and conservative, is more than likely, unless educators exhibit courage and intelligence, to become synonymous with the most vicious form of chauvinism.   Already the pressure to teach "Americanism" is one aspect of the arrant nationalism in our unhappy half-century.

In view of our need for a cultural dynamic we cannot postpone the problem indefinitely.   That problem is to find some practical, popular means of combining two disparate elements, each involved in emotion, into a single educational aim which shall receive both critical and emotional loyalty: the implanting in the younger generation of a real enthusiasm for the theory and practice of democracy; and the securing at the same time a real and an intelligent toleration of other outlooks than the western one, provided that these philosophies are not aggressive and authoritarian.   All this demands a profound readjustment of attitudes and evaluations.   How to accomplish this task is the dominant educational problem of the United States in the twentieth century, one that must be solved by more vigorous tactics than a simple return upon the past of western man.[28]

C.   Education in Relation to the Social Sciences

The purpose of this volume is to treat education more broadly than it has been treated ordinarily in text materials used in teacher preparation.   We are attempting a different approach to the study of education not only for the student who is preparing to teach, but for the general education student as well.   We desire

---

28 Howard Mumford Jones, *op. cit.,* pp. 111–112.

to shift the emphasis from teaching as an occupation to education as a field of study.   It is due to much more than mere fashion that educational leaders now speak of the "education of teachers" and "teacher preparation" instead of "teacher training."   Since the establishment of the first normal school in this country, teacher preparation has exhibited in large measure the characteristics of trade training or vocational education, instead of those of general education.   That is, the emphasis has been placed on the acquisition of skills and techniques and devices that will be useful in specific classroom situations and on the actual subject matter that will be studied by the pupils.   With the coming of exploratory courses, pupil guidance, integration of subject matter, and the activity curriculum, teachers and school administrators have felt the need for a broader, richer educational background.   Increased demands upon the schools to participate in social and community enterprises and to interpret political and economic and international issues force the teachers to seek a better understanding of social and industrial forces.   It may be said that the prospective teacher does not learn to teach ; he is considered instead a student of education.

This development makes a new definition of education necessary.   We need to think of education as a social force.   We have already discussed the many agencies that, in a multitude of ways, serve as educative influences.   In the preceding section we gave serious consideration to the school as an agency for improving the social order.   All persons, whether they be teachers or not, are concerned about the aims of education.   We need to study education in relation to other social forces.   The study of education thus becomes the study of a social science or, at least, it is pursued in relation to the other social sciences.   Professor Melvin tells us that :

. . . one must gain a vision of the public school as a grand mission of human liberation.   Unless one can see the events which have been the upward striving of men, one does not know what the schools have done, or dream of what they can do.   The hardheaded fight of the Puritans for schools to deliver their children from gross ignorance was only a beginning. Today total childhood swarms into schools each morning and is delivered back to the community in the afternoon. The children dwell in houses made by men and learn what society would have them learn. These public schools are the mighty buttresses of human liberty.[29]

Before proceeding further, let us turn to the social scientists themselves. Professor E. R. A. Seligman, the editor of the *Encyclopedia of the Social Sciences*,[30] wrote an introduction for it entitled, "What Are the Social Sciences?" First, he contrasts the physical sciences and the social sciences, after which he states, "The social sciences may thus be defined as those mental or cultural sciences which deal with the activities of the individual as a member of a group." Then he classifies them into three groups. First, the purely social sciences: politics, economics, history, jurisprudence, anthropology, penology, and sociology. Second, "side by side with them fall the semi-social sciences. They are social in origin and retain in part their social content." In this group are ethics, education, psychology, and philosophy. Third, sciences with social implications include biology, geography, and medicine. Dr. Seligman states the case for education a little more fully and pointedly, thus:

While pedagogics deal with the unfolding of the individual mind and the strengthening of the individual aptitude, it has always been recognized that isolation is incompetent to achieve the desired results. The activity of the individual in the group and the reactions of the group on the individual are of signal importance. Not in vain have schools and classes been invented; not lightly to be dismissed are the educational functions of play, of song and of dance, all of which connote a social origin. Education is thus partly social in aim, partly social in method, partly social in content, and may therefore be deemed a semi-social science.

There is much support here for the notion that education needs to be studied as one of the social forces, as one of the influences

29 A. Gordon Melvin, *Education—A History* (New York: John Day, 1946), pp. 3–4.
30 E. R. A. Seligman, Editor, *Encyclopedia of the Social Sciences* (New York: Macmillan, 1930), Vol. I, pp. 3–7.

that shape and mold society. It also confirms and approves the socializing tendencies in school practices. This is an important point. If the school is to participate in society as one of the social agencies, its procedures should naturally harmonize with those in the life about it.

Another well-known authority, Dr. Charles A. Beard, was asked to discuss the background for the objectives prepared by the Commission on Social Studies of the American Historical Association. This he did in a book entitled *The Nature of the Social Sciences*, which contains many references to education. They furnish some good arguments for treating education as a social science. The social sciences, he says, "are concerned with the actualities of human societies in development. . . . They all deal with the same subject, man, or, to speak more concretely, men, women, and children, within the framework of their environment." [31] Education has within the last generation or two become increasingly interested in the social group, as well as in the individual. At another point, Dr. Beard says, "As ethical sciences, they (the social sciences) are concerned with good or better conduct and good or better material and social arrangements." [32] So is education. Better conduct has always been one of education's chief aims, but better social conditions have come into the educator's sphere of interest only recently. He also indicates that trends in the social sciences "all point in the direction of concerted and collective policy and action," [33] and reminds us that the major problem is "closer coordination and more effective integration of the swiftly changing elements in American social life, which must be brought into living relation with education in the public schools, if that education is to be kept abreast of contemporary ideas and interests." [34] This is a telling argument for the philosophy of change that was advocated in the preceding section.

---

[31] Charles A. Beard, *The Nature of the Social Sciences* (New York: Scribner's, 1934), p. 3.
[32] *Ibid.*, p. 44.
[33] *Ibid.*, p. 155.
[34] *Ibid.*, p. 156.

Professor Finney goes even further in contending that education is a social process and that this principle is being recognized by the educators themselves. ' The schools turn to the social sciences for their facts. They take the initiative in attempting to interpret the changes that are constantly occurring in society. This point of view is elaborated as follows:

> Education may function as an important guiding factor in social evolution, especially in periods of critical transition like the present— not absolutely, to be sure, but to a degree that has never been sufficiently capitalized by an aspiring society. And that throws a new and enlarged responsibility upon educators, to which it is high time that they awake. Potentially, the school is the steering gear of a democratic society. If society is to be engineered on the basis of ascertained knowledge and general enlightenment, instead of on the basis of superstition, sentiment, and personal ambition, the scholars and educators must proceed to take their place at the wheel.[35]

This idea of education as a form of social engineering is defended by Kimball Young, who insists that education is indispensable to all social progress:

> Clearly urbanized mass society, as we have described it, cannot carry on without extensive use of the school and other means of teaching and indoctrination. Within the limits of normal mental-emotional capacity to have a place in society, every individual will require (1) essential intellectual tools of a literate man, (2) provision for good health, (3) basic vocational training so as to take his place in helping to operate a complex technological, economic, and political system, (4) information or knowledge about the world and (5) a basic value system— a set of beliefs, convictions, or philosophy of life.[36]

This quotation raises two exceedingly important questions. The first one has to do with those who are guiding education. Education cannot contribute to the improvement of society if its leaders are not convinced of their responsibilities. Educational

---

[35] Ross L. Finney, *A Sociological Philosophy of Education* (New York: Macmillan, 1928), p. 116.

[36] Kimball Young, *Sociology—A Study of Society and Culture* (New York: American Book Company, 1942), p. 478.

leaders must not be controlled by nor fearful of the disapproval
of those who, for their own selfish interests, would maintain relationships as they now exist. The second question is concerned
with the objectives of education. Who will formulate them? How
can we determine whether they are valid and worthy? The answer is to be found in the social sciences; it will be firmly established in a sound social philosophy. Educational leaders must be
found who understand social forces and who are able and willing
to think beyond the development of tools and skills. Italy under
Mussolini furnished a good illustration of the need for giving attention to those who control education and the objectives they set
up. An able correspondent evaluated the situation there prior to
World War II in this fashion: "Italy is one vast full-time school
in which every boy and girl, from infancy to maturity, is taught
one lesson: to believe, to obey, to fight." [37] If society does not
find its ablest leaders and authorize them to prepare for socially-
minded leadership, then we may expect self-appointed leaders to
assume the role.

Man is a social being. That is the chief reason why education
should be studied as a social science. As an individual, considered
biologically, man is not greatly different from the lower animals.
It is when we consider man in relation to other men that the most
significant differences appear. Animals are trained as individuals,
almost never in groups. Man is educated as a member of a group
and in relation to the needs of the group. Of course, man learns
as an individual, and it is as such that the psychologist studies
him. The educator takes the findings of psychology concerning
the learning process, and, in the light of social needs, directs his
education along socially useful lines. At least, that is what should
be done if education is to render the best service in society. It
would not be correct to say that the schools have given too much
attention to the technical aspects of learning; but we are justified
in contending that too little has been directed to the social ob-

---

[37] Anne O'Hare McCormick, "The New Italy—Fact or Phrase," *New York
Times Magazine,* May 17, 1936, p. 25.

jectives of education. We find support for this position in the
following quotation from Kimball Young:

> Not only are we more or less constantly in contact with our fellows,
> but from birth on our very survival is dependent on what others do
> for and to and with us. Normally the newborn infant gets his first
> training from his parents. Later relatives, neighbors, and friends add
> to this teaching. Without such social care and direction he would not
> only perish, but he would not become a human being at all. In our
> particular society so much stress is put on individual effort and attain-
> ment that we sometimes forget that all through our lives we remain
> enmeshed in a web of contacts—direct and indirect—with those about
> us. Our individualism itself is a social-cultural product.[38]

The philosophy of change as well as the social point of view
that we have been advocating finds confirmation in a statement
from Coe:

> Education, then, is to aim at variability in the student, a cultivated
> variability! The youth brings to high school and college the precious
> treasure of youth, a feeling that the world is not finished and done, but
> in the making. . . .
> How shall we ever have a deliberate, thought-guided social evolution
> —as against, perhaps, revolution, certainly as against social flounder-
> ing—unless our educational system, from the bottom to the top, is
> reorganized with reference thereto?[39]

We have undoubtedly made the mistake in the past of conducting our schools as though we were trying to make all individuals
alike; our aim certainly has not been toward a "cultivated vari-
ability." We have even tried to stamp it out when it occurred
naturally. Realizing that this was done during the period that
society was apparently regarded as static, it is easy to see why the
school's objectives became so far removed from the reality of life.

Professor Harold Rugg has for many years been in the front
ranks among those who would have the schools assume a major
role in guiding society. He assumes that social reconstruction is

---

[38] Kimball Young, *op. cit.*, p. 3.
[39] George A. Coe, *What Ails Our Youth?* (New York: Scribner's, 1924), p. 45.

inevitable and that educators will participate in it.   He answers
his own question "What will be the educator's strategy?" as follows:

> To me the answer emerges from the foregoing analysis. The Ameri-
> can way of controlled social change follows the democratic method of
> building consent among the people. But this can be done only by
> educating the people to an understanding of and participation in their
> collective affairs. The educator, then, is as vitally concerned with the
> American mind as is the student of politics. Both are strategists of
> practical social reconstruction. Both formulate their policy program
> around the real, not the assumed, concepts and loyalties of the Ameri-
> cans today. Let the educator, therefore, make his own direct study
> of the American climate of opinion and found his strategy of educa-
> tional reconstruction upon it. Let him be aware of the findings of
> earlier students of culture, but let him never, for long at a time, allow
> his attention to swerve away from the crucial conditions and problems
> of his own people and his own times.[40]

Have we been mistaken in the past in keeping the schools out of
politics?   It would seem so.   We have had too little share, as a
result of that policy, in shaping the policies of the state.   Our
pharisaical attitude of aloofness has rendered the schools incapable
of effecting desirable social changes.   Politics have fallen into
disrepute, and the term has become one of opprobrium.   The
school can, and is really obligated to, raise the level and dignity of
politics until they will command the respect and interest of us all.
It is the process by means of which we can all participate in the
state.   One of our great educators, Henry Suzzallo, who was
famous as a phrase maker, expressed the ludicrous result of our ill-
advised hands-off policy pithily when he said, "Sprinkle a majority vote on a plumber—at election—and he becomes a states-
man."   We have allowed those without the preparation to do so
to control our social planning, and what is worse, we have not been
particularly careful to see that our citizens learned to be intelligently critical of the process.

---

[40] Harold O. Rugg, "The American Mind and the Class Problem," *Social
Frontier*, II:142, February, 1936.

The Education Policies Commission was established by the National Education Association and the American Association of School Administrators in 1935 for the purpose of defining guiding policies for American education. Its publications [41] have exerted a considerable influence upon American education, especially in the matter of clarifying the role of education in our democratic society. It is important to note that in the United States, where there is no national system of education, there is an especially significant place for voluntary agencies in the field of policy formulation. The Educational Policies Commission has no authority over any teacher, school, or school system. Yet its proposals receive respectful consideration from educators and laymen.

We have tried in this section to defend the thesis that education should be studied as one of the social sciences; that it should be understood by all persons, whether teachers or not, as a potent social force, on the grounds that: (1) Man is essentially a social animal. (2) Virtually all of his problems are of a social origin. (3) The school's main function is to induct the young members of society into the group. (4) Education is also obligated to further the interests of the society of which it is a function. All these situations demand the understanding of social phenomena and the utilization of social processes.

D. Using Education to Attain National Objectives

We can get a better understanding and appreciation of the significance of education in society when we examine the practices of strong nationalistic governments. In them we shall see how education was used as an agency for molding the character and forming the attitudes of the people. The most striking examples are to be found in Germany, Italy, and Japan, prior to their defeat in World War II. It should be clear that education is always employed, more or less consciously, by a country for the attainment of its national objectives. If the policy of the gov-

---

[41] Published by the National Education Association of the United States, 1201 Sixteenth Street, N. W., Washington, D. C.

ernment is highly nationalistic, aggressive, and militaristic, education under that regime will reflect these tendencies. The more highly centralized the government, the more easily and surely will it control its educational establishment. It is important to note, in this connection, the fact that in the United States we have no national system of education. Education is recognized by tradition, and by interpretation of the Constitution of the United States, as a responsibility of the respective states. Consequently, it would be difficult, although perhaps not impossible, for the Federal Government to gain control of education in this country. When we observe what certain highly nationalistic governments have done to pervert education to unworthy purposes, it is not difficult to understand why many thoughtful citizens resist strenuously any possible changes looking toward Federal control of American education.

Let us consider briefly education in Germany, Italy, and Japan.

1. Germany

The people of Germany have long had faith in education, as the high store that Martin Luther set by education demonstrates. In the early days of Prussia seventeen teachers were sent to Switzerland to study with Pestalozzi. They followed his teachings only to a degree because they soon realized that a liberal and comprehensive education would give the people a taste for independent thinking that was not congenial to the type of patriotism their rulers desired. In Unit II we saw how subject matter and method were blended to serve the interests of the Hohenzollerns, who were in power just prior to World War I. It was the intention of the founders of the German Republic in 1919 to make the educational system thoroughly democratic, and much progress was made in that direction. Its leaders were trying to capture the enthusiasm and the spirit of freedom of the Youth Movement. All this changed with the coming of Hitler. "This Germany is to have only one goal, one party, one conviction [he might have added one fiction, one race, and one religion], and this state organization is to be identical with the nation itself." [42]   The whole life of the state became one vast "educational" enterprise, with a Minister of Propaganda at the head.   Censorship was rigid, and a great many activities were subject to complete governmental control. The schools were completely subordinated to the will of the state —a state headed toward aggressive war.   Teachers who were "unsafe" were purged.   There was no academic freedom.   Only military defeat was able to break the hold of Hitler on the German people and their educational establishment.

It is significant to note that our political and military leaders responsible for the occupation of Germany have recognized fully the necessity for "denazifying" German education.   There appears to be no tendency to underestimate the power of education. Perhaps one of the few gains resulting from the war is the belated recognition by the American people of the terrific force of education—a force that may as readily be utilized for developing race hatred, warlike aggressiveness, and brutality, as for developing democratic ideals and for implementing the great ideal of the brotherhood of man.

2. Italy

The one compelling motive in Italy under Mussolini was Fascism. Mussolini found his opportunity in the poverty, illiteracy, corruption, inefficiency, and class distinction rife in Italy.   He capitalized on an intense love of country that dates back to the "grandeur that was Rome."   From the time his black-shirted mob marched on Rome, there was a steady advance toward the nationalistic goal that was intended to restore Italy to its former place of world prominence.   The schools were "improved" under Fascist domination.   Let us examine some aspects of that improvement.   Illiteracy was greatly reduced.   The Minister of Public Instruction in the first Mussolini cabinet expressed the belief that the schools should be employed for "strengthening the

---

[42] I. L. Kandel, "Education and Politics," *Kadelpian Review*, 14:113–20, January, 1935.

nation and making Fascists. . . . The state is, as it ought to be, a teacher. . . . In the school, the state comes to a consciousness of its real being." [43]   An attempt was made to influence the children through the primers, from which they were to repeat: "We children must salute the King, Mussolini, and our own great country, Italy." [44]

By certain kinds of superficial standards, Mussolini certainly improved education in Italy.   He also was widely credited, and perhaps correctly, for making the trains run on time in Italy. Perhaps some day we may learn not to make these superficial judgments about education and teaching.   Regardless of the efficiency with which the activity is conducted, it is the educational outcome that is important.

3. Japan

Japan was another aggressive and militaristic nation that utilized education for the achievement of her nationalistic purposes. She did this with great efficiency.   With education and all other media of communication and information in Japan subordinated to the will and the objectives of the central government, there was no means short of military defeat of reversing the trend.   Today capable American educators are laboring valiantly with the Japanese teachers in an effort to help them democratize education in that unhappy country.   The prospects for success appear to be somewhat better there than in Germany.

4. Scandinavian Countries

For purposes of contrast, let us consider briefly the Scandinavian countries, and their utilization of education to attain national objectives.

---

[43] Giovanni Gentile, quoted by Shepard B. Clough in R. G. Tugwell and L. H. Keyserling, *Redirecting Education* (New York: Columbia University Press, 1935), p. 189, by permission of Columbia University Press.

[44] Francesco F. Nitti, "Fascist Education," *School and Society,* 36:824–6, December 24, 1932.

In few parts of the world prior to the German invasion in 1940 could we have found a social philosophy permeating the activities of a people to the extent to which those of Norway, Sweden, and Denmark were thus permeated. These small independent countries did a remarkably effective job in social planning, and their program was accomplished through education, not by means of force and coercion. Old age pensions, care for the defectives and delinquents in society, and coöperative enterprises of many types are typical illustrations of the fruits of this social planning. Denmark furnishes a particularly good example. Hemmed in on all sides by warring neighbors in the post-Napoleonic era, her leaders realized that no military force that they could muster would prevent their small country from being swallowed up. In the middle of the nineteenth century Bishop Grundtvig sensed the national degradation that was taking place. His efforts to correct it led to the establishment of the folk high schools, which, with other later educational developments, made possible the fashioning of a thriving coöperative state that withstood the effects of World War I, a world-wide economic depression, and World War II with remarkable success. The Germans were able to occupy Denmark, but they were not able to convert her people to Nazism, nor to break their will to resist. The Danes had developed a way of life that was theirs because they had created it, and they did not lose confidence in it even in their darkest days. Education had served them well. In *Denmark, a Cooperative Commonwealth*, C. Howe tells us that:

Denmark seems to me to be quite the most valuable political exhibit in the modern world. It should be studied by statesmen. It should be visited by commissions. Denmark is one of the few countries in the world that is using political agencies in an intelligent, conscious way for the promotion of the economic well being, the comfort and the cultural life of the people.[45]

---

[45] Quoted by John H. Wuorinen, in Tugwell and Keyserling, *Redirecting Education* (New York: Columbia University Press, 1935), Vol. II, p. 213, by permission of Columbia University Press.

E.   Problems and References for Collateral Study

Problems for Students

1. Attack or defend the proposition that the home today is less effective as an educational agency than formerly.

2. In the light of your own experience indicate how the church could be more effective as an educative agency.

3. Compare the contents and policies of two or more newspapers (or of newspaper chains) to determine the type of education each is providing.

4. Make a critical analysis of the radio offering for a period of time to determine its value as an educational medium.

5. Keep a record of the motion picture offering for a period of time to determine the range and scope of education provided.

6. Study the theater for a season in order to evaluate its worth when compared with other educative agencies.

7. Catalog our contemporary dramatists according to the type of problems treated by their productions.

8. Prepare an appraisal of what you learned from the associations and the organizations with which you have been affiliated.

9. Make a critical analysis of one advertising medium (radio, magazines, billboards) to determine its educational value.

10. Assemble data regarding the various types of propaganda to which an ordinary citizen is exposed.

11. What kind of education would an individual have if he never attended school at all (assuming that one could disregard the compulsory attendance laws)?

12. What is the school attempting to teach that it might better leave to other agencies?

13. Enumerate the skills or knowledges that an individual needs and for which the school should assume a greater responsibility.

14. Prepare a list of current issues or questions concerning which the school would be justified in pursuing a policy of indoctrination.

15. Attack or defend the proposition that education is one of the social sciences.

Selected References

Alexander, W. P., *Educational Needs of Democracy.* London: University of London Press, 1940.

Beard, Charles A., *The Nature of the Social Sciences.* New York: Scribner's, 1934.

Breed, F. S., *Education and the New Realism.* New York: Macmillan, 1939.

Britt, S. H., *Social Psychology of Modern Life.* New York: Farrar and Rinehart, 1941.

Brown, Francis J., *Educational Sociology.* New York: Prentice-Hall, 1947.

Bruce, W. F., *Principles of Democratic Action.* New York: Prentice-Hall, 1939.

Charters, W. W. (editor), *Motion Pictures and Youth,* Payne Fund Studies. New York: Macmillan, 1933, 13 vols.

Cohen, J., and R. Travers, *Educating for Democracy.* New York: Macmillan, 1939.

Dale, Edgar, *Audio-Visual Methods in Teaching.* New York: Dryden Press, 1946.

———————, *How to Appreciate Motion Pictures.* New York: Macmillan, 1933.

Ernst, Morris L., *The First Freedom.* New York: Macmillan, 1946.

Fallaw, Wesner, *The Modern Parent and the Teaching Church.* New York: Macmillan, 1946.

Federal Communications Commission, *Public Service Responsibility of Broadcast Licensees,* Washington, D. C., 1946.

Furnas, J., and others, *How America Lives.* New York: Holt, 1941.

Hoban, Charles F., Jr., *Focus on Learning.* Washington, D. C., American Council on Education, 1942.

———————, *Movies that Teach.* New York: Dryden Press, 1946.

Hutchins, Robert M., and others, *A Free and Responsible Press.* Chicago: University of Chicago Press, 1947.

John Dewey Society, *Democracy and the Curriculum.* New York: D. Appleton-Century, 1939.

———————, *Teachers for Democracy.* New York: D. Appleton-Century, 1940.

Jones, Howard Mumford, *Education and World Tragedy.* Cambridge, Mass.: Harvard University Press, 1946.

Kilpatrick, William H., *Group Education for a Democracy.* New York: Association Press, 1940.

Landis, Paul, *Social Policies in the Making.* Boston: D. C. Heath, 1947.

Landry, R. J., *Who, What, Why is Radio?* New York: Stewart, 1943.

Levenson, William B., *Teaching Through Radio.* New York: Rinehart, 1945.

Lewin, W., *Photoplay Appreciation in American High Schools.* New York: D. Appleton-Century, 1934.

MacDougall, Curtis D., *Newsroom Problems and Policies.*   New York: Macmillan, 1941.

Melvin, A. Gordon, *Education—A History.*   New York: John Day, 1946.

Moley, Raymond, *The Hays Office.*   New York: Merrill, 1945.

NEA Educational Policies Commission, Washington, D. C.:
Education and Economic Well-being in American Democracy, 1940.
Education and the Defense of Democracy, 1940.
Policies for Education in American Democracy, 1946.

Pittenger, B. F., *Indoctrination for Democracy.*   New York: Macmillan, 1941.

Villard, Oswald G., *The Disappearing Press.*   New York: Knopf, 1944.

Waples, Donald (editor), *Print, Radio, and Film in a Democracy.* Chicago: University of Chicago Press, 1942.

Wieman, Regina W., *The Modern Family and the Church.*   New York: Harper, 1937.

Woelfel, Norman, and I. Keith Tyler, *Radio and the School.*   Yonkers, N. Y.: World Book Co., 1945.

Young, Kimball, *Sociology—A Study of Society and Culture.*   New York: American Book Company, 1942.

Contemporary Problems Challenging Education

In this unit the writers have selected some of the major problems that confront the society of our day, and with which education must be concerned, directly or indirectly. An attempt has been made, not to present a complete list of such problems, but rather to present enough of them to give the student a realization of the close interrelationship that must exist between education and the society in which it functions. Some consideration will also be given to the question of the contribution that education may be expected to make toward the solution of some of these problems.

A.   Reconstruction of the Social Order

Probably few persons would disagree with the statement that society must always be in a process of reconstruction or change. New conditions, some the acts of nature, such as volcanic eruptions, earthquakes, or glacial action; inventions, such as the steam engine, the cotton gin, the internal combustion engine, or the harnessing of atomic energy; discovery and exploration, which open up new continents, new trade routes, and introduce new customs; war, and the willful acts of powerful leaders—these are only a few of the major factors that dictate and determine social change. Society must always be in a process of adjusting itself to these powerful forces. Indeed, it probably is not too much to say that the very existence of a society depends upon its ability to make satisfactory adjustments quickly enough to stave off disaster. This problem of how to effect quick changes and adjustments to new conditions is especially serious in a democratic society. In periods of extreme emergency we solve it by granting unusual temporary emergency powers to the chief executive officer. The problem was well illustrated by our difficulties in making the transition from a peacetime to a wartime economy at the outbreak of World War II, and again in our efforts to make a quick and orderly shift from wartime to peacetime economy after the war.

Just as there are these powerful and sometimes irresistible forces demanding change and reconstruction, so are there almost equally powerful forces resisting change. Society organizes itself for the discharge of essential social functions into a large number of social institutions or agencies, such as the family, the church, the school, business, and many others. These institutions become powerful and develop traditions and practices that are not easily changed. Furthermore, the very size of some of these agencies, such as the church and the school, makes change difficult. Organized society, then, tends to be conservative and to resist change.

There also must be considered the human factor in connection with these social institutions and agencies, for the latter could not exist independently of human beings. In all of these institutions there are vested interests, held in large or small part by many people. The individual holding such a vested interest usually views any proposal for change from the point of view of its probable effects upon his personal fortunes. When proposals are made to socialize medicine, for example, a large share of the medical profession, particularly those members who enjoy a lucrative private practice, organize the opposition to such proposals. Similarly, private utilities interests oppose the development of publicly owned and operated electric plants. The capitalist opposes socialism. In all of these, and in many similar instances, the true reason for the opposition is seldom stated, and the public is usually confused by a barrage of propaganda, often false and misleading, which conceals, rather than reveals, the true issues involved.

Sometimes the changes that are proposed are sound and defensible. Sometimes they are not. The forces of right are not always on the side of change. Sometimes the advocates of change may wish to move too rapidly, even though the direction in which they wish to go is the right one.   It has been said that probably the greatest contribution of certain left-wing political parties in this country is to be found, not in the possibility that they may be elected to office, but in their education of the public relative to needed reforms and changes that are advocated through their platforms and speeches.   Many of these reforms are later adopted by the major political parties.

1.   Control of the Factors of Production and Distribution

One of the ever-changing and ever-present problems with which our society is confronted is that of maintaining a proper balance between production and distribution.   Economists and social reformers have been disturbed about this problem for many years. One of the best known of the earlier writers on this subject was Thomas Robert Malthus, who in 1798 presented to the world "An Essay on the Principle of Population as It Affects the Future Improvement of Society."   He began with the assumption that population is necessarily limited by the means of subsistence, and that population invariably increases where the means of subsistence increase, unless prevented by some very powerful checks.   It was his contention that population would increase in geometrical proportion, and productivity of human necessities only in arithmetical proportion.   Men of his day drew many and diverse conclusions from Malthus' theories, such as that it was useless to attempt to do anything to alleviate the condition of the poor, as all efforts must necessarily result in failure.

Since Malthus' day, many changes have occurred that have radically modified, if not entirely discredited, his theories.   The Industrial Revolution, a greatly accelerated rate of invention, the application of power to the machine, and the perfection of mass production techniques in many fields are among the major influences.   One way of expressing the total effect of these changes is to say that we have changed from an economy of scarcity to an economy of abundance.   Among present-day economists, Stuart

Chase is the foremost exponent of the abundance theory.[1] A
pioneer advocate of the newer economic theories, and one from
whom Stuart Chase and many other experimental economists of
the present day received inspiration, was Thorstein Veblen
(1857–1929). In *The Engineers and the Price System* (1921),
he suggested putting technicians and engineers in control of
industry, with authority to plan and manage production in the
interests of society. It was in this proposal that Technocracy
had its origin.

It is the contention of the adherents of the abundance theory of
economics that, owing to such changes as those enumerated above,
our present major problem is one, not of production, but rather
of distribution. They held that we now have it within our power
to abolish poverty and to provide an abundance for all. They
point out that capitalism served well the needs of an economy
based upon scarcity, when there was not enough to go around,
and that perhaps the best method of distribution under those
conditions was one based upon competition, in which the individual
was encouraged to scramble for the little that was available for
distribution. They hold that such a system is highly inconsistent
under present conditions, and that it results in restricting, rather
than in facilitating, distribution. They point to poverty in the
midst of plenty, to unemployment when factories are idle and
when the output of those factories is badly needed by the people.
They point to the steady decline in the importance of human
labor as a factor in production, owing to the development of
technological processes.

There are disagreements among economists and other expert
students of the problem relative to how high a living standard could
be maintained if the productive machinery were free to operate for
the satisfaction of human needs, rather than for profit. The

---

[1] Stuart Chase, *The Economy of Abundance* (New York: Macmillan, 1934);
Goals for America—A Budget of Our Needs and Resources (New York:
Twentieth Century Fund, 1942); *Where's the Money Coming From?* (New
York, Twentieth Century Fund, 1943); *Democracy Under Pressure* (New York:
Twentieth Century Fund, 1945).

problem is a complicated one.   Such questions as the following must be taken into consideration: What is America's capacity to produce?   What is America's capacity to consume?   Can a satisfactory and workable system of distribution be devised to replace the present one, which, it is generally admitted, is far from perfect? Would the productive machinery be slowed down by the removal of the profit motive, and if so how greatly?   We know that our wartime production during World War II was far in excess of previous estimates of our ability to produce.   Whether we can attain and maintain such production in peacetime remains to be demonstrated.

There is widespread disagreement among thoughtful people relative to the workability of the socialist formula: "To each according to his need; from each according to his capacity."   It is not the purpose of the writers to attempt to provide the reader with answers to these and similar questions, but rather, if possible, to provoke thought and discussion concerning them.   We believe it is obvious that if society is to move toward a coöperative and away from a competitive organization, education must play an important role in effecting an orderly transition.   This point will be discussed more fully in the section dealing with the contribution of education to the solution of contemporary problems.

2.   Providing a Guarantee of Economic Security

This problem is closely related to the one we have just considered.   The fact that economic insecurity exists is largely an admission that the distributive system has not functioned properly. Here we are concerned with unemployment, which occurs for a variety of reasons, with economic insecurity due to illness and accident, and with economic insecurity during old age.   The depression which began in 1929 in the United States, and which reached its greatest depths in 1932, made the people more keenly aware than ever before of the necessity for taking constructive action regarding the problems of economic insecurity.   Many people expect an even worse economic collapse to follow World War II.

There has always been some unemployment. Some people will not work. Others, owing to mental or physical handicaps, are incapable of working, and must be supported by relatives and friends, by charity, or by the public. This was a familiar problem before the depression, and it was handled more or less adequately by organized charity and by the provision of public institutions, such as almshouses and poor farms, usually supported locally. It was only during the depression, when we found ourselves with fifteen million persons unemployed in the United States, that we became aware of the seriousness of the problem. At the beginning of the depression the problem was regarded as one for the local communities, since local communities always had cared for their own unemployed. Later, it was recognized that the states, and then that the Federal Government, would have to act. The problem became so great that only the resources and the credit of the Federal Government were adequate to meet it. Even then it was considered by most persons to be a temporary emergency problem, and it was so handled. More recently there has been a growing conviction in the minds of many persons that unemployment is no temporary problem, and that we must make long-time constructive plans for its solution.

The United States has lagged far behind other advanced countries, such as England, in providing unemployment insurance and provisions for the retirement of the superannuated. As a substitute for the emergency measures taken during the depression, belated efforts have been made to meet these problems through legislation by the Federal Government in coöperation with the states. In the meantime many plans, most of them unsound, have attracted the attention of millions of people. Perhaps the major contribution of the unofficial groups that have sponsored weird and unworkable proposals has been to focus attention upon the need for prompt constructive action.

The goal to be attained is reasonably clear. It is to provide the greatest possible degree of economic security for all people. For those who are able to work this means guaranteeing that there will be the opportunity to work, and at such a rate of pay as will provide a decent standard of living. For those who are unable to work, whether by virtue of sickness and accident or of super-annuation, it means the provision of a decent standard of living without dependence upon charity. The goal is more easily stated than reached. Such a program admittedly will be costly. Con-sequently, many persons and organizations are in opposition to it.

The widespread labor-management strife that has followed the end of hostilities in World War II is intimately related to this problem of economic security. Such issues as retirement funds, health and accident insurance, a guaranteed annual wage, seniority, the relating of wages to profits, and the demand that labor be permitted to participate with management in the determination of certain vital policies, are indications of this relation. It is almost incontrovertible that no one is opposed to high wages, high living standards, and economic security for everybody. The sharp differences relate almost entirely to the means of securing these benefits. Almost all agree as to the necessity of securing them if our present economic system is to endure.

B. Perpetuating the Ideals of Democracy

An overwhelming majority of the people of the United States are in favor of democracy. In fact, until very recently, and for a long period of time, democracy was something we just took for granted. We knew that we had it; we knew that we should always have it; we knew that it was the best form of government for us; and we were convinced that it would also be the best form of government for all other countries, if they could only be persuaded to try it. That was before the disillusionment following the First World War, which we entered with the slogan: "To make the world safe for democracy." Czarist Russia and Imperial Japan were on our side in that conflict. How amused they must have been at our slogan! A similar period of disillusionment has followed World War II. Again we have learned that winning a war did not make the world safe for democracy. It never does.

The First World War marked a turning point in the history of nations. In its aftermath the swing toward democratic, popular government of free peoples was checked. Powerful dictatorships, openly contemptuous of democracy, came into being, and were signally successful in conquest and diplomacy. The League of Nations, up to that time the world's most ambitious and idealistic experiment in the extension of the democratic principle to international relations, was utterly unable to cope with certain economic-political situations that arose, such as aggression by stronger members of the family of nations against those incapable of their own defense. It was unable to prevent the world from again going to war. Now, following World War II, the weak and inadequate League of Nations has been superseded by the United Nations. It remains to be seen whether or not the peoples of the world and their leaders will be wise enough to build a United Nations structure that will be able to avert a third world conflagration. The future of civilization is at stake.

The net result of the depression at home and of the domestic and world situation following World War II has been to cause many Americans to question seriously how our democratic institutions can be preserved. A net gain, however, is the fact that we are no longer so greatly inclined to take democracy for granted. We now know through the experience of other countries that democracy can be lost if the people are not vigilant and alert in its protection. Furthermore, through studying the experiences of the peoples under modern dictatorships, we are able to understand what would be involved in the loss of democracy.

At the present time we appear to be in the process of expanding our conception of the meaning and scope of democracy. A common dictionary definition of democracy is that it is government by the people. We have expanded that definition to read, somewhat idealistically, "government of the people, by the people, and for the people." What we have, to be more nearly accurate, is a representative democracy, probably the only type that could function successfully in a country as large as ours in area and in population. By tradition we have thought of democracy almost wholly in political terms. In these terms it was concerned with the right to vote, to hold office, and to participate in the making of the laws. It was also concerned with the protection of the civil rights of the individual. The extension of the democratic principle has been largely in the direction of extension of suffrage, such as the removal of property qualifications for voting and the giving of the vote to women.

It is not astonishing that in our earlier history democracy should have been conceived in political terms. The need that was felt was for political liberty and for equality of political opportunity. Our country was established and our Constitution was adopted in a period when individuals did not feel as they do today the need for guarantees of equality of economic opportunity. The closing of the frontier, our development into an industrial nation, the concentration of wealth and economic power, and the rapid strides of technology, all have contributed to focus attention increasingly upon the need for the development of an industrial and economic democracy paralleling our political democracy.

In the light of modern conditions, it appears that certain generalizations may safely be made relative to democracy and the problems involved in perpetuating the ideals of democracy. These are:

1. A democracy demands the active and intelligent participation of its citizens.

2. A democracy demands active coöperation among its members.

3. A democracy demands that its finest and ablest citizens should be elected to positions of leadership.

4. A democracy demands the exercise of initiative and independence of thought on the part of its citizens.

5. A democracy demands that all its citizens be given the best possible training for service, both to self and to society.

6. Continuous social change, with the purpose always of achieving the greatest good for all, must be a major objective of a democracy.

In all of these, it is apparent that the main bulwark of a democracy is an informed and an intelligent citizenry, trained in active participation in government. The teaching of this citizenry is the major task of education in a democracy.

C.   Developing International-Mindedness

One does not need to be especially sensitive to what is going on around him to realize that one of the most fundamental developments of our day is the action of science and invention in bringing the peoples of the world into ever closer physical relationship to each other.   In August, 1947, William P. Odum flew around the world, a distance of 15,596 miles, in 73 hours, 5 minutes, 11 seconds.   Presently men will do it in half that time.   On September 21, 1947, an American Air Force Douglas C-54 Skymaster with a "mechanical brain" took off from Stephenville, Newfoundland, with 14 crew members and observers aboard.   Ten hours and 15 minutes later the plane landed at Brice Norton, near London, after a flight of 2,400 miles.   No human hand touched the controls for the takeoff, the flight, or the landing.   In communication the advances have been even more amazing.   Wartime advances in wireless transmission include speeds of 800 words a minute.   By the end of the war more than 360 radio transmitters located in more than 50 countries were sending more than 2,000 words a minute round the world in more than 40 languages. Advances in speed of transportation, combined with new inventions applied to communication, now make it possible to fly whole pages of magazines in cellophane mat form to printing plants all over the world, thus making possible the simultaneous publication on five continents of a complete magazine forty-eight hours after the material has been written.   Contrast these accomplishments with the fact that our greatest victory in the War of 1812 was won by General Jackson at New Orleans on January 8, 1815, while the treaty of peace which officially ended the war was signed at Ghent on December 24, 1814.

The net result of these and other changes is that it has become clearly impossible for any part of the world to exist in isolation. We are forced to the conclusion that for peace, prosperity, and economic security, we are dependent not alone upon our own actions and those of our own people and of our own government, but also upon the actions of the peoples and the governments of

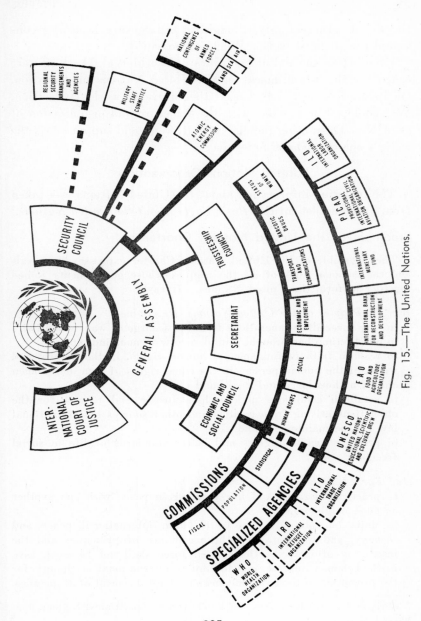

Fig. 15.—The United Nations.

235

the world. Increasingly, thoughtful citizens are becoming convinced that it must be One World or no world.

Even before the end of hostilities in World War II, steps were taken for the establishment of the United Nations organization. On its success may well depend the future of world civilization. We should all be familiar with the structure and organization of the UN. Then, being familiar with it, we should support it as the world's one great hope for peace.

United Nations Organization

The following information about the United Nations was taken from the pamphlet entitled *Basic Facts About the United Nations.*[2]

Preamble of the United Nations Charter

The Preamble of the United Nations Charter expresses the ideals and the common aims of all the peoples whose governments joined together to form the United Nations. It says:

We, the Peoples of the United Nations, Determined
  to save succeeding generations from the scourge of war, which twice in our lifetime has brought untold sorrow to mankind, and
  to reaffirm faith in fundamental human rights, in the dignity and worth of the human person, in the equal rights of men and women and of nations large and small, and
  to establish conditions under which justice and respect for the obligations arising from treaties and other sources of international law can be maintained, and
  to promote social progress and better standards of life in social freedom,

And For These Ends
  to practice tolerance and live together in peace with one another as good neighbors, and
  to unite our strength and to maintain international peace and security, and to ensure, by the acceptance of principles and the institution of methods, that armed force shall not be used, save in the common interest, and to employ international machinery for the promotion of the economic and social advancement of all peoples,

---

2 Prepared by the Department of Public Information, United Nations, January, 1947.

Have Resolved to Combine Our Efforts to Accomplish These Aims. Accordingly our respective Governments, through representatives assembled in the city of San Francisco, who have exhibited their full powers found to be in good and due form, have agreed to the present Charter of the United Nations and do hereby establish an international organization to be known as the United Nations.

Membership

Membership of the United Nations is open to all peace-loving nations which accept the obligations of the United Nations Charter and, in the judgment of the Organization, are able to carry out these obligations.

(There were fifty-one original members. Other countries can be added by the General Assembly upon the recommendation of the Security Council.)

Organs

Six main organs make up the United Nations. They are:

The General Assembly
The Security Council
The Economic and Social Council
The Trusteeship Council
The International Court of Justice
The Secretariat

Subsidiary organs may be set up as necessary.

The General Assembly

The General Assembly is composed of all member states. Each member shall have not more than five representatives in the Assembly. Each country decides the way in which it chooses its representatives.

The functions of the General Assembly are:

to consider and to make recommendations on the principles of international co-operation in the maintenance of peace and security, including the principles governing disarmament and the regulation of armaments;

to discuss and make recommendations on any world problem except a dispute or situation currently being discussed by the Security Council;

to initiate studies and make recommendations to promote international political co-operation, the development of international law and its codification, the realization of human rights and fundamental freedoms for all, and international collaboration in economic, social, cultural, educational and health fields;

to receive and consider reports from the Security Council and other organs of the United Nations;

to make recommendations for the peaceful settlement of any situation, regardless of origin, which might impair friendly relations among nations;

to approve trusteeship agreements and supervise their execution;

to elect the six non-permanent members of the Security Council, the eighteen members of the Economic and Social Council, and to take part in the election of the judges of the International Court of Justice;

to consider and approve the budget of the United Nations and to examine the budgets of specialized agencies.

Voting on important questions, such as recommendations on peace and security, election of members to organs, admission of new members, trusteeship questions and budgetary matters, is by a two-thirds majority. On other questions, it is by a simple majority.

The General Assembly meets once a year. Special sessions can be convened at the request of the Security Council or by a majority of members of the United Nations.

The budget of the United Nations was approved at $19,230,000 for 1946 and $27,450,000 for 1947.

The Security Council

(The Security Council is composed of five permanent members: China, France, the Union of Soviet Socialist Republics, the United Kingdom, and the United States, and six non-permanent members, elected by the General Assembly for a two-year term.)

The functions of the Security Council are:

to maintain international peace and security, in accordance with the Purposes and Principles of the United Nations;

to investigate any dispute or situation which might lead to international friction;

to recommend methods of adjusting such disputes;

to formulate plans for the establishment of a system to regulate armaments;

to use economic or military sanctions to prevent or stop aggression;

to submit reports to the General Assembly.

The Security Council acts on behalf of all the Members of the United Nations, who all agree to carry out its decisions and to undertake to make available to the Security Council at its request armed forces, assistance and facilities necessary for the maintenance of peace and security.

Voting in the Security Council on all matters other than questions of procedure is by an affirmative vote of seven members including the concurring votes of the five permanent members. This constitutes the so-called "veto" right of the permanent members, and means that no important decisions can be taken unless the five permanent members are in agreement about them. On questions of procedure, voting is by affirmative vote of any seven members.

The Security Council functions continuously and a representative of each if its members must be present at all times at the headquarters of the United Nations. Countries which do not belong to the Council may take part in its discussions when the Council considers that a country's interests are specially affected or when it is a party to a dispute under consideration by the Council.

The Military Staff Committee, composed of the Chiefs of Staff of the five permanent members, advises and assists the Security Council on such questions as the Council's military requirements for the maintenance of peace, the strategic direction of armed forces placed at its disposal, the regulation of armaments and possible disarmament.

The Atomic Energy Commission, although not directly dependent on the Security Council, reports to that body and is accountable to it on all matters affecting security. All the members of the Security Council are represented on it, and in addition Canada, at times when that country is not a member of the Security Council. The Commission was established on January 24, 1946 by the General Assembly. Its functions are:

to inquire into all phases of the problem of the control of atomic energy, and to make recommendations on them;

to extend between all nations the exchange of basic scientific information for peaceful ends;

to make proposals regarding the control of atomic energy so as to ensure its use only for peaceful purposes; for the elimination from national armaments of atomic weapons and other weapons of mass destruction; and for effective measures of inspection.

Economic and Social Council

The Economic and Social Council is composed of eighteen members elected by the General Assembly. Its functions are:

to be responsible for the economic and social activities of the United Nations; to make studies, reports and recommendations on international economic, social, cultural, educational, health and related matters;

to promote respect for and observance of human rights and fundamental freedoms for all;

to call international conferences, to prepare draft conventions for submission to the General Assembly on economic and social matters;

to coordinate the activities of the Specialized Agencies;

to provide advice and technical assistance to members of the United Nations upon request.

(Voting in the Economic and Social Council is by a simple majority.)

The Council works through Commissions and Committees. Nine commissions have so far been set up. They are:

Economic and Employment Commission
Transport and Communications Commission
Fiscal Commission
Statistical Commission
Population Commission
Social Commission
Human Rights Commission
Commission on Status of Women
Commission on Narcotic Drugs

A temporary sub-commission on economic reconstruction of devastated areas has also been established. Sub-commissions are also to be set up on employment and economic stability; economic development; statistical sampling; freedom of information and of the press; protection of minorities; protection against discrimination.

(It is the Council's responsibility to coördinate the work of specialized agencies. Through the Council's Committee on Negotiations with Specialized Agencies, draft agreements defining this relationship are being negotiated with each specialized agency.)

Non-governmental organizations are consulted by the Economic and Social Council on questions with which it is concerned. The Council recognizes that these organizations should have the opportunity to express their views and that they often possess special experience of technical knowledge which will be of great value to the Council in its work. So far four non-governmental organizations have been given "consultative status." They are:

The World Federation of Trade Unions
The International Co-operative Alliance
The American Federation of Labor
The International Chamber of Commerce

Trusteeship Council

The United Nations have accepted as a sacred trust the obligation to promote the well being of dependent peoples and their progressive development towards self-government and independence. They have accordingly set up an International Trusteeship System for the administration of territories placed under United Nations supervision through individual trusteeship agreements.

The Trusteeship Council is composed of countries administering trust territories; permanent members of the Security Council; and enough other countries (elected by the General Assembly for three-year terms) to make an equal division between countries which administer trust territories and countries which do not. Its functions and powers are:

to consider reports from administering authorities;

to examine petitions;

to make periodic inspection visits;

to check conditions with an annual questionnaire on the political, economic, social and educational advancement of the inhabitants of trust territories.

International Court of Justice

The International Court of Justice meets at The Hague, Holland. Its purpose is to act as the principal judicial body of the United Nations. It is a Court of Law and deals with legal questions only, not with political disputes. All countries parties to the Court can refer to it any case they wish. In addition, the Security Council may refer a legal dispute to the Court, and all the organs of the United Nations can ask the Court for an advisory opinion on any legal question. Individuals cannot refer cases to it.

The Court consists of fifteen judges elected by the General Assembly and the Security Council. No two judges can be nationals of the same state. The judges serve for a term of nine years and may be re-elected. The judges are chosen on the basis of their qualifications, not on the basis of their nationality. Care is taken, however, to see that the principal legal systems of the world are represented on the Court.

The jurisdiction of the Court is optional, that is, cases are brought before it only with the consent of the parties concerned. States themselves must decide over what cases the Court is to have compulsory jurisdiction. This can be done either by separate agreements or by signing the optional clause of the Court's Statute. *The optional clause,* if signed by a State, provides that that country recognizes as compulsory the jurisdiction of the Court in all legal disputes concerning: the interpretation of a treaty; any question of international law; the existence of any fact which, if established, would constitute a breach of an international obligation; the nature or extent of the reparation to be made for the breach of an international obligation. The first four countries to sign the optional clause were: China, the Netherlands, the United Kingdom, the United States.

The Security Council can be called upon to back decisions of the Court.

Secretariat

The Secretariat is composed of a Secretary-General appointed by the General Assembly upon the recommendation of the Security Council and "such staff as the organization may require." It is the Secretary-General's job to be the chief administrative officer of the United Nations. He is authorized to bring to the attention of the Security Council any matter which in his opinion threatens peace and security.

The present Secretary-General of the United Nations is Trygve Lie, former Foreign Secretary of Norway. He is assisted by an international staff recruited on the basis of their qualifications.

Specialized Agencies

These organizations are international in scope and their members are Governments. The General Assembly has approved agreements governing the relationship of the United Nations with the Food and Agriculture Organization, the International Labor Organization, the Provisional Civil Aviation Organization, and the United Nations Educational, Scientific and Cultural Organization (UNESCO). Agreements will be negotiated with the other specialized agencies.

Food and Agriculture Organization of the United Nations (FAO)

FAO originated in the hope, expressed in the Atlantic Charter, to see established a peace which will afford assurance that all men in all lands may live out their lives in freedom from want. Its purpose is to raise levels of nutrition and standards of living; to secure improvements in the efficiency of the production and distribution of all food and agricultural products; to better the condition of country dwellers; and by these means, to contribute to an expanding world economy.

International Bank for Reconstruction and Development

Its purposes are to assist in the reconstruction and development of territories of members by facilitating the investment of capital for productive purposes; to promote private foreign investment and to provide loans out of its own capital for productive purposes; to promote the balanced growth of international trade and the maintenance of equilibrium in the balance of payments.

International Labor Organization (ILO)

Its purposes are to contribute to the establishment of lasting peace by promoting social justice; to improve, through international action, labor conditions and living standards and to promote economic and social stability.

(The ILO was established on April 11, 1919, when its Constitution was adopted as Part XIII of the Treaty of Versailles. It

was one of the most useful and successful of the agencies associated
with the League of Nations, and one of the few survivors of that
organization.)

International Monetary Fund

Its purposes and functions are: to promote international monetary
co-operation and the expansion of international trade; to promote exchange stability, maintain orderly exchange arrangements among members, and to avoid competitive exchange depreciation; to assist in the
establishment of a multilateral system of payments in respect of current transactions between members and in the elimination of foreign
exchange restrictions which hamper the growth of world trade.

International Refugee Organization

Its purposes are to assist in the repatriation or resettlement of refu-
gees and displaced persons; to protect their rights and legitimate interests and give them care and assistance until their repatriation or
resettlement can be carried out.

International Trade Organization

Its purpose is to promote the expansion of world trade and the
removal of trade barriers.

Provisional International Civil Aviation Organization

Its purpose is to study problems of international civil aviation and
the establishment of international standards and regulations for civil
aviation.

United Nations Educational, Scientific and Cultural Organization

UNESCO was established November 16, 1945, when its Constitution
was adopted by a Conference of forty-three nations in London.   It
was created in order to advance, through the educational and scientific
and cultural relations of the peoples of the world, the objectives of
international peace and of the common welfare of mankind for which
the United Nations was established and which its Charter proclaims.

(A detailed statement of the purposes of UNESCO is given on
pages 251–54 as a part of the section of this unit concerned with
the development of international-mindedness.)

World Health Organization

Its purpose is the attainment by all peoples of the highest possible level of health.

D.   Contribution of Education to Solution of These Problems

There are marked differences of opinion among educators and the public concerning the proper role of education in a democratic society.   There are many who believe that education should avoid controversial issues, such as those that have just been discussed. They point to the large and important field of service that is open to the school in giving training in the fundamentals, in health education and health habits, in character education, and in good citizenship.   They believe that youth so trained will meet adequately the problems it will be called upon to solve when adult.   They hold that the school will alienate much of its support if it introduces the consideration of controversial issues.   In general, those who hold these views are conservatives who prefer that social change should proceed at a slow tempo rather than at the greatly accelerated pace demanded by some liberals and by radicals.

Still others hold that it is folly for the school to fail to acquaint youth with the perplexing and fundamental issues and problems confronting our society.   They point out that modern society is confronted by many difficult problems that demand prompt and positive action.   They recognize that our schools, in neglecting the consideration of these controversial issues in the past, have been responsible in large measure for the fact that the present generation of adults is poorly equipped to face intelligently the new problems that demand fundamental changes in the social order for their successful solution.

Along with this change in policy relative to the education of youth, there also is advocated an extension upward of educational opportunity to include adult education.   It is held to be highly inconsistent in a rapidly changing society to say, in effect, to youth upon graduation: "Your education is now completed.   You are equipped to meet the problems of life.   Society in your lifetime will change so slightly that your preparation will not become obsolete." Yet that is substantially what our policies have indicated. Until recently most people have believed that the capacity to learn diminished rapidly after about the age of twenty-five. Studies by Thorndike and others have disproved this belief. Adult education, which formerly consisted chiefly of Americanization classes and classes in English for foreigners, is now conceived as a social necessity for a". Two major purposes would be served through adult education with reference to the problems under consideration in this section: (1) The present generation of adults would be brought up to date and reoriented in their social, economic, and political education. (2) As a result of this process, the resistance of the public to the changes suggested above in the education of youth would be removed.

Some educators take a more extreme position than that just outlined. They believe that under present conditions we must have a definitely planned society. They would entrust to boards and commissions, consisting of those persons best equipped for the tasks involved, the responsibility for the redirection of our society. It would then be the task of the school and of education to plan an educational program in harmony with this charted course for social reconstruction. There are certain important differences between this position and the one described above. This one clearly involves indoctrination. The other involves a consideration of all aspects of the problems under consideration, with the individual free to make choices.

This question of indoctrination is one of the most important of the many problems that teachers must face. A dictionary defines indoctrination as follows: "To instruct (in) or imbue (with), as principles or doctrines; to teach." The definition just quoted was written several years ago. Many persons have pointed out that teaching has always been a process of indoctrination, but that the indoctrination has been in favor of the status quo. So long as it took this form few persons objected to it. To the new form, indoctrination in favor of a changed social order, strenuous objections are raised by many persons and powerful interests and organizations. For example, a law enacted by Congress in 1935 forbade the teaching of communism in the public schools of the District of Columbia. Doubtless a large number of the Congressmen who voted for this bill considered teaching to be synonymous with advocating. It appears to be highly important that teachers and the public should draw a distinction between teaching and indoctrinating. We should realize that teaching means, not advocating, but giving information about something. It seems inconceivable that teachers in the District of Columbia, or elsewhere, should have been forbidden to give information about communism to their classes. It seems perfectly right that they should not be permitted to advocate it in the classrooms. Our practices need to be changed and the dictionary definition of indoctrination revised, so that indoctrination is not made synonymous with teaching.

What, then, should be the contribution of education toward the solution of the persistent and challenging problems of society? In the judgment of the writers these problems should be very much the concern of education, and education should make a major contribution toward their solution. Let us consider first the role of the public school, below the college level. Much has been spoken and written in recent years relative to socializing the curriculum. This term may be defined as the selection, organization, and treatment of curriculum materials so as to make the maximum possible contribution to social good. Educators, and the term includes teachers, are largely responsible for the selection, organization, and treatment of curriculum materials. It is not difficult to identify the major persistent problems and issues confronting society. Since decisions relative to the curriculum must be made, they may be made in terms of these problems and issues.

1. Perpetuating the Ideals of Democracy

Most schools are not very democratic, either in the relations between administration and teachers, or in the relations between teachers and pupils. It appears to be highly inconsistent for the school, which is supposed to be the most important agency of a democracy for the perpetuation of its ideals, to be organized and administered along autocratic lines. The school should be the most democratic of our social institutions rather than one of the most autocratic, as it is at present. Children should have experience in the selection of leaders, and should learn the importance of wise choices; they should participate in the determination of policy as rapidly as their degree of maturity will permit. They should grow up in a democratic environment, and in one that encourages the exercise of citizenship.

We shall give one other illustration of what the school can do. There is excellent justification for the belief that our society should move still further in the direction of a coöperative and away from a highly competitive society. To do this involves the developing of incentives to labor other than those of profit and competition. The schools can make a major contribution here. At present the principal incentives to labor in the schools are marks, fear of nonpromotion, and competitive awards and distinctions, such as honor rolls. It is interesting to note that children in kindergartens, where marks and fear of nonpromotion are not in evidence, usually work more enthusiastically than do older pupils who have these incentives. When a certain school of education abandoned the giving of marks, many teachers of long experience who were taking courses in that institution registered a complaint with the head of the institution. They stated that since there were no marks, they had nothing to work for. But if this artificial incentive had never existed, they would have had sufficient incentive in the value they derived from their courses. Some progressive school systems have now abolished marks and nonpromotion, with results that are highly satisfactory and without sacrificing standards.

At the college and university level, education should play an important part in the solution of the major problems of contemporary society. It has been said that higher education, particularly scientific and technical education, appears to create more problems for society than it solves. Trained intellects, not exclusively, but largely, the products of modern higher education, are greatly responsible for the rapid technological advances of the past few decades. It is reasonable to expect that these advances will con-

tinue.   Undoubtedly every major advance in technology precip-
itates important social problems.   Higher education has been
criticized, and perhaps justly, for having failed to contribute
sufficiently to the solution of these social problems that it has had
a hand in precipitating.   There are several reasons for the failure
of higher education to contribute as greatly to the solution of
political, social, and economic problems as it has to the solution of
technological ones.   It may be profitable to consider briefly some
of these reasons.

The scientific method and the great generalizations of science have
made possible the astounding technological advances of recent
years.   Hyman Levy, in *The Universe of Science*,[3] has listed the
great generalizations of science from which most of our physical
apparatus could be reconstructed.   These are:

Newton's Law of Motion.

Newton's Law of Gravitation.

Faraday's and Maxwell's Laws of Electromagnetic Action.

The laws governing the conservation of matter and energy—
the first and second laws of thermodynamics.

The atomic theory.

The theory of evolution.

The Mendelian theory.

The electronic constitution of the atom.

The theory of evolution and its generalization concerning the
nature of time and space.

Technological education thus has a body of tested generalizations and principles upon which it is based.   Those who seek to
contribute to the solution of social problems have no such sure
base from which to start.   Sir Norman Angell, in *From Chaos to
Control*,[4] has pointed out that the layman is able and willing to
follow the advice of the medical experts, but not of the economic
experts, because we adopt a scientific attitude toward medical mat-

---

3 Hyman Levy, *The Universe of Science* (New York: D. Appleton-Century
Co., 1933).

4 Sir Norman Angell, *From Chaos to Control* (New York: D. Appleton-Century Co., 1932).

ters and physical phenomena that we do not adopt toward the study of social, economic, and political phenomena. This attitude is due in part to the lack of an accepted scientific basis for the solution of many of these problems, in part to disagreement among the experts, but probably chiefly to failure of the schools to develop a scientific attitude on the part of their students toward social, economic, and political problems. In the consideration of these matters we are guided and swayed by prejudice, emotion, oratory, and propaganda, rather than by facts and by the best judgments of the experts.

There is considerable evidence to the effect that the colleges and universities are becoming more keenly aware of their neglect of the social sciences, and of their obligation to contribute to the solution of social problems. The major engineering societies have indicated clearly during the past few years their conviction that the engineer should be made aware of the social implications of his technology. There is now a marked tendency in higher education and in all professional education to provide a broad general curriculum in which a liberal time allotment is made to the social sciences.

President Dodds [5] of Princeton calls our attention to a great weakness in liberal or general education:

A liberal education should be an education for use. It not only should cultivate a desire in the student to apply his education to the world about him; it should also teach how he can so apply it. It is not enough to teach merely the content of the academic courses. How what is learned can be used must be taught also. . . . Now the subject matter and the methods of analysis and the criteria with which the classroom deals are equally useful and valid when applied to the actual situations of life. But the student may never become aware of this; he may never bridge the gap between learning about something in an academic way and applying his academic knowledge to the problems of later life. . . . What is taught in the classroom remains in the "classroom compartment" of a young man's mind because he has never been taught how to use it.

---

[5] Harold W. Dodds, *Out of This Nettle Danger* . . . (Princeton: Princeton University Press, 1943), pp. 54–55.

2. Developing International-Mindedness: UNESCO

A glance at the diagram (Fig. 15) on page 235, showing the United Nations organization, discloses that UNESCO is one of the specialized agencies of the United Nations. Probably it should have occupied a more prominent place in the organizational structure, since the ultimate success or failure of the United Nations must inevitably rest largely upon the degree of success with which UNESCO discharges its functions. It is essential that we be acquainted with the organization and purposes of UNESCO, and that we find effective ways of coöperating with it in the achievement of its purposes. As a contribution toward that end, the introductory statement and Article I of its constitution are reproduced here:

Constitution of the United Nations Educational, Scientific and Cultural Organization

The Governments of the States Parties to This Constitution on Behalf of Their Peoples Declare

that since wars begin in the minds of men, it is in the minds of men that the defences of peace must be constructed;

that ignorance of each other's ways and lives has been a common cause, throughout the history of mankind, of that suspicion and mistrust between the peoples of the world through which their differences have all too often broken into war;

that the great and terrible war which has now ended was a war made possible by the denial of the democratic principles of the dignity, equality and mutual respect of men, and by the propagation, in their place, through ignorance and prejudice, of the doctrine of the inequality of men and races;

that the wide diffusion of culture, and the education of humanity for justice and liberty and peace are indispensable to the dignity of man and constitute a sacred duty which all the nations must fulfill in a spirit of mutual assistance and concern;

that a peace based exclusively upon the political and economic arrangements of governments would not be a peace which could secure the unanimous, lasting and sincere support of the peoples of the world, and that the peace must therefore be founded, if it is not to fail, upon the intellectual and moral solidarity of mankind.

For These Reasons,

the States parties to this Constitution, believing in full and equal opportunities for education for all, in the unrestricted pursuit of objective truth, and in the free exchange of ideas and knowledge, are agreed and determined to develop and to increase the means of communication between their peoples and to employ these means for the purposes of mutual understanding and a truer and more perfect knowledge of each other's lives;

In Consequence Whereof

they do hereby create the United Nations Educational, Scientific and Cultural Organization for the purpose of advancing, through the educational and scientific and cultural relations of the peoples of the world, the objectives of international peace and of the common welfare of mankind for which the United Nations Organization was established and which its Charter proclaims.

Article I

Purposes and Functions

1. The purpose of the Organization is to contribute to peace and security by promoting collaboration among the nations through education, science and culture in order to further universal respect for justice, for the rule of law and for the human rights and fundamental freedoms which are affirmed for the peoples of the world, without distinction of race, sex, language or religion, by the Charter of the United Nations.

2. To realize this purpose the Organization will:

   a. collaborate in the work of advancing the mutual knowledge and understanding of peoples, through all means of mass communication and to that end recommend such international agreements as may be necessary to promote the free flow of ideas by word and image;

   b. give fresh impulse to popular education and to the spread of culture;

   by collaborating with Members, at their request, in the development of educational activities;

   by instituting collaboration among the nations to advance the

ideal of equality of educational opportunity without regard to
race, sex or any distinctions, economic or social;

by suggesting educational methods best suited to prepare the
children of the world for the responsibilities of freedom;

c. maintain, increase and diffuse knowledge;

by assuring the conservation and protection of the world's
inheritance of books, works of art and monuments of history
and science, and recommending to the nations concerned the
necessary international conventions;

by encouraging coöperation among the nations in all branches
of intellectual activity, including the international exchange of
persons active in the fields of education, science and culture
and the exchange of publications, objects of artistic and scientific interest and other materials of information;

by initiating methods of international coöperation calculated to
give the people of all countries access to the printed and published materials produced by any of them.

De Palma photo from Black Star

Fig. 16.—These Two Young Ladies Have Caught the Spirit That UNESCO
Seeks to Promote.

3. With a view to preserving the independence, integrity and fruitful diversity of the cultures and educational systems of the States Members of this Organization, the Organization is prohibited from intervening in matters which are essentially within their domestic jurisdiction.

What can colleges, teachers and students do to strengthen and to work with UNESCO? The statement that follows was prepared by the Association of American Colleges, and is reproduced here with the permission of the Association.

What the Individual College Can Do

The substantive program of UNESCO will afford opportunities for American educators to participate in international projects both as individuals, through their professional organizations, and through the colleges themselves. We now ask what steps can be taken by an individual college to promote UNESCO's purpose "to advance the intellectual and moral solidarity of mankind." Among the objectives to which the individual college should direct its efforts are:

A. To prepare itself by appropriate administrative action to participate as an institution, and through its faculty members, in the international program of UNESCO.

B. To consider whether its curriculum can be improved so as to further the basic purposes of UNESCO.

C. To promote student activities which will contribute to a better understanding of the peoples of the world and of their cultures, and activities which best support UNESCO in its efforts to promote this better understanding.

D. To render services to its community in order to develop within the local and regional areas that sense of participation and dedication and that habit of coöperation without regard for race, class, or creed that must ultimately prevail throughout the world.

1. *General administration.* Some administrative action may be necessary before a college can participate adequately as an institution in the program of UNESCO. A committee at the Estes Park Conference considered this problem and suggested the following steps:

a. Secure the formal recognition of UNESCO by governing boards and faculties, and approve the inclusion of UNESCO in the recognized activities of each institution.

b. Make budgetary provision for such activities.

c. Appeal for contributions to expand UNESCO activities.

d. The college faculty members should adopt a definite policy of encouraging activities as individuals. Such encouragement may take the form of granting leaves of absence to faculty members participating in foreign interchange and in research projects suggested by UNESCO, providing funds for the interchange of faculty members and students, and fostering faculty membership in international organizations interested in UNESCO.

e. The college should appoint a faculty liaison UNESCO officer or UNESCO committee or both. Such an officer or committee should coördinate and initiate campus UNESCO activities, should serve as information officer, and should be designated as the agent of the college in all relations with the National Commission and UNESCO.

f. The faculty should be granted opportunity and assistance for attendance at summer schools in foreign countries, and at conferences on and off campus.

g. Interchange of personnel should be stimulated by the appointment of a committee to examine the areas of the college program in which exchange and visiting teachers could be most effectively used; to communicate with the appropriate national or international committees; and to provide for participation in the selection of such persons.

h. The establishment of bi-lateral relations with a particular foreign university should be considered. The objective of these relations would be to secure a better appreciation of their cultural and other achievements. Such a relationship, moreover, should stimulate the interests of that institution in corresponding American achievements at the point where reciprocal studies would be initiated.

i. The college should provide an adequate program of orientation and counselling for foreign students.

j. As an institution, the college should undertake research projects recommended by UNESCO, including the assignment of faculty members to such projects.

k. International, national, and regional conferences should be sponsored and supported.

l. In the college itself, foreign lecturers may be invited to speak before college assemblies. Art exhibits, music recitals, and museum collections will likewise stimulate interest in UNESCO and through it in the various cultures of the world. Other agencies which deal with international understanding also may contribute to this program.

m. Publicize the colleges' participation in UNESCO through all appropriate media, including a column in the Alumni Magazine.

2. *Curriculum adjustment.*

a. The college curriculum should be carefully examined in light of the need for eliminating national prejudices, strengthening devotion to the principles of justice and fair play, increasing the basic understanding of other peoples and their cultures, and expanding the meaning of "human rights" and "dignity of man." Special attention should be given to the incorporation of these principles into American citizenship and other political science courses.

b. Adequate courses in international relations should be offered in every college.

c. In all fields of study the ideas, ideals and aspirations common to all people should be emphasized.

d. Courses in comparative literature, music, art, education, history, economics, and human geography should be offered.

e. Subject matter relating to the United Nations should be used in themes, speeches, scripts written in radio classes, etc.

f. Renewed emphasis should be placed on the need for a second language, especially for those interested in foreign service or study abroad, and new techniques of teaching languages should be developed and studied. The intensive instruction program of the A. S. T. P. and the U. S. Navy Language Schools should be examined for valuable methodology which might be adapted to college classroom use. Use of exchange students as language assistants, special schools taught in the foreign language, and intensive evening classes for adults going abroad also deserve wider recognition on college campuses.

g. Area study programs might also be considered both with a view to increasing the immediate value of the language and with the purpose of heightening the appreciation of the culture in which the language is rooted.

h. Textbooks must be closely examined in the light of the ideals expressed by UNESCO. College teachers, who write American textbooks, should be encouraged to give proper international emphasis in their writing, especially directing attention to international questions and organizations in social science textbooks.

i. Experiments and other evaluational procedures to determine relative effectiveness of various textbooks in teaching international understanding should be devised and instituted.

j. Study abroad should be encouraged, preferably by summer schools and workshops abroad or on an exchange scholarship basis since both the student and the institution profit from these experiences.

k. Utilization of visiting professors, traveling panels, and available radio, phonograph, and film material will also serve to increase international understanding as well as stimulate student interest and increase the practical value of instruction.

l. Project-research programs recommended by UNESCO should be incorporated in courses and seminars wherever possible. Such research might include problems in specific countries or areas on such matters as family life, health, housing, community planning, education, and economics.

m. Colleges should strive to increase their library holdings of international relations materials, especially translations of significant foreign works in all fields, and should urge reading assignments among these works.

3. *Student activities.* Student activities can be a most helpful instrument for arousing the interest of the student body in UNESCO. For this reason the encouragement of these activities by the faculty and administration are very important. Following are examples of student activities:

a. Active campus organizations with objectives similar to UNESCO, such as the International Relations Clubs, should be stimulated.

b. Autonomous United Nations Youth Groups might be established which would have an interest in the activities of UNESCO, and international student movements with similar purpose should be encouraged.

c. Students of each college and university should be encouraged to establish correspondent relations with one or more foreign institutions, for the purpose of furthering mutual understanding.

d. News about UNESCO and the United Nations should appear regularly in campus papers.

e. Students should be interested in raising funds for foreign scholarships, perhaps to aid students from their correspondent institutions in whom the students would have a special interest.

f. Active participation of students in a campus "UNESCO Week" will increase the effectiveness of that activity.

g. Should adverse political events threaten the existence or the program of UNESCO, students should be interested in writing their Congressmen, the State Department, or otherwise making known their beliefs and desires.

4. *Service of the individual college to the community.*
   a. Each college and university should take the initiative in developing on a community basis (local, state, or regional, as its influence permits and conditions require) such agency or agencies as seem best calculated to stimulate, facilitate, and coördinate activities designed to advance the goals and objectives set forth in the constitution of UNESCO and the resolutions of the preparatory commissions.   This agency should represent all of the significant groups and organizations in the community interested in UNESCO studies and activities.   In communities enjoying the service of more than one college or university, the closest coöperation among those institutions is essential in the development of an effective community agency.
   b. The college should assume responsibility for providing adequate information services about the agencies of the United Nations. All important documents should be readily and quickly available to all interested persons in the community.   The UNESCO liaison officer should study existing information services in the community, and recommend action to support and strengthen them, or to establish an information service at the college.
   c. Since the possession of information without the skill of effective utilization is of little value to community leaders, colleges and universities (in coöperation with the community UNESCO agency) should study the techniques of teaching and group leadership in order to develop an effective program of special short courses designed to train officers and leaders of organized groups in group leadership techniques and in the preparation and delivery of effective written, spoken, and artistic presentation.
   d. The college and university and the community UNESCO agency should devote special attention to youth organizations, on and off campus, both those specifically concerned with increasing international mindedness and those organized for work in one of the fields related to UNESCO.
   e. Close coöperation of colleges and universities with primary and secondary schools in the development of special programs and general curricula with international focus is urged.
   f. Both college-owned and privately-owned radio should be used in promoting UNESCO objectives.   Among the means available to colleges might be the following:
      1. Development of live programs for local and network broadcast, either on a sponsored or sustaining basis.

2. Preparation of transcriptions for tne use of local stations at suitable times, and for distribution to stations outside the area where the college is located.

3. Encourage introduction into as many existing radio programs as possible of commentaries on the international implications of the music, newscast, or other material broadcast.

4. Extend an invitation to local newscasters and commentators as well as program executives to consult with the faculty and college committees on suitable material for use in their programs.

5. Make newscasts available for students in their student union buildings, coffee shops, and other public places where students congregate.

g. In the use of films, the college might:

1. Develop film libraries of educational films and documentaries.

2. Increase the use of existing projectors by providing mobile units that can be used off campus and before local groups.

3. Make special efforts to see that foreign-made pictures are exhibited both on the campus and in the community, and that suitable publicity be given to their showing.

4. Examine the feasibility of using shorts, trailers, and end-clips carrying UNESCO messages.

h. The Press may be brought into this program more closely by the colleges in the following ways:

1. Invite the local editors or publishers to serve on special committees on public information to be appointed by the colleges and universities.

2. Encourage members of the faculty to write quasi-popular news and feature articles for the newspapers on topics affecting international affairs.

3. Emphasize UNESCO in releases prepared by public relations officers.

i. Effective displays and exhibits have important community influence and should therefore be carefully considered. The college can:

1. Enlist the coöperation of the art departments in the development of posters and other graphic materials illustrating international problems.

2. Seek the coöperation of outdoor advertising agencies in the use of 24-sheet billboards on particularly important issues.

    3. Develop special exhibits for department stores, movies, lob-
bies, railroad, airline, and bus depots, post offices, schools,
county and state fairs, conventions, etc.

j. Conferences.   The college can:

    1. Arrange special conferences of students, the general public,
or specialists on current problems of world affairs.

    2. Plan to provide speakers, graphic materials and exhibits for
other conferences that may be held within the community,
where a presentation of problems of international scope
might be relevant.

    3. Develop institutes of international relations in collaboration
with other colleges and universities, and with representative
economic and social groups in the community.

    4. Sponsor and publicize guest speakers on UNESCO or other
international matters for community meetings.

k. UNESCO Week.   All countries are urged by UNESCO to observe a UNESCO Month or UNESCO Week at the time when
the General Conference of UNESCO is in session. Each college should plan to observe a UNESCO Week (or Month), and
to initiate or to support observance in the community.   A special
effort should be made to enlist the support of the local press, radio
and motion picture agencies.

    The purposes common to UNESCO and other agencies of the
United Nations should be stressed.   Dramatic pageants, displays and exhibits, lectures, conferences, and news stories about
UNESCO, should demonstrate how international understanding
can contribute to international peace.[6]

    The realization of the necessity and urgency for the achievement
of international understanding and coöperation was heightened by
the development and use of the atomic bomb.   The very existence
of man on this earth depends on our ability to establish an effective
international control of the development and use of atomic energy,
and to bring about the outlawing of the atomic bomb by effective
inspection and enforcement machinery.   Without such international control under the United Nations, no nation, not even our
own, can feel secure.   With atomic energy effectively controlled,

---

[6] Ben M. Cherrington and others, "UNESCO: A Challenge to Higher Education in America," *Association of American Colleges Bulletin,* Vol. XXXII, No.
3, October, 1946.

and utilized for the welfare and happiness of mankind, a new and glorious era in the history of the world will unfold. It awaits only the practical application on a worldwide basis of the great ideal of the brotherhood of man.

E. The Question of Academic Freedom

The preceding section, which dealt with the contribution of education to the solution of present-day social problems, leads quite naturally to a consideration of academic freedom. This is one of the most important and most highly controversial questions with which education is now faced. Probably at no other time in our history have teachers and associations of teachers been as keenly aware as they are today of the need for vigorous action in the interest of academic freedom. Seldom, if ever, has there been as great activity on the part of pressure groups to restrict academic freedom as there is today. The concern of the teachers and the activities of the pressure groups are due to the fact that we are clearly in one of the most critical periods of our country's existence. Important decisions are being made. In the judgment of many, the old order is passing, and a new social order is emerging. In such a period, many powerful individuals and groups that have a vested interest in the old order and a strong affection for it exercise their right to try to stem the tide of change. That such action is not peculiar to the present situation is well illustrated by a resolution that was adopted by the trustees of the Lane Theological Seminary before the Civil War. Perhaps the events that followed shortly also demonstrated the futility of attempting to prevent change by forbidding people to talk about it. The resolution read: "From this date the subject of slavery shall not be discussed by students or faculty in the classrooms or on the campus of the Lane Theological Seminary."

An editorial by Dr. Kandel in *School and Society* is reproduced here because it helps to explain the current situation in regard to academic freedom, and because it contains so much good American common sense:

To those who recall the imposition of loyalty oaths on teachers, the hasty revision by state departments of education of directives on the teaching of history, the scrutiny of textbooks, and the requirement that teachers in the District of Columbia must state under oath that they had not "taught" Communism, which followed World War I, the current wave of concern about the loyalty of American citizens will not come as a surprise. What is surprising is that so little has been learned from past experiences about the effects of making martyrs of small groups which are assumed to be disaffected. Nor has the lesson been learned that a better method of counteracting bad ideas is to emphasize good ideas as emphatically and as vigorously as possible. In intellectual matters Gresham's law works in reverse—good ideas can be relied upon to drive out bad.

When this Republic was founded George Washington urged his fellow citizens to establish institutions for the dissemination of knowledge, for, as he said, "in proportion as the structure of government gives force to public opinion, it is essential that public opinion should be enlightened." As far as the development of that enlightenment is concerned, American schools still have a great task ahead of them. Nor has Lincoln's statement that democracy means "agreement to disagree" been given the attention that it deserves, particularly in its implication that a foundation must be established in agreement before disagreement can begin.

A reference to the fact that the Japanese authorities in the twenties engaged in the wholesale arrest of students for "harboring dangerous thoughts" is sure to bring a smile to the faces of an American audience; to go on from there and refer to the creation in the Japanese Ministry of Education of a "Bureau of Thought Supervision" is certain to make the audience rock with laughter, without any realization that our own methods of dealing with "subversive activities" are not very different.

In the days when the conflict between science and religion was hotly debated, a group of students in a denominational college informed its president that they were planning to organize a society of atheists. "Fine," said the president, "put my name down as a charter member." The society was not organized. There is a profound lesson in this story—suppression and martyrdom, which are too often invited or expected, will not work.

To paraphrase John Stuart Mill's statement that "you cannot make men sober by law," a statement which it would have been well to remember when this country embarked on its own glorious experiment —"you cannot make men loyal by law" or by police methods. Suppression creates martyrs, and martyrs may win sympathy in the most unexpected quarters. What is actually being accomplished by the current wave of hysteria is to give publicity to ideas that we do not like on the assumption that the ideas and ideals which we wish to maintain and preserve will somehow or other take care of themselves.[7]

The National Education Association in a Memorandum on Academic Freedom, issued by the Research Division in June, 1935, made the following statement regarding the position of the N. E. A. on the subject of academic freedom and loyalty oaths:

ACADEMIC FREEDOM, THE CHILD'S RIGHT TO UNFETTERED TEACHING

Teachers should have the privilege of presenting all points of view, including their own, on controversial issues without danger of reprisal by the school administration or by pressure groups in the community. Teachers should also be guaranteed the constitutional rights of freedom of speech, press, assembly, and the right to support actively organized movements which they consider to be in their own and the public interest. The teacher's conduct outside the school should be subject only to such controls as those to which other responsible citizens are subjected. The sudden singling out of teachers to take an oath of allegiance is a means of intimidation which can be used to destroy the right of academic freedom.

This question of academic freedom is so complicated and so far-reaching in its implications that it may be many years before it is definitely settled. Society, which owns and controls the public schools, has the right to prescribe what may be taught and what may not be taught in those schools. It may require teachers to teach that the earth is flat if it so desires. Indeed, there are states which impose requirements just about as ridiculous as that. We question, not the right to impose such requirements, but the wisdom of imposing them. Society may deny to teachers the right to mention Russia in the classroom. That is just about what actually happened in the District of Columbia. Again, it is a question, not of right, but of the wisdom, of such action. Since

---

[7] I. L. Kandel, "Hysteria Repeats Itself," *School and Society*, Vol. 65, No. 1686, April 19, 1947, p. 277.

society has the right to impose such requirements, just as it has the right to deny tenure to teachers, and, in nontenure areas, to dismiss teachers for inadequate reasons, or for no reasons at all, the problem would appear to be largely one of educating the public.

Teachers have an important responsibility in this matter of educating the public along these lines. Individually, the teacher is helpless, and can do little either in the direction of protecting his own interests or in changing the attitude of the public. A strongly organized teaching profession with capable and vigorous leadership can do much. If teachers will unite in demanding tenure and academic freedom, they will get them. There is just one important qualification which must be placed upon this statement. It is that tenure and academic freedom must clearly be in the public interest. In other words, teachers must assume responsibility for not abusing such important privileges. As was pointed out in an earlier section, they must teach and not advocate.

It should be obvious that academic freedom is dependent on tenure. The teacher who can be dismissed at the will of the employing board feels so insecure that he literally has no academic freedom. This relationship between academic freedom and tenure is fully recognized in the following statement jointly subscribed to by the American Association of University Professors, the Association of American Colleges (an employer group), and the American Association of Teachers Colleges (an employer group):

The purpose of this statement is to promote public understanding and support of academic freedom and tenure and agreement upon procedures to assure them in colleges and universities. Institutions of higher education are conducted for the common good and not to further the interest of either the individual teacher or the institution as a whole. The common good depends upon the free search for truth and its free exposition.

Academic freedom is essential to these purposes and applies to both teaching and research. Freedom in research is fundamental to the advancement of truth. Academic freedom in its teaching aspect is fundamental for the protection of the rights of the teacher in teaching and of the student to freedom in learning. It carries with it duties correlative with rights.

Tenure is a means to certain ends; specifically: (1) freedom of teaching and research and of extra-curricular activities, and (2) a sufficient degree of economic security to make the profession attractive to men and women of ability.   Freedom and economic security, hence tenure, are indispensable to the success of an institution in fulfilling obligations to its students and to society.

The teacher is entitled to full freedom in research and in the publication of the results, subject to the adequate performance of his other academic duties; but research for pecuniary return should be based upon an understanding with the authorities of the institution.

The teacher is entitled to freedom in the classroom in discussing his subject, but he should be careful not to introduce into his teaching controversial matter which has no relation to his subject.   Limitations of academic freedom because of religious or other aims of the institution should be clearly stated in writing at the time of the appointment.

The college or university teacher is a citizen, a member of a learned profession, and an officer of an educational institution.   When he speaks or writes as a citizen, he should be free from institutional censorship or discipline, but his special position in the community imposes special obligations.   As a man of learning and an educational officer, he should remember that the public may judge his profession and his institution by his utterances.   Hence he should at all times be accurate, should exercise proper restraint, should show respect for the opinions of others and should make every effort to indicate that he is not an institutional spokesman.

After the expiration of a probationary period teachers or investigators should have permanent or continuous tenure, and their services should be terminated only for adequate cause, except in the case of retirement for age, or under extraordinary circumstances because of financial exigencies. . . .

Termination for cause of a continuous appointment, or the dismissal for cause of a teacher previous to the expiration of a term appointment, should, if possible, be considered by both a faculty committee and the governing board of the institution.   In all cases where the facts are in dispute, the accused teacher should be informed before the hearing in writing of the charges against him and should have the opportunity to be heard in his own defense by all bodies that pass judgment upon his case.   He should be permitted to have with him an adviser of his own choosing who may act as counsel.   There should be a full stenographic record of the hearing available to the parties concerned.   In the hearing of charges of incompetence the testimony should include that of teachers and other scholars, either from his own or from other institutions. Teachers on continuous appointment who are dismissed for reasons not involving moral turpitude should receive their salaries for at least a year from the date of notification of dismissal whether or not they are continued in their duties at the institution.

Termination of a continuous appointment because of financial exigency should be demonstrably *bona fide*.[8]

The American Association of University Professors has done and is doing an excellent job of protecting the academic freedom and tenure of college teachers. Equal protection for the great body of public elementary and secondary school teachers is a much larger and more difficult matter. It is one, however, on which the National Education Association has been working with considerable success in recent years. The major long-time effort has been devoted to securing the enactment of tenure laws by state legislatures. Even in the absence of statutory protection of tenure, however, the National Education Association, working through its Tenure Committee, its Department of Classroom Teachers, and its Commission for the Defense of Democracy Through Education, has been able to protect many teachers against unjust dismissal, and, in some instances, to bring about the reinstatement of teachers who had been unjustly dismissed.

A case in point is that of Miss Kate Frank, who was dismissed from her teaching position in the Muskogee, Oklahoma, public schools in the spring of 1943, just before time for the schools to close for the summer vacation. Miss Frank had been a teacher in Muskogee since 1919. She was dismissed without a hearing and with no charges preferred against her. In this case, following an investigation, and after unsuccessful efforts to persuade the Muskogee Board of Education to reinstate Miss Frank, the N.E.A. Commission for the Defense of Democracy Through Education and the N.E.A. Department of Classroom Teachers announced the establishment of a Kate Frank Defense Fund. Miss Frank remained in Muskogee, her salary being paid from this fund, and did teacher organization work. It was necessary to have Miss Frank

---

[8] Quoted from the *Twenty-second Yearbook* of the American Association of Teachers Colleges, 1943.

remain in Muskogee in order to keep the issue alive until the next school board election, which took place in the spring of 1945. The result of this strategy was reported to the N.E.A. Delegate Assembly by the Chairman of the Commission for the Defense of Democracy Through Education, at the Annual Convention of the N.E.A. in Buffalo, July, 1946:

Miss Frank . . . was reappointed to her former position by the school board early in 1945 (before the school board election) and with no strings attached to the reappointment.

Thus the organized teachers of America, operating through the Kate Frank Defense Committee organized by the Department of Classroom Teachers and the Defense Commission, have effectively served notice on boards of education that they do not intend to permit capable members of the teaching profession to be dismissed without just cause.

It seems to me that equally heartening was the action of the citizens of the town of Muskogee at the polls following the belated action of the Muskogee School Board in reinstating Miss Frank. The citizens turned out that board of education for their atrocious behavior in having fired her in the first place.[9]

The protection of the academic freedom and tenure of teachers is complicated not only by the fact that thousands of local boards of education exercise the right to hire and fire teachers, but by the further fact that hundreds of pressure groups, representing a great variety of vested interests, exert pressures to have the teachers teach what they want to have taught and refrain from teaching what they do not want to have taught. Some of these groups are large and powerful organizations. Some are one-man organizations. Large or small, they have the effect of exerting pressure on boards of education, school administrators, and teachers. With the establishment of the N.E.A. Commission for the Defense of Democracy Through Education in 1941, the teaching profession gained an agency for the investigation of charges against schools and teachers, and when investigation warrants it, for the exposure of individuals and organizations making such charges.

---

9 *Summary of Reports of Committees, Commissions and Councils,* Annual Convention, 1946, National Education Association, Washington, D. C.

The following quotation from the *Defense Bulletin* sets forth its policy and its advice to teachers about "witch hunting":

LET'S KEEP THE WITCH HUNTERS OUT OF THE SCHOOLS

Following a pattern all too familiar at the close of World War I, witch hunters are again trying to undermine public confidence in the schools by making blanket charges against the loyalty and patriotism of the teachers. Charges of radicalism, communistic teaching, plots to undermine our government, and other subversive activities are being raised against the teachers of America who, by and large, are more patriotic than any other group. A number of attacks which have come to our attention recently are without foundation or proof. They are of such a nature as to seriously injure the schools at the time when they need every possible support in order to carry out their heavy responsibilities.

In this postwar period the Defense Commission urges members of the teaching profession to be on the alert for unwarranted and destructive attacks against the schools and to report such attacks to the Commission. One of the first activities of the Commission when it was set up in 1941, was to re-establish the confidence of American leaders in the teaching profession, which had been badly shaken by the unjustified charges of radicalism made against the schools after the first world war.

By prompt and vigorous action the teachers can bring to public attention the underlying motives of those individuals who are attempting to discredit the schools. They can insist that such attacks come out into the open and submit proof against specific offenders. The contribution of teachers to the defense of our democracy, both before and during the war, leaves no doubt that the teaching profession deserves full confidence and support.[10]

F.   Problems and References for Collateral Study

Problems for Students

1. What should be the contribution of education to the solution of the problems of postwar reconstruction?

2. Trace the changes which have occurred during your lifetime in any one or two of the social agencies with which you are acquainted.

---

[10] *Defense Bulletin* No. 18, September, 1946. Issued by the National Commission for the Defense of Democracy Through Education, National Education Association, Washington, D. C.

3. In parallel columns, endeavor to itemize or characterize the living standards of three families in your community, one a poor family, one a family in comfortable circumstances, and one a family that is wealthy, at least relatively.

4. Defend or oppose the workability of the socialist formula: To each according to his need; from each according to his capacity.

5. What should be our attitude toward proposals for additional amendments to the Constitution of the United States?

6. What are the arguments for and against the development of industrial and economic democracy, paralleling our political democracy?

7. Just how internationally-minded are you? What do you propose to do about it?

8. What should be the attitude of the school toward controversial issues?

9. What should be the attitude of teachers toward academic freedom? What obligations should the extension of academic freedom impose upon the teacher?

10. How have pressure groups influenced your education?

Selected References

SOCIAL CHANGE

Arnall, Ellis, *The Shore Dimly Seen.* Philadelphia: J. B. Lippincott, 1947.

Chase, Stuart, *Rich Land, Poor Land.* New York: McGraw-Hill, 1936.

Conant, James B., *On Understanding Science.* New Haven: Yale University Press, 1947.

Elliott, W. Y., *The Need for Constitutional Reform.* New York: Whittlesey House (McGraw-Hill), 1935.

Hecht, Selig, *Explaining the Atom.* New York: Viking Press, 1947.

Merriam, C. E., *The New Democracy and the New Despotism.* New York: McGraw-Hill, 1939.

Raup, B., *Education and Organized Interests in America.* New York: G. P. Putnam's Sons, 1936.

Toynbee, Arnold J. (Abridgment by D. C. Somervell), *A Study of History.* New York: Oxford University Press, 1947.

PRESERVING DEMOCRACY

Bode, Boyd H., *Democracy as a Way of Life.* New York: Macmillan, 1937.

Marshall, James, *The Freedom to be Free.* New York: John Day, 1943.

Developing International-Mindedness

Burnham, James, *The Struggle for the World.* New York: John Day, 1947.

Dallin, David J., *The Real Soviet Russia.* New Haven: Yale University Press, revised to 1947.

Fischer, John, *Why They Behave Like Russians.* New York: Harper, 1947.

Jones, H. M., *Education and World Tragedy.* Cambridge, Mass.: Harvard University Press, 1946.

NEA Department of Elementary School Principals, "Learning World Goodwill in the Elementary School," *Twenty-fifth Yearbook,* 1946.

NEA Educational Policies Commission, Washington, D. C.:
The Purposes of Education in American Democracy, 1938.
Education and Economic Well-Being in American Democracy, 1940.
The Education of Free Men in American Democracy, 1941.
Policies for Education in American Democracy, 1946.

Snow, Edgar, *Stalin Must Have Peace.* New York: Random House, 1947.

U. S. Department of State, *Report of the United States Education Mission to Japan, Submitted to the Supreme Commander for the Allied Powers.* Washington, D. C.: Superintendent of Documents, 1946.

Welles, Sumner, *The Time for Decision.* New York: Harper, 1944.

Academic Freedom

American Academy of Political and Social Science, *Freedom of Inquiry and Expression.* Philadelphia: The Academy, 1938.

American Civil Liberties Union, *What Freedom for American Students?* New York: The Union, 1945.

Beale, Howard K., *Are American Teachers Free?* New York: Scribner's, 1936.

——————, *History of Freedom of Teaching in American Schools.* New York: Scribner's, 1941.

John Dewey Society, *Educational Freedom and Democracy,* Second Yearbook. New York: D. Appleton-Century, 1938.

Necessary and Impending Changes in American Education

In the preceding unit attention was given to some of the current problems in society and to the part that education may be expected to play in their solution. It is apparent that outmoded educational machinery and inadequate school facilities will greatly hinder social progress. In many parts of the country educational progress is retarded because there are still too many small, inefficient school districts. Gross inequalities exist in the financial support of education. Many well-equipped schools with good teaching corps suffer for lack of able, constructive, professional leadership, or the teachers are unable to do their best work for fear of losing their positions. It will be difficult for the schools to guarantee equality of opportunity to all children, or to further the cause of democracy, until some needed changes in the educational structure and program are effected.

This treatise is based on the belief that education will assume a more important role during the next generation or two than it has during the past. The American people have been so largely occupied for three hundred years with the task of meeting frontier problems and with getting an industrial society established that they have had comparatively little time for planning. Indeed, they have not felt the need for planning until recently. Everyone was busy trying to catch up with the procession in order to take full advantage of the seemingly limitless opportunities. For several decades now the pace has been slowing up. We find ourselves confronted with new problems. The frontier, in the physical sense, no longer exists. That kind of pioneering is past. There are no more wild animals or Indians to fight, no wilderness to win, no free lands to settle. Instead, we have to contend with dust storms, soil erosion, flood control, conservation of resources, unemployment, social security, national defense, and similar problems. Our pioneering must be done now in the social and economic realm. Our former society was individualistic; our present one is highly complex and social in nature, demanding coöperative endeavor. This change implies the need for a new kind of education.

This new education will be more vital and dynamic and will function more effectively. When men wrested their living from the soil or forests or mines, and when there was little interdependence among men, a simple education that provided the tools of learning was sufficient. Now that millions are crowded into large cities, and depend upon the whims of the fluctuating markets for demands sufficient to provide work, a new education for social living is required. Education must touch man's life as he is living it now, not as it was when our educational machinery was set up and put in motion. The old framework will not meet all present-day needs. We shall enumerate some of the changes that will be necessary, many of which are already under way.

A. Needed Administrative Changes

A large proportion of the new demands upon the schools place a heavy burden upon the present administrative machinery. That machinery was designed for fairly simple community relationships in a day when there was comparatively little interdependence among districts. Each town was a law unto itself, as was, indeed, each family. In many situations now we find the sovereignty of the local district a real hindrance to progress. A realignment of forces and factors will be necessary before the school can make its maximum contribution to the society that supports it. From the administrative point of view the changes most needed are larger school districts and more equitable bases for financial support. These changes are rather closely related and are, in fact, complementary. If any thoroughgoing modifications are to be effected, these two changes must go hand in hand.

1. Larger Units of Administration

The most pressing need in many parts of the country is a larger school district. Most of the desirable reorganizations could be more economically and more effectively carried out if more children were available and if there were more wealth to support the program. It is impossible to provide a varied educational program to meet the needs of different types of children with the limited enrollments in many small districts. For example, special classes for atypical children cannot be provided, nor can instruction in many special fields be offered. If two or more districts could join forces, from among them the requisite number of children could be found, and the combined resources of all would provide ample support for the program.

The solution to this problem may be approached in two ways. First, two or more school districts could be consolidated into one larger unit for all school purposes. The new district would be completely unified and integrated and would retain the sovereignty and autonomy of the present smaller districts. That is the form this reorganization movement has taken in most places, although there are many types and varieties of organization. Second, a more flexible arrangement would be to allow local districts to remain substantially as they are now, with some needed relocation of boundary lines, but to permit the formation of larger units for specific purposes, such as for technical or special education, or for better high schools or junior colleges. The several coöperating districts would simply join forces to support a program that no one of them alone could afford. The latter solution has much to commend it, and it gives promise of helping to solve many of our problems. Both plans have much to offer, so we shall study each one more carefully.

a. *Forming larger districts by consolidation.* The first plan is usually referred to by the term *consolidation* of schools, a movement which began with the passage of a law in Massachusetts in 1869 permitting school children to be transported at public expense. By 1890 the movement was well under way throughout

New England, and by 1910 thirty-eight states had passed legislation making consolidation possible by vote of the districts involved.
The types of organizations that resulted may be grouped into
several distinct classes:

Photo from Black Star

Fig. 17.—A Bookmobile Brings the Library to the Children.

Several one-room rural districts combine to form a consolidated
district with a central high school, the elementary grades being left
as they were.

Similar consolidations with central elementary and high schools
are sometimes effected, provision being made for the transportation
of all children.

In many places this consolidation takes the form of township
districts, to which some or all of the children are transported at
public expense.

Joint or union districts are formed in many states; under this plan two or more boroughs or townships retain their own organization for elementary schools but unite to support a high school and, in some places, junior colleges.

One or more outlying districts are frequently annexed to an adjacent borough or city school system.

Complete county units are found in some states—in Maryland, for example, and, in a modified form, in a number of other states.[1]

The need for some type of consolidation into larger districts is seen readily in the statistics for school districts or on maps showing the boundary lines of districts. A glance at any map showing school districts will reveal that in many instances there is nothing logical or rational about the location of the boundary lines. They were established in the pioneer days when little thought was given to planning and no account was taken of ultimate growth and development. Improved transportation facilities and hard-surfaced roads and industrial developments have completely changed the situation with respect to the location of schools. Mountain ranges sometimes divide a district, or a new highway may isolate a small community. Theoretically, the districts were so organized that no pupil would need to travel more than two miles to reach a school, but actual study of the situation reveals that gross inequalities exist in the sizes of districts. Frequently, although a pupil could attend a well-equipped, modern school by crossing the street and walking two blocks, he has to be transported or walk a mile or more to a poorer school, because the street that passes his home happens to be the dividing line.

This fact suggests one of the most difficult hurdles in the move toward larger districts. The existing boundary lines cannot be disregarded; nor can they be changed without the greatest difficulty, community feuds, lawsuits, and court decisions frequently being involved. Consolidation laws usually provide for treating existing school districts as distinct entities and make no provision

---

[1] Complete county units are found in Alabama, Florida, Georgia, Kentucky, Louisiana, Maryland, New Mexico, North Carolina, Tennessee, Utah, Virginia, and West Virginia, according to Bulletin 45; United States Office of Education.

for parts of districts. It would be much more logical to reorganize the districts in terms of communities and industrial or trade or commercial centers and transportation routes, rather than in terms of the arbitrary boundary lines as they now exist.

Considerable progress was made, in the period between the two world wars, in reducing the number of one-teacher schools [2] in the United States, in increasing the number of consolidated schools, and in increasing the number of pupils transported to school. The following table tells the story. It may confidently be anticipated that this progress will be resumed.

Year	Number of One-Teacher Schools	Number of Consolidated Schools	Number of Pupils Transported	Amount Spent for Pupil Transportation
1919–20	190,655	11,890	800,000	$14,537,754
1923–24	169,718	12,674	995,961	29,627,402
1927–28	156,066	13,852	1,650,574	39,052,680
1931–32	143,390	15,945	2,362,566	58,077,779
1935–36	131,101	17,531	3,250,658	62,652,571
1939–40	113,600	......	......	......
1943–44	96,302	......	4,410,362	107,754,467

The little red schoolhouse and the "deestrict" school have attained a mythical, romantic fame in song and story all out of proportion to their true significance. The truth is that this love and devotion to the only school that our parents and grandparents knew is now an almost insurmountable obstacle in the path of the progress of public education. There was a time when a candidate for almost any office could be assured of success at the polls if he could claim a log cabin as his birthplace and a one-room country school as his one and only alma mater. Both of those landmarks have lost their glamour and fascination for those who are now

[2] *Are the One-Teacher Schools Disappearing?* Pamphlet No. 92, 1940, U. S. Office of Education, Washington, D. C., p. 5; "Biennial Survey of Education in the United States," *Statistics of State School Systems,* 1943–1944, Federal Security Agency, United States Office of Education, 1946.

forced to share their hospitality and enjoy their comforts. Not much glory adheres to them in the eyes of one who sees all about him the benefits of the more progressive schools of his more enlightened neighbors. The automobile, the concrete highway, and the radio have just about disarmed the demagogue, robbed him of his most effective weapon; he can no longer appeal to his constituents by pointing with pride to his primitive upbringing.

b. *Joint or coöperative districts.* Let us now turn our attention to the more flexible plan for enlarging the administrative unit. If we stop with combining districts as they now exist, there still remains the difficulty of fixed, arbitrary boundary lines. Many new opportunities for constructive improvements will be open to us if we think in terms of larger units for specific purposes, but not necessarily for all school purposes. There is already plenty of precedent for such a program. In California and Illinois, for example, all local districts provide for elementary education. In the case of the smaller districts, two or more of them may unite to organize a central high school, with the administration and control of elementary and secondary education entirely separated. These joint high school districts, in turn, may join forces to support a junior college. Although a richer educational program may be provided by such arrangements, it should be pointed out that wider separation and less articulation among the units of the school system are almost certain to result unless serious efforts are made to avoid them.

Many states have passed legislation permitting two or more districts to employ the services of special teachers or supervisors, or even the superintendent, jointly. Many districts have thus been able to secure such special services as those of school nurses, music supervisors, or industrial or home economics teachers that could not have justified the program otherwise, either in terms of the number of pupils or the cost. Even with such permissive legislation we have made comparatively little progress; but there have been a few noteworthy attempts. For example, the superintendents in the suburban areas surrounding St. Louis have joined forces to secure handwriting supervision, primary supervision, visual education, sight-saving classes, and curriculum revision in several fields.   There are two areas in which such a program offers promise of reward, namely, in technical or vocational education and in the junior college.

Provision for more challenging offerings in these areas, available to more people, would go far toward helping the later adolescents, those persons from 16 to 25 years of age, to make a more satisfactory adjustment to the changing economic and social structure facing them.   Most of them cannot leave home to attend a college or university, and they have reaped all the benefit they can from attendance at the local high school.   If they have been graduated, they find little to draw them back as postgraduates, and if they left before graduation, it was doubtless because they found the curriculum unsuited to their needs and abilities.   The diagram in Figure 18 shows the place of these technical schools and the junior colleges in the public school program.

4	TECHNICAL or VOCATIONAL	COLLEGE (Academic)		TECHNICAL or VOCATIONAL	JUNIOR COLLEGE	2
				SENIOR HIGH SCHOOL		3
4	SECONDARY			JUNIOR HIGH SCHOOL		3
6	ELEMENTARY			ELEMENTARY		6

Fig. 18.——Chart Showing Place in Public School Program of Technical Schools and the Junior College, Particularly When an Expanded Program Is Made Possible by Formation of Larger Districts.

In this scheme the technical schools would be definitely vocational and terminal in nature. They would not necessarily be preparatory to some other higher institutions, but there would undoubtedly be value in organizing the work so that a few of their students who so desired could be admitted to technical courses in universities. But the vast majority who entered them would do so for the specific purpose of attaining vocational proficiency in some specific field. An institution of this character would offer training in a variety of vocational lines, and would not be restricted to the skilled trades for boys and home economics for girls, as is the case today. The 6-4-4 setup shown in column one in Figure 18 would start the work at the eleventh grade and continue it for four years or more. Column two shows how the program would be adjusted for those who complete a regular 6-6 or 6-3-3 program. The vocational preparation would thus be based upon or would parallel the upper years of a good high school course. That arrangement would represent gain over the present one in which the vocational students get comparatively little of the usual high school curriculum.

Such a school could offer its technical training on a higher plane and with more emphasis upon vocational proficiency, and its graduates could compete on an equal footing with the graduates of private business colleges and trade schools. The offering should include commercial and secretarial courses, institutional as well as domestic home-making, beauty culture, salesmanship and merchandising, auto mechanics, radio technology, practical and applied arts, photography and laboratory techniques. In fact, anything could be offered that students now study in short courses in the private institutions. This program would not include, of course, the two-year agriculture and forestry courses offered by universities. But there is no reason why an institution supported by public funds could not do as well in preparing, say, beauty parlor operators as do the commercial institutions. In 1947 in one Eastern state there were seventy-two private beauty schools licensed.

With respect to the junior college, a similar situation exists.

Uncounted hundreds of students finish high school who are not sure whether they want to go to college or what they would study if they were to go.   Or they cannot afford to go away from home for college, and there is too much risk involved for most of them to borrow the necessary funds or to try to earn all their expenses by working part time.   Two years of college-grade work at home will furnish these students with additional opportunities for self-discovery.   It is a much more economical arrangement, viewed from any angle, than the conventional one.   The junior college may be considered either as a terminal course for those who cannot or should not pursue formal education further, or as a foundational preparation for those who wish to pursue cultural or professional training in a university.   The fact that California supports forty-two public junior colleges attests to the demand that exists where provision has been made for them.

Either of these institutions—the technical school or the junior college—would require the combined resources of several school districts.   Few except the very large school districts could afford such a program.   But all the districts surrounding an industrial or commercial center could unite forces and establish technical schools and junior colleges that would meet the needs of all the students within a radius of fifty miles.   We have thought too long in terms of confining educational offerings within the limits of school districts.   We need now to study the possibilities of pooling the resources in a given trade territory and providing an educational offering in harmony with the needs of the young people of that area.   A few years ago a state superintendent of a Midwestern state was considering the establishment of a public junior college within reach of every high school graduate in the state. At that time there were eight or ten already in existence, and it was his plan to use those and the seven or eight state institutions as the nucleus for such a program.   It was and is an entirely sound idea, and we shall doubtless see many states moving in that direction during the next decade or two.   New York has a few technical schools that are above the secondary school level and not of strictly collegiate grade.   They are similar to the junior technical schools found in so many European countries. If there is a need for special and more advanced education beyond the present limits of the public school curriculum, and there is abundant evidence in support of that position, then the only satisfactory solution seems to lie in a larger unit of school administration.

Summary. The benefits from larger units may be summarized as follows:

1. Economy results, since the overhead cost per pupil is lowered.

2. More varied program is possible because of larger number of teachers and pupils.

3. Larger numbers give more stimulation to teachers and pupils.

4. Better prepared teachers are attracted by higher salaries.

5. Inequalities among small districts are minimized.

6. More able professional leadership can be obtained.

7. Many features can be introduced that several districts with limited resources cannot consider.

It is also to be pointed out that there are some difficulties and disadvantages:

1. Transporation of pupils always presents problems and requires careful planning.

2. The local community must relinquish some of the control over its schools. (With good leadership this need not be a disadvantage; in fact, it can be a distinct advantage in many cases.)

3. The total cost of education may increase, chiefly because a better program is offered, and frequently because more adequate buildings and equipment are provided.

2. Better Professional Leadership for Schools

The solution of educational problems depends in large measure upon the leadership in the field of education. The satisfactory adjustment of education to meet the changing needs of society requires able leaders who are professionally trained and free from political domination and control. So long as laymen, who may be motivated by selfish or minority group interests, are able to dictate educational policies, we may expect the schools to contribute to the betterment of society only with great difficulty. When local politicians can put in office school directors or school board members who function as political henchmen in employing superintendents and teachers and who determine all educational policies in terms of the political consequences, we may be certain that whatever service the schools may render will be in spite of the leadership rather than because of it. This situation represents one of the most serious questions facing American citizens today.

This problem has its roots imbedded in one of the earliest traditions of American education, the universal belief that education is a local matter. The prevailing practices illustrate, in theory at least, the best functioning of the democratic ideal. In many parts of the country, school directors are elected annually at an assembly of the people of the district, after the fashion of the New England town meeting. If these directors are men or women truly representative of the community and motivated by a high ideal of service, then in their administration we have democracy at its best. Such school boards, knowing their limitations and lack of training, will employ the services of professionally trained educators to plan their educational programs. But we see popular government at its worst when scheming politicians control the elections and use school directors as mere tools, automatons who do as they are told. All too frequently lay control of education in America has resulted in poor schools, inefficient instruction, low morale among teachers, and, frequently, graft and corruption in buying supplies and equipment and in the granting of teachers' contracts.

School boards are primarily legislative bodies. Their functions have to do chiefly with business and financial matters. Virtually all educational matters should be entirely delegated to the superintendent of schools. His function is to formulate policies, organize the schools, and administer the program. He is the executive officer to whom the board delegates the authority to act. Just as the board of directors of a corporation selects the president, general managers, and other executives, and then leaves to them the management of the business, so should school boards leave to the superintendent the educational program of the schools. No person seeking employment in a bank or industrial concern would think of running around to see the members of the board of directors to make application in person. It is just as illogical to interview school board members to secure teaching positions. It is absurd for salesmen of floor brushes, school supplies, and textbooks to think of trying to sell their products to individual members of the board. Their dealings should be with the superintendent or the purchasing agent or business manager.

Lay members of school boards can render a great service in society by trying to understand better the needs of society and the wishes of the community, and by endeavoring to refine those desires and aspirations. There is plenty of work for them to do if they are to find the ablest educational leader available and provide the financial support necessary for the best schools the community is able to afford. Occasions will arise when they will need to serve as a check against the unbridled enthusiasm of the superintendent, but as a rule they will function best in encouraging and stimulating and approving the efforts of the leader selected by them. Trouble is certain to follow and poorer schools will be the inevitable result when lay members usurp the educational prerogatives of professional leaders. It is suggested occasionally that school board members be elected for longer terms and be paid for their services, the argument being that men and women of higher caliber would thus be called into service. But it is doubtful if that would be a satisfactory solution of the problem. What we need is an awareness on the part of the citizens generally of the function of education in society and an alertness to the necessity of preventing selfish lay leaders from assuming control over the schools. The importance of freeing educational leaders from political and factional domination constitutes the justification for including this topic in this unit.

A good illustration of the evils of political manipulation for selfish reasons is shown in the following newspaper account of factional control of a school board:

The board took summary action last night with only six days left before the deadline, and terminated the contracts of forty teachers. . . .

The motion was approved by all directors, with the exception of the secretary, who cast the only dissenting vote.

The dismissed teachers took their case to the courts, where they secured an injunction preventing the board from filling their places, the judge stating emphatically that it is not within the rights of school directors to dismiss teachers for purely political reasons. This case was a clear-cut one of a school board punishing teachers who failed to line up politically and of getting revenge on the lone member of the board who refused to go along.

3. Democratization of School Administration

Superintendents are not blameless in this matter of proper relations among school employees. They, too, sometimes fail to share their responsibilities and to delegate authority to principals and teachers. It is exceedingly difficult, if not impossible, for the schools to teach democracy if they are not administered democratically. It is incongruous, indeed, to think of an autocratically controlled institution making a contribution to democracy. Much progress along this line has been made in the last few years, but administrative autocracy still remains as one of the factors hindering educational progress.

The chief difficulty here lies in the fact that autocratic and dictatorial administration tends to curb initiative and stamp out originality among teachers. Much of the supervision, particularly that done by special subject supervisors, has apparently been aimed toward securing uniformity in practice. This aim is all right up to a certain point. If it leads to higher standards of attainment and a richer program, well and good, but if it limits and throttles the more aggressive teachers, then the effect is harmful. The authors knew of one district where four special supervisors wielded so much power that all the elementary teachers were kept busy working for them and larger objectives were neglected.

When teachers are fearful of superior officers and never have a part in determining policies or programs, they become mere cogs in a machine, like workmen at an assembly line in a mass production scheme. The relationships in teaching are much too personal to permit our dealings to sink to that level. The personality of the teacher is far too important to allow it to be molded into a pattern or made ineffective by uniform routine practices dictated by a superintendent or principal or supervisor. Teachers worthy of their positions can assist materially in the formulation of policies, modification of programs, and curriculum revision. A coöperative effort is needed. It is seldom good administration for a superintendent to uproot and eliminate some part of the program without consulting the teachers and departments concerned, or to initiate a radically different program without securing the coöperation of the teachers in preparation for the change. In one district considerable progress had been made in transferring dull and retarded pupils to opportunity rooms, and much effort had gone into securing community approval for the program. A new superintendent, who was elected, by the way, as a result of political upheaval, eliminated the special education program and put the children back in the regular rooms, more maladjusted than when they were taken out. This step was taken without consultation with teachers and to the consternation and disgust of everyone concerned. Few changes in schools are so urgent that they must be made without taking time to secure the coöperation and approval of the persons who will be affected by them. Democratization of society will be more easily attained as our schools become more democratic in spirit.

4. Security, Tenure, and Retirement for Teachers

The type of service we are expecting the public schools to render in society calls for a teaching staff that is not fearful of their positions. That fact suggests the need for a modification in existing practices before the school can make its maximum contribution. Teachers need to be relieved of the worries of economic insecurity and dependence in later life, particularly in localities where they live in fear of losing their positions because of the dictates of a few controlling interests in the community. Some states have attempted to solve this problem by legislation providing for permanent or indefinite tenure and old age retirement pensions. In those states teachers may be dismissed only for incompetency or immorality, and may retire on pensions at the age of sixty to sixty-five, or earlier, if they become disabled. Even under these circumstances, however, teachers are not so free as they need to be to take their places as participating citizens in the social and civic life of the community. We cannot expect to recruit the ablest young people for lifelong service in the schools until we can guarantee some larger measure of economic security than teachers have enjoyed in the past.

In discussing this problem, President G. W. Frazier of the Colorado State Teachers' College proposed that "if teachers are to be most effective, they must have some well-developed freedoms." [3] In addition to academic freedom he suggested that the most pressing problem is:

. . . financial freedom, which includes such things as the following: An adequate salary schedule, an adequate retirement allowance, a twelve-month payment plan, flexible and usable credit, sick leave with pay, cooperative buying, and intelligent tenure.[4]

Four guarantees of security and welfare should be provided for teachers:

1. Guaranteed salaries
   a. Adequate minimum salaries
   b. Annual increments of increase
2. Indefinite tenure
3. Retirement
4. Sick leave benefits

These guarantees are necessary if teachers are to attain a status in society comparable with that of other professions, of government workers, or even of the majority of workers employed by large industrial concerns. The continuation of our system of free public schools in the democratic tradition requires that teachers

---

[3] G. W. Frazier, "Meeting New Demands Through Organization," *Pennsylvania Education Bulletin,* 4:109, May 4, 1936.
[4] *Ibid.*

enjoy prestige and recognition as professional workers, while receiving salaries that furnish a "cultural" as well as a "living" income. Legislative enactment on a state-wide basis is the best way to provide these guarantees, and such legislation has been enacted in various ways throughout the United States. Moreover, many cities have established regulations relating to these guarantees in states where statutory provisions have not been passed on a state-wide basis. The following summary of conditions throughout the country was prepared from materials furnished by the Research Division of the National Education Association:

Twenty-nine states and one territory are listed as having minimum salary laws of one kind or another. There are various types of minimum salary prescription. The simplest provides that all teachers be paid a certain minimum salary, but makes no guarantee of increments for experience. Another type sets a minimum salary and provides definite increments for experience. The third type is a combination salary and state subsidy measure that provides a certain basic amount for each classroom unit.

There are also great variations with respect to tenure laws. In seven states no legislation has been passed guaranteeing tenure. Eighteen states have mandated tenure or protective continuing contracts. Twenty-one other states make guarantee concerning tenure within certain districts or for parts of the state.

The NEA reported in the spring of 1947 that all states now have either a pension plan or a retirement law. Three states have the pension type; the others have retirement laws of varying degrees of soundness in terms of actuarial and other standards.

Sick leave is guaranteed by state law in one form or another in thirteen states. In this respect teachers have suffered by comparison with other professional and even industrial workers. Government and state employees have a certain amount of sick leave annually, and in some instances it is accumulative. But although many school districts have made generous provision for absence from school because of illness, it is only recently that there has been a concerted move to secure sick-leave benefits on a state-wide basis.

Throughout the country the smaller towns and rural areas generally do not provide these reassuring guarantees.

B.   Equalization of Financial Support

In the third unit we suggested that an ideal of "equality of opportunity" is fundamental in the American school system.   We have held it before us an an ideal, but it has been difficult of attainment.   The attitude of the typical citizen toward two important problems must be fundamentally changed before we can provide anything like equality of opportunity.   First, the financial support of education must be equalized.   Second, the educational offering must be differentiated to meet the needs of all the children. Equality does not imply uniformity.   Educational opportunities at present depend too much upon the accident of birth—that is, geographic location or economic or social position, and our administrators should take steps to offset those factors.

The organization of schools in America has always been a local matter and their development and improvement a matter of community pride.   The initiative has come from the local community. The character of the schools has depended upon the enlightenment of the people and their ability and willingness to provide adequate support.   In the early days of our Republic it did not make much difference what kind of education was offered; if the people of a community were satisfied with poor schools, that was considered their own affair.   Of course, that was never the intention of the founders of our government, of men like Thomas Jefferson and James Madison, who saw the need for a well-educated and informed citizenry.   Such an indifferent attitude toward education was altogether out of harmony with the ideal of those who favored a public school system, but such indifference was not so serious a problem during the pioneer days as it would be now.

Numerous individuals, as well as organized groups such as Taxpayers Leagues, frequently make violent attacks upon school budgets, stressing the mounting costs of education.   School costs have increased, it is true, but we are likely to overlook the chief reason for the increase.   The following extract from a bulletin from the Public Relations Committee of a State Teachers Association furnishes the answer in every-day language:

IT'S THE KIDS' FAULT

What makes the schools cost more? Why are they helping to "up" my taxes? Why can't they be run as cheaply as they were when I went to school?

Well, Mr. Citizen, I was just wondering about that myself. Being a curious soul, I've been nosing around to find out. . . .

It's the doggone kids—bless 'em!

They're too numerous. They're too persistent. They're too hard to satisfy. Charge everything you can to better equipment, decreased purchasing power of the dollar, higher salaries, lengthier curriculum and all other causes, and still you can't avoid the conclusion that much more than half the boost in school costs is the fault of those youngsters.

Now they all go to school. Time was when a good share of them dropped out, when they were 10 or 12, and went to work. . . .

We can save ten or fifteen dollars a year apiece on our school taxes by making half of them drop out in the sixth grade, and by cutting down the high school course to what it was in 1898. What d'ye say we do?

No, no—neither would I.[5]

1.   Support of Schools a State Responsibility

When people began to move freely from one place to another, we came to the realization that education was a state function and not merely a local matter. Rapid increases in population due to immigration and the tendencies for people to move into large industrial and commercial centers during the last half century make apparent the need for universal public education. The community content to get along with inadequate educational facilities or unable to support a minimum program can no longer be justified in its attitude. It becomes a matter of concern to the entire region or possibly to the nation at large. A poor educational foundation may not be such a serious handicap for the person who remains in the unprogressive and unenlightened community that failed to provide for him more adequately, but those deficiencies

---

[5] From *Education Bulletin* of the Pennsylvania State Education Association, March 20, 1933

become a liability indeed, and he himself may become one, in the new community where he seeks employment or establishes his residence. These arguments would not hold true for every community at any given moment; but over a long period of time and for the country as a whole, it may safely be said that poor educational facilities in any area constitute a liability for the state.   For example, the Southern planter was excusable, as he saw it, if he provided the barest minimum of education or none at all for the Negroes.   But during the last three or four decades the Northern states have been seeing the effects of this neglect with the increasing migration of the Negro to the industrial centers of the North and East.

This argument suggests that the cost of education should be equalized; that the educational facilities of a locality should not depend entirely upon its own resources.   The state cannot afford to allow isolated sections or impoverished areas to suffer from poorly equipped schools and inadequately prepared teachers and the consequent low-grade instruction.   The only solution is some plan by which the wealth of the state, wherever it happens to be located, is made available to support schools wherever they are needed.   Such a plan would, of course, require the state to assume a larger share of the cost of education, taking the income from the areas where the wealth is concentrated and distributing it to the poorer districts where it is needed the most.

The need for reorganization of school districts and revision and overhauling of the tax machinery is clearly indicated in the following statement from W. T. Markham, State Superintendent of Kansas:

The present situation is the fault of no one except the Legislature. Our school system needs revision.   There isn't much that can be done until the state is re-districted and changes made in our tax program. The present situation has been aggravated by the depression.   We have 1,266 school districts where the property value is $100,000 or less. The highest possible sum that can be raised in these districts is $600 a year if all the taxes levied are collected.   That must pay the teacher and all the costs of running the school.[6]

---

[6] Quoted in *School and Society*, 44:237, August 22, 1936.

a. *Local school costs need to be reduced.* The agitation for the state to bear relatively more and the local community less of the cost of education has become more pronounced during the past ten or fifteen years. The fundamental argument is that since the state as a whole reaps the benefits of a good educational program, or suffers from a poor one, it should assume the responsibility for equalizing the burden. There are two aspects of this problem. The first is implied in the foregoing discussion, the problem of making more money available to the poor districts. The solution of this problem involves a program for collecting state revenues in sufficient amounts to add a considerable portion of the cost of schools to the cost of the other functions of state government. That would be difficult to do in some states because of constitutional limitations of one kind or another. In most states it would necessitate additional taxes or the tapping of hitherto untouched sources of revenue. Many states have allocated definite portions of specific funds, such as those derived from gasoline sales, or income taxes, to educational budgets. Most students of school finance do not favor such ear-marking of specific sources, but would rather see school funds taken from the general revenue. In any event, such revenue reforms are difficult to achieve because of selfishness, vested interests, political maneuvering and lobbying, and because the public in general and state and legislative leaders in particular have not become convinced of their soundness.

b. *State-wide tax revision necessary.* An even more difficult question is seen in the second aspect of the problem. It is the need for lessening the burden on real estate and increasing it on other forms of wealth. That task presents a more difficult problem because it involves a thorough overhauling of our entire tax-collecting machinery. For the country as a whole, taxes on real estate furnish the larger proportion of the total revenue, although other forms of property represent the bulk of the wealth. Real estate has been the source of a disproportionate share of the support for education. When that realization is coupled with the fact that the local community has hitherto borne most of the cost of schools, it is easy to see why tax revision is necessary. The reason for the present dilemma can be traced to the tradition, established at a time when there was little wealth except real estate, for all the support for schools to be secured locally. If we recall that the vast majority of our state constitutions were first written in an era when those conditions prevailed, we can more easily appreciate the difficulty to be encountered in making the needed changes. Four fundamental changes need to be made in our taxing machinery before we can equalize the cost of education.

First there is the change mentioned in the preceding paragraph, namely, the removal of some of the burden from real estate. At present from 80 to 90 per cent of the local support for education is derived from real estate taxes.

TABLE 21

Rate of Assessment Among School Districts of One County [7]

Rate			Number of Districts
100	per cent	....	2
90–99	"	"	4
80–89	"	"	3
70–79	"	"	15
60–69	"	"	15
50–59	"	"	6
40–49	"	"	4
30–39	"	"	6
20–29	"	"	1

Second, a uniform, state-wide system for assessing property for taxation should be worked out. No system of distributing state aid can be satisfactory so long as such differences in assessment rates as those shown below are found in one county.

In addition to these differences among districts, we find gross injustices in one locality. For example, in one instance a property valued at $6,500 was assessed at 70 per cent of its value, while other properties valued as high as $30,000 were assessed at only 37 per cent of their value.

Third, more efficient tax collection procedures are imperative.

---

[7] From *Public Education Bulletin,* State Department of Public Instruction, Harrisburg, Pennsylvania, September, 1934, p. 3.

The need for improvement here is shown in figures released in Pennsylvania.[8]

TABLE 22

Per Cent of School Taxes Collected in Pennsylvania, 1928 to 1937

YEAR	PER CENT COLLECTED	YEAR	PER CENT COLLECTED
1928	92.8	1933	76.5
1929	90.5	1934	73.1
1930	90.7	1935	75.8
1931	89.0	1936	80.6
1932	83.8	1937	81.9

One district collected only 22 per cent in 1935. Too much laxity exists on the part of tax collectors and other officials toward exoneration for nonpayment.

Fourth, most states need a complete revision of their system for distributing state aid. Practices vary from certain flat rates for specific items to graduated scales for reimbursing districts according to need. In the survey made in Pennsylvania,[9] it was found that the poorest district had back of each pupil $213 assessed valuation; the richest, $39,944. In the former a five-mill property tax yielded $20 per teacher; in the latter, $3,625. Yet, the poorer district received only fifty per cent more state subsidy than the wealthy district. There can be little defense for such inequalities as are shown in the following ratios for two neighboring districts:

TABLE 23

Ratios Showing Inequalities Between Two Adjoining Districts

	DISTRICT A	DISTRICT B
Number of pupils	4	1
Total wealth	1	10
Tax rate	5	1
State aid	1.5	1

Note: These numbers represent the ratios between these two districts for each of the four items.

---

[8] Ibid.
[9] Ibid.

c. *Proportion of state support needs to be increased.* Several states have tried to work out equalization plans, one of the first being New York. Under the direction of Professor Paul R. Mort of Columbia University, a system was worked out that attempted to distribute state aid on the basis of two fundamental principles. The first of these is the principle of need, expressed largely in terms of the number of children to be educated. The second is the principle of ability, meaning the wealth available for the support of education. Many other states have tried to effect revisions along similar lines. Such a plan would work somewhat like this: The state department of education would make a thorough study of costs to determine what would be considered a minimum educational program. Let us say that this minimum is set at an expenditure of $100 per year per pupil in average daily attendance. Any district that could meet that standard without exceeding the uniform minimum tax rate would receive no subsidy from the state. A poor district that could raise locally only $55 per pupil would be reimbursed to the extent of $45; another, still poorer district, whose taxes yielded only $42 per pupil, would receive $58 from the state. If, in addition to these equalization funds, each school district received a stated amount for each teacher-pupil unit, the local district could be relieved of most of the burden. The state would assume the responsibility for providing the major portion of the support and would distribute it equitably.

The only fair plan for reducing the burden on real estate and relieving local districts of some of the cost of education is to increase the proportion of school support by the state. This plan is usually accomplished by a method of distributing school subsidies to school districts on the basis of the number of pupils and the taxable wealth of each district. These subsidy procedures are usually referred to as "Equalization" plans.

There are several difficulties in the way of such a program. The one that looms largest is inherent in the fact that many people just naturally resist all change. The public generally is afraid that any change will result in worse conditions, and is particularly fearful that taxes will be increased. Second, not many states possess the educational leadership and political statesmanship necessary to work out such a plan. The third difficulty is closely akin to the second, and is due to the fact that we try to make sweeping changes too suddenly; a much longer period of preparation and education should precede the actual introduction of such measures in the legislature. Fourth, tax collectors and others holding lucrative positions under the present system offer formidable opposition and seem able to control more votes than do those working for the change. Finally, there lurks the ever-present threat that with state support there will go an accompanying amount of state control. That threat is real, but actually state control may be either an advantage or a disadvantage. A certain amount of it is justifiable in the interest of maintaining minimum educational standards.

2. Equalization by Means of Federal Aid

As we have used the term *state*, we have meant it to refer to the forty-eight commonwealths. At present, it is the individual commonwealth that is the supporting unit for education. The arguments in favor of equalization of educational opportunity, however, could be applied just as logically to the nation as a whole. A glance at Table 24, which shows the per pupil cost of education in the several states, indicates clearly the need for such equalization.

Equalization on a nationwide basis means Federal aid for education, a moot question in this country for several decades. As in the several states, the chief objection has been the fear of centralization of control. Except for an emergency grant to the states during the depression, and for an emergency appropriation in 1941 to provide school facilities in communities suddenly overcrowded as a result of the defense program, no Federal money has been appropriated directly to support general education. These emergency grants and the subsidies for vocational education that followed the Smith-Hughes and subsequent legislative measures represent the only Federal appropriations for direct benefit to the

TABLE 24

Current Expense Per Pupil in Average Daily Attendance [10]
(Not including interest)

STATE	1929–30	1933–34	1937–38	1943–44
Alabama	$ 37.28	$ 30.09	$ 34.27	$ 54.17
Arizona	109.12	77.11	94.16	120.10
Arkansas	33.56	22.60	31.62	52.36
California	133.30	109.83	131.43	164.79
Colorado	110.76	78.30	87.41	125.44
Connecticut	102.58	82.12	104.47	151.09
Delaware	95.12	92.85	104.64	131.54
District of Columbia	132.39	107.30	123.05	161.73
Florida	50.61	40.73	59.91	82.76
Georgia	31.89	28.34	37.71	55.70
Idaho	86.86	57.09	75.00	102.12
Illinois	102.56	78.18	103.77	158.02
Indiana	91.66	60.20	77.01	111.27
Iowa	96.10	65.44	81.15	116.08
Kansas	92.81	60.19	72.84	114.58
Kentucky	46.23	33.37	44.49	75.28
Louisiana	48.19	36.12	54.09	90.57
Maine	69.89	52.09	60.36	83.17
Maryland	80.15	68.64	78.93	110.51
Massachusetts	109.57	95.69	109.81	161.00
Michigan	114.76	67.68	89.31	124.21
Minnesota	101.29	75.15	91.92	134.29
Mississippi	36.13	23.55	28.19	42.25
Missouri	70.28	60.27	70.68	100.58
Montana	109.73	79.24	104.12	159.11
Nebraska	93.08	57.48	70.67	112.01
Nevada	136.18	117.90	133.89	149.30
New Hampshire	92.77	79.67	92.13	119.66
New Jersey	124.90	102.53	125.53	185.07
New Mexico	77.21	60.19	71.30	113.52
New York	137.55	124.13	147.65	185.12
North Carolina	42.85	24.18	39.59	65.16
North Dakota	99.55	67.32	74.85	118.88
Ohio	95.69	72.51	86.23	124.86
Oklahoma	65.48	43.70	63.25	88.71
Oregon	103.31	68.90	87.88	132.96
Pennsylvania	87.81	75.04	92.82	131.14
Rhode Island	95.74	86.97	98.49	148.87
South Carolina	39.98	27.14	36.52	58.22
South Dakota	95.36	62.29	90.90	130.82
Tennessee	42.66	34.62	41.61	62.21

[10] *Statistics of State School Systems,* U. S. Office of Education, Washington, D. C., October 9, 1946.

TABLE 24 *(Continued)*

Current Expenses Per Pupil in Average Daily Attendance

STATE	1929–30	1933–34	1937–38	1943–44
Texas	54.57	46.63	65.42	88.15
Utah	75.08	58.71	74.86	111.87
Vermont	84.24	59.76	77.70	111.97
Virginia	44.25	37.51	42.31	75.30
Washington	100.45	69.16	103.83	146.57
West Virginia	76.16	48.54	60.55	93.06
Wisconsin	94.17	71.99	90.39	127.31
Wyoming	128.59	88.70	105.91	150.17
Total states	86.70	67.48	83.87	116.99

public schools since the land grants in the early days of the Republic. For a decade following 1918 there was considerable clamor for a secretary of education in the president's cabinet, and numerous bills were introduced to that effect. Some of them received favorable consideration and one or two presidents expressed approval of the idea. The objections to it were always the same, fear of Federal control over the schools, although the proponents of the measure tried to allay the fears on that score.

Since the days of the depression the agitation has taken a different turn. We have heard less about a secretary of education in the cabinet and considerably more about direct Federal aid as a means of equalization. Every session of Congress in recent years has considered one or more Federal aid bills.[11] The Eightieth Congress (1947) had before it Senate Bill 472, a bi-partisan measure sponsored by eight senators: Robert A. Taft (R), Ohio; H. Alexander Smith (R), N. J.; John S. Cooper (R), Ky.; Charles W. Tobey (R), N. H.; Lister Hill (D), Ala.; Elbert D. Thomas (D), Utah; Allen J. Ellender (D), La.; and Dennis Chavez (D), N. M. Action was postponed until the final year of the session.

a. *Provisions of Federal Aid Bill.*[12] In its essential provisions, the bill:

1. Authorizes Federal funds up to $250,000,000 a year to assist public schools in the neediest states.

---

11 National Education Association, "Our Public Schools," Washington, D. C., 1947.

12 *Ibid.*

2. Apportions these funds on the basis of need, which is to be determined by the number of children and the wealth of a state.

3. Guarantees that every child in every school district of every state shall have at least a $40 per year education.

4. Guarantees local control of the public schools.

5. Provides for fair distribution of the Federal funds in the education of minority races.

b. *Arguments for Federal aid.* The National Education Association has for two decades or more vigorously urged the passage of such national legislation as that exemplified by Senate Bill 472. At various times the NEA has also had the support of such national organizations as the American Legion, the Federal Council of the Churches of Christ, and the National Congress of Parents and Teachers. The arguments for equalizing educational opportunities by the granting of Federal aid have been summarized as follows:

1. American children are entitled to a fair start in life. They are not all getting it.
   a. Some children go to school in safe, comfortable buildings. . . . others in ugly, dangerous shacks.
   b. Some children have a chance to go to high school. . . . for others no school is provided beyond the eighth grade.
   c. Some children go to school ten months a year. . . . others only six.
   d. Some children have college-trained teachers. . . . others are taught by teachers who have not finished elementary school.
   e. Some communities spend sixty times as much for the education of their children as others do!

2. Wealth is unevenly distributed. The people of the richest state have five times as much income per child as the people of the poorest state. Much of the wealth created in the nation flows to great manufacturing and business centers. Many of the states helping to create the wealth therefore have no power to tax it for the support of their schools.

Only the Federal government has the power to tax wealth, wherever it is, for the education of children, wherever they live.

3. Children are unevenly distributed. Some states have twice as many children per 1,000 population as other states have. They are not the wealthiest states. In fact, if some states spent all their normal revenues for education, they could not support their schools as well as the average school of the nation is supported. Their children, therefore, will never have equality of educational opportunity unless the Federal government helps pay for the schools.

c. *Arguments against Federal aid.* These arise chiefly from two sources:

1. Those who are fearful that distribution of Federal money will destroy local control.
2. Certain groups that are opposed to further increases in support for public education for all children.

A great deal more is involved in the problem of equalization of educational opportunities than merely equalizing the financial support. Larger school districts and revised finance programs will help. These administrative measures provide a variety of educational offerings that form the best basis for equalization, but they do not furnish the entire solution. The use of a single program would provide equality of opportunity only if all children were alike, which, of course, is never true. There are several groups in our schools who will enjoy some measure of equality of opportunity only if special arrangements are made. A few of these groups will be enumerated in the next section.

C. More Adequate Provisions for Exceptional Children

British educators who have visited our schools have been quick to point out that the American schools do a good job of providing for the average or mediocre children, but that we neglect the superior students and do not adequately take care of the duller ones. There is much truth in this criticism. Our philosophy of "education for all" is in such marked contrast to that of England, where so much effort is made to locate and educate the superior student, that we would naturally expect that observation from English critics. It is true that only in recent years have we given serious attention to the problems of children who are atypical mentally. The first impetus in this movement came from the studies of individual differences. It was not until we devised suitable measuring instruments that we were able to determine the character and the amount of the differences that exist among school children.

For this discussion, those children who are not able to take full advantage of the offerings of the school, the Exceptional Children —comprising those who are exceptions to the general rules—are classified into two large categories:

1. Children who are exceptional mentally.
2. Physically handicapped children.

1. Children Who Are Exceptional Mentally

Children who differ from the average in mental ability will be discussed under four headings:

a. *Mentally retarded, or slow learners.* Let us consider first the problems of those children who are slow to learn, those with intelligence quotients in the neighborhood of 70 to 80. These children are like other children in most respects. They differ only because they are mentally retarded; they must learn at a slower rate, and their ultimate mental development will be on a lower level. Their lot in the school is a difficult one because they cannot engage in most children's activities with success and sometimes with distinction. They cannot do their classroom work with speed or satisfaction, and they become discouraged and develop habits of failure. Their parents frequently fail to understand them, and they are sometimes scolded or punished because they do not receive good marks. What they need is sympathy and kindness and learning tasks adjusted to their individual learning rates and mental levels. But there still persists in the minds of most people the notion that all children should be able to progress through the schools at the normal rate. It has been exceedingly difficult to persuade school boards to provide a suitable program for those who cannot do so with success.   In fact, many teachers find it inconvenient and distasteful to modify the ordinary group procedures of the classroom to allow a maximum of opportunity for slow learners.

Any resourceful teacher could do more than is customarily done for these children, but administrative devices of one sort or another make it much easier.   That is why the Rochester Plan and the Winnetka Plan are valuable.   Another program designed to meet the needs of dull pupils is often referred to as the Coaching Teacher Plan, in which one or more teachers in a building devote all their time to individual instruction of pupils sent to them from the regular classes.   This coaching may be done in one subject or in several subjects and for the length of time necessary for the pupil to become adjusted to his class.   There is no good reason for expecting all children to go through school at the same rate.   It is most unfair to stigmatize and penalize those who will secure more satisfactory results if they are permitted or encouraged to proceed at a slower rate.   Such a program is much easier to explain to parents and children if the objectives are stated in terms of certain goals to be reached, rather than in terms of time spent or work covered.   There never was any logical or rational explanation of an eight- or a six-year elementary school course.   Equality for the retarded group demands that the tempo of the program be adjusted to a pace that they can maintain.

"School Dull and Life Right" [13] was the title of a convincing address by the State Commissioner of Education of Connecticut on the problems of the slow learner.   He made a stirring plea for the type of pupil who does not do well in school but who achieves success in later life.   Certain children cannot do successfully the regular classroom work at the same rate as the majority of children, especially work in the academic subjects.   Some of them, those who deviate from the average in the greatest degree, can best be provided for in "special classes," sometimes called Opportunity Rooms or Òrthogenic Groups.

b. *Superior children.*   Mentally superior children are frequently

---

[13] E. W. Butterfield, "School Dull and Life Bright," *NEA Journal,* 20:111–14, April, 1931.

referred to as the really underprivileged children of the public schools. Of course, they get along and achieve success frequently in spite of, rather than because of, the teacher's efforts, but usually at a level or rate considerably below their maximum capacity. They are permitted to develop habits of indifference and indolence and become satisfied with mediocre work because they can do all of the required work with so little effort. As in the case of the slow learners, they suffer because the pace is not adjusted to their rate of achievement with maximum success and satisfaction. In too many cases the schools have tried to provide for them by promotion or skipping grades. That is only a temporary solution. Although a child thus accelerated finds himself with children more nearly of his intellectual level, he frequently learns that his associates are much more mature socially, and he becomes unhappy and discontented, sometimes seriously emotionally disturbed. A more satisfactory adjustment for most superior children seems to be a rich and varied program, calling for more difficult work and larger measures of responsibility, and opportunities for limited specialization and independent study. Here again progressive tendencies permit a flexible program that provides more of a challenge for the brighter pupils.

In all these efforts to provide more adequate opportunities for atypical children of all classes, the first step is a change of attitude on the part of the teachers toward them. It is necessary that teachers become interested in and learn how to diagnose an individual pupil's difficulties. Sympathy and interest in the problem must precede the working out of administrative details leading to a solution. The task calls for a combination teacher, personnel worker, and diagnostician.

c. *Mental illness.* Mentally diseased children present another type of problem in the public schools. Unlike those who are mentally defective, there is much that medical and psychological science can do for them. It has been estimated that of the thirty million public school children, about a million and a half will at some time in their lives become inmates of an institution for mental disease. That is five per cent, or two out of every classroom of forty children.   Although many cases of mental disease are traceable to hereditary predispositions, the majority are "due to the social environment of the individual, the stresses and strains to which the personality has been exposed.   The minor fears and jealousies and prejudices and uncertainties which hamper us all are of much the same stuff as that of which mental disease is made." [14]

The problem of the teacher in this connection is twofold.   First, the early detection and treatment of such cases is of primary importance, and teachers may be trained to recognize symptoms in the earliest stages, even though the treatment will generally be delegated to physicians or psychiatrists.   The second obligation is to provide a wholesome, healthful classroom environment that eliminates fears and inhibitions and removes the cause of the conflicts.   In the beginning, such conditions are essentially emotional. The nervous, shrinking, shy, timid, self-conscious youngster whom the teacher formerly considered a model pupil generally represents a more serious problem than the "bad boy" who is mischievous and causes the teacher the most trouble as a behavior case.   Here we have one of the best arguments for the Activity Curriculum, which substitutes coöperative endeavor in genuine social situations for the fear-arousing, competitive, question-answer recitations and formal drill.   Just as in the case of treatment of physical ills, the first task is to remove the cause.

The essential thing in dealing with any behavior problem is to find out, if possible, what the child lacks—to what subtle and unconscious aims his efforts are being misdirected; and to help him find the satisfaction which every human being needs, in a way that is intrinsically sound and socially constructive.[15]

2.   Facilities for Physically Handicapped Children

Only with considerable difficulty and effort can the typical public school offer educational advantages to the children who are

---

14 "The Problems of Mental Disease," Metropolitan Life Insurance Company *Health Bulletin,* Vol. VII, No. 9, May, 1936, New York.
15 *Ibid.*

suffering from physical handicaps and defects.   Special provisions
are frequently necessary, and again we see the need for a larger
unit of administration.   Such children compare favorably with
other school children in ability to do schoolwork and frequently
have a great deal more incentive and drive for their work, a seem-
ing compensation for their handicap.   These children include
crippled children, those handicapped by congenital deformities as
well as those who were injured by accidents or disease, those with
sight or hearing or speech defects, and those suffering from organic
or functional ailments, such as heart and lung conditions or glandu-
lar disturbances.

TABLE 25

*Showing the Number and Per Cent of Exceptional Children in the
Total School Population of 26 Million* [16]

Defects of Children	Number	Percentage	Benefited by Special Education
(1)	(2)	(3)	(4)
Sight (Blind & Partially Sighted)	130,000	.5	14,745
Hearing (Deaf & Hard-of-Hearing) ..	520,000	2.0	28,151
Speech	520,000	2.0	126,146
Crippled	130,000	.5	25,784
Delicate (Heart, Nutrition, Tubercular)	520,000	2.0	26,792
Mentally Retarded	780,000	3.0	120,222
Mentally Superior	780,000	3.0	3,255

The accompanying table shows the approximate number of
school children suffering from the various handicaps and defects,
and the proportions which these are of the school population.

Approximately 50 per cent of young men registering for selective
service in 1941 were rejected by local board and induction board
examiners as unfit for general military service.   These rejections

---

[16] Columns (1) and (4) are taken from the *Biennial Survey of Education
in the United States:* 1938–40, Volume II, page 11, "Statistics of Special
Schools and Classes for Exceptional Children," 1942.   Columns (2) and (3)
are from surveys issued by Division of Special Education, Lester N. Myer,
Chief, State Department of Public Instruction, Harrisburg, Pennsylvania.

exceeded in percentage those of World War I. It would not be correct, however, to draw the conclusion that the health status of American young men was lower in 1941 than in 1917. The standards of selection employed in 1941 were different and more rigid. Many of the defects leading to rejection were remediable (eyes and teeth), and not of such a nature as to unfit the man for civilian pursuits. Actually, the health status of the American people was better in 1941 than in 1917. Nevertheless, it is clear that society and education must take more seriously their responsibilities in this matter of health protection and correction of physical defects.

D. Problems and References for Collateral Study

Problems for Students

1. Secure from your local superintendent (or county superintendent) information concerning the need for a reorganization of the school districts in your county.

2. Prepare maps and charts that will show how existing school-district boundary lines are no longer consistent with commercial and industrial developments and educational needs.

3. Cite instances that have come to your knowledge of harmful effects of lay control interfering with professional leadership of schools.

4. Collect data for your school district concerning the school costs compared with those of other similar districts and with the averages for the state and nation.

5. For a school district with which you are familiar compute the revenues that would be available if school costs were equalized on the basis of $100.00 per pupil as explained in this unit.

6. From interviews with teachers and school officials ascertain what proportion of the children are physically handicapped and compare with the percentages shown in Table 24.

7. Secure information from school officials concerning the efforts being made to adjust the school work to meet the needs of exceptional and handicapped children.

8. Prepare a critique of the provisions that are made for superior children in elementary or secondary schools.

9. What data would you need if you were responsible for determining whether several districts in a locality should join forces in organizing a central technical or vocational school?

10. For a county with which you are familiar ascertain the benefits of consolidation or joint district employment of special services.

11. Submit evidence that children from different economic levels do (or do not) have equal educational opportunities in public schools.

12. What major educational changes have been produced by the war?

Selected References

American Association of School Administrators, "School Boards in Action," *Twenty-fourth Yearbook,* The American Association of School Administrators, 1946.

Baker, Harry J., *Introduction to Exceptional Children.* New York: Macmillan, 1945.

Ewing, I. R., and A. W. G. Ewing, *Handicap of Deafness.* New York: Longmans, 1938.

Frampton, M. E., *Education of the Blind.* Yonkers, N. Y.: World Book Company, 1940.

————, and H. G. Rowell, *Education of the Handicapped.* Yonkers, N. Y.: World Book Company, Vol. I, 1938; Vol. II, 1940.

Gossard, A. P., *Superior and Backward Children in Public Schools.* Chicago: University of Chicago Press, 1940.

Heck, A. O., *Education of Exceptional Children.* New York: McGraw-Hill, 1940.

Johnson, W., *Education of the Handicapped.* Iowa City: University of Iowa, 1939.

Kirk, S. A., *Teaching Reading to Slow-Learning Children.* Boston: Houghton Mifflin, 1940.

Lowenfeld, V., *Nature of Creative Activity.* New York: Harcourt Brace, 1939.

Mort, Paul R., and W. C. Reusser, *Public School Finance: Its Background, Structure, and Operation.* New York: McGraw-Hill, 1941.

Sears, Jesse B., *Public School Administration.* New York: Ronald Press, 1945.

Stafford, G. T., *Sports for the Handicapped,* 2nd ed. New York: Prentice-Hall, 1947.

Promising Educational Activities Today

"The schools aren't what they used to be," we frequently hear our elders say. True enough, and we should consider it a cause for rejoicing. We may memorialize the "little red school house," but there is no denying that it has had its day. We are forcibly reminded that the proverbial "three R's" no longer suffice as a description of the curriculum. In spite of the demands in recent years to eliminate the fads and frills from schools, the enriching experiences and creative activities are here to stay. In this unit the student will get a glimpse of some of the challenging educative activities that are being provided, not only for boys and girls, but for adults as well. Some of the newer movements, such as speech education and guidance activities, will tend to reduce the inequalities that prevent some pupils from taking full advantage of the opportunities that are available.

A. Beyond the School

The title of this section suggests that the boundaries of the school are being extended, or that educational facilities are being provided for a wider age span. We are so accustomed to thinking of education only in terms of formal schooling from the first grade through high school or college that we need to remind ourselves of the possibilities beyond these limits. In fact, legislative enactments or state constitutions frequently make it extremely difficult to provide educational offerings at public expense except for persons between the ages of six and twenty. We shall consider some of the newer developments in those areas beyond the customary school years.

1. Preschool Education

Two to six,[1] the title of a book on child development, might very well be used as the caption for this topic. We are concerned here with a child's growth and development before he enters school, an area of investigation that has only recently commanded the attention of educational and psychological research workers. Preschool education is a comparatively new idea. The child study movement flourished during the latter part of the last century under the inspiration of G. Stanley Hall and others. To a large extent the impetus for that movement came from the work and teaching of Pestalozzi, Rousseau, and, particularly, Froebel. From that influence came the kindergarten and later the attention given to adolescence. In more recent years we have seen this interest in child development move in two somewhat divergent directions —the establishment of nursery schools and the scientific study of infant behavior.

a. *Kindergartens.* These we shall discuss first because they represent the early efforts to provide for the education of children before formal schooling begins. We do so at the risk of criticism from those who would question including the kindergarten in a preschool classification since it is frequently considered an integral part of the school system. "Children's garden" is a literal translation of *kindergarten,* and it was Froebel's idea that young children should carry on constructive play activity amid pleasant surroundings provided with flowers, fountains, sand boxes, toys, and pets. The main purposes of the kindergarten are the formation of good health habits, attainment of emotional control, development of coöperative attitudes in social situations, and participation in creative activities. Public school teachers were quite skeptical about the kindergarten in the beginning, fearing that the habits of freedom and self-activity developed there would cause them trouble when the children reached the first and second grades. For this reason the kindergarten was slow in coming into the schools, and when it did it suffered from traditional influences, becoming a

---

[1] Rose H. Alschuler, *Two to Six* (New York: Morrow, 1933).

bit fixed and rigid and formal in its program. In recent years, however, the pendulum has been swinging in the other direction and the kindergarten has exerted a fine, wholesome, stimulating influence upon the school. The healthy, happy learning situations and the original creative activities of the lower grades are traceable in large measure to the kindergarten influence. Numerous research studies have attempted to discover the effect of kindergarten attendance upon achievement in the early years of the elementary

Photo from Black Star

Fig. 19.—Good Kindergartens Are a Sound Educational Investment.

school. One of the most extensive of these studies was made in a number of Ohio cities under the direction of Dr. B. R. Buckingham, then the director of the Bureau of Educational Research at Ohio State University.[2]

The number of kindergartens in public schools is not increasing very rapidly; in fact, in the retrenchment programs of the early thirties many of them were eliminated. This tendency has been checked considerably by the recent rapid growth of the private kindergarten. Many parents, seeing the benefits obtained from

---

[2] Josephine H. MacLachy, *Attendance at Kindergarten and Progress in the Primary Grades* (Columbus: Ohio State University Press, 1928).

kindergartens, are now urgently requesting boards of education to provide for them in the school budget. We may reasonably expect that public kindergartens will increase in number and eventually become an established part of the graded ladder scheme. One hindrance at present is that many state constitutions fix the legal school age at six years, a fact that makes many school boards hesitate about providing education for five-year-olds at public expense.

A study [3] in the Pittsburgh school calls attention to the behavior traits that seem to be traceable to the kindergarten experience.

b. *Nursery schools.* In many European countries before the war nursery schools were provided to take care of the children of mothers who found it necessary to work, but had no one at home with whom they could leave the children. The same need lay behind the establishment of nursery schools in this country. The development of nursery schools on a broader basis in the United States came during the depression years, when a considerable portion of Federal Emergency Relief funds was allocated to community nursery schools on a temporary and experimental basis. These nursery schools thoroughly justified their existence in terms of providing good care and diet to little children, many of whose parents were unable to provide adequately for them; in providing socially useful work to unemployed teachers and dieticians; and in testing and demonstrating the social usefulness of nursery schools.

Nursery schools as laboratories for the study of child growth and development have been established in many colleges and universities. The nursery school aims to provide a natural, wholesome environment in which children can learn to adjust themselves in social situations. This opportunity is particularly valuable to children who have few or no playmates in their homes or neighborhoods. The children are under the close observation and guidance

---

[3] "Survey of Behavior Traits in Kindergarten Pupils," *Bulletin of Pittsburgh Schools,* Vol. X, No. 5, May, 1936.

of skilled supervisors who attempt to check the development of undesirable personal traits and qualities and to provide activities that will develop desirable social attitudes and habits.

The employment of many thousands of married women in war work created a new demand for nursery school facilities. Some of these wartime nursery schools were established with public funds, while others were established by war plants. Unquestionably these wartime nursery schools made a great contribution to production, by freeing for war work many women who otherwise would have been required to remain in the home. The experience of the public with nursery schools, first during the depression, and then as an important aid in wartime production, has dissipated the older idea that a nursery school is a place where bridge-playing mothers can park their children if they can afford to pay a high fee for the privilege. It seems safe to predict that the nursery school will find a permanent place in our educational establishment. In the nursery school the emphasis is upon the growth of personality, poise, and emotional control. This fact suggests the next topic.

c. *Study of infant behavior.* Here we have one of the most promising fields of research. Such investigations as those of Bird T. Baldwin at the University of Iowa on the physical growth of children; of John B. Watson, whose critical observations of infants furnished support for behavioristic psychology; and of Stanford University's Lewis M. Terman, who studied the mental abilities of hundreds of superior children, have contributed richly to the scientific knowledge of child life. More recently the Child Guidance Clinic at Yale University under the direction of Dr. Arnold Gesell has supplied much exceedingly valuable information relative to the characteristic behavior of infants. There is now very little justification for guesswork concerning the backgrounds and potentialities of children. This development is of special importance to persons who wish to adopt children as members of their families. The majority of recent studies indicate that personality traits have their origins in early childhood, a result emphasizing the extreme importance of more scientific knowledge and more careful observation. Comparatively safe predictions for the future may be made as a result of the knowledge gained from young children relative to their health, mental capacity, and personality.

The following newspaper account [4] of a long-term investigation is a good example of the benefits derived from the study of the behavior of young children:

Children who are likely eventually to join the unemployed can be selected at the age of 6 years by first-grade teachers in the public schools, according to the findings of Dr. J. W. M. Rothney of the Harvard Graduate School of Education, following a study of 1,700 recent high school graduates in three Massachusetts towns.

Back in 1922, the Harvard School of Education began a "growth study" of 3,500 pupils starting in school in the first grade, and teachers in that first year were asked to rate the students according to qualities of leadership, behavior, concentration, intelligence and scholastic standing in the class.

This group has been the subject of study as to physical and mental development through all their school years, until high school graduation in 1934.

Dr. Rothney, working with Professor Walter F. Dearborn, director of the growth study, recently questioned 1,700 of these students on their employment record and mental attitude toward the work.

In reply to his questionnaire, he received answers from 88 per cent of the group, an all-time high for surveys of this kind, and the results show conclusively that in every respect on which the rating was made in the first grade the young people who are now out of jobs received lower marks on the average. He found that the first-grade rating was more accurate for boys than for girls.

2.   Adult and Part-time Education

With education assuming the importance in society that is suggested in this volume, it is obvious that we cannot think of it as being synonymous with schooling. Much of the program attempted by the school will need to be completed in later life. This statement implies the necessity for adult and part-time education. Just as the pre-school influences are significant in determining what the school will attempt, so the after-school years will figure largely in having these efforts bear fruit.

---

[4] Special to the *New York Times*, March 8, 1936.

The philosophy of change that we advocated in an earlier unit will be attained as a goal only if we can set up an organization that will provide systematically directed educational experiences for those who have left school. It will need to be on a part-time basis if it is to be of maximum benefit to those who are employed. This movement has been accelerated by scientific studies by Thorndike and others that refute the notion that learning efficiency declines rapidly after physical maturity, that "you can't teach an old dog new tricks." Thorndike's [5] conclusions were to the effect that maximum learning efficiency is not reached until about age twenty-five and that there is comparatively little diminution in learning ability until the age of forty to forty-five. We may, with confi-

TABLE 26

Summary of Public Participation in WPA Classes and Related Activities, October, 1940 [6]

Program	No. of Classes or Units	Number of Participants			
		Total	White	Negro	Other
Adult Education Classes (Total)	47,565	1,014,624	810,162	197,848	6,614
Literacy Classes	9,946	161,244	91,470	68,863	911
Naturalization Classes .	3,491	84,242	83,220	369	653
Vocational Training Classes (Total)	8,027	182,768	162,530	19,423	815
Homemaking and Parent Classes	7,981	170,836	123,616	45,594	1,626
Other Adult Education Classes	18,120	415,534	349,326	63,599	2,609
Nursery Schools	1,330	37,667	29,982	6,962	723
Correspondence Courses ...		18,095			
Lectures, Forums, Discussion Groups, etc.	1,982	103,004			
Adult Education Classes under Workers' Service Program	405	21,167	17,246	3,897	24

Number of Persons employed on the WPA Education Program as of October 1940 28,541

[5] E. L. Thorndike, *Adult Learning* (New York: Macmillan, 1928).
[6] Prepared by Division of Education, Works Progress Administration, L. R. Alderman, Director, Washington, D. C. Released March, 1941.

dence, expect much broader, richer adult and part-time education in the future, and these innovations will to a much greater extent be articulated with the public school system.

Great impetus was given to the adult and part-time education movement by the emergency education program of the Federal Government, set up for the purpose of training men and women for war work. Again, as in the case of nursery schools, the WPA, NYA, and CCC programs that had been initiated during the depression paid enormous dividends when it became necessary to organize our society to produce for war. Some notion of the extent of the WPA educational program is given in the table on page 313. It is an interesting commentary on our society to observe that only a severe economic depression or war has been able in recent years to cause us to engage in creative endeavor to develop our human resources through education.

   a. *Americanization or immigration education.* This usually means the teaching of English and other tool subjects to non-English-speaking immigrants, but of late it has come to have a much broader significance. Citizenship training is implied also, although that is a very elusive term. What is meant is some sort of educative experiences that will provide opportunities to think constructively about the rights, privileges, duties, and responsibilities of citizens. These efforts are frequently made just before a group of aliens apply for naturalization papers, but are often continued over longer periods of time and in a broader scope. In the latter case the program is so organized that tactful, trained workers carry on systematic constructive study and recreational activities in foreign settlements, with the aim of instructing the foreign-born residents in the traditions and customs of the locality and of inculcating ideals of loyalty and patriotism. This work, too, is frequently done by public school teachers and in public school buildings. Its nature is well illustrated by the following statement on citizenship education in Chicago:

Some 75 teachers are engaged in the teaching of adult aliens in Chicago. There are approximately 350 classes distributed throughout the city in over 150 teaching units, and the estimated enrollment of all these classes is 15,000. The majority of these classes meet twice a week in periods of an hour or longer. The expenses of these classes are borne entirely by the Chicago Board of Education and teaching materials are furnished by the Immigration and Naturalization Service.

On June 15, 1944, approximately 1,000 graduates of these classes participated in a graduation exercise at the Field Museum. They had passed an examination at about the 8th grade level which is given each year in citizenship and English. This program, which has been going on for 27 years, is recognized by the Immigration and Naturalization Service as one of the outstanding programs of its kind in the United States.[7]

b. *Removal of illiteracy.* This represents another task that has been receiving much attention lately. The percentage of persons who can neither read nor write has been steadily decreasing, but there are still large areas containing disgracefully large numbers of illiterates. The United States Office of Education has been keenly alert to the necessity of removing illiteracy, and has promoted or lent encouragement to many fine programs looking in this direction.

The Emergency Educational Program of the Works Progress Administration also attacked the problem. A press release for May, 1936, stated that 6,602 formerly unemployed teachers were conducting 21,493 classes in which 266,630 people were learning to read and write. Plans were laid to increase the number of students to nearly half a million, a figure that was estimated to represent about one-eighth of the country's approximately four million illiterates. Curtailment of WPA appropriations, and eventual elimination of that agency, prevented the consummation of these plans.

The Bureau of the Census has estimated that 3.7 per cent of the American public were illiterate in 1940, as against 20 per cent in 1870 and 10.7 per cent in 1920. There appears to be good reason to believe that the estimates of the Census Bureau as to the amount of illiteracy—in 1940, at any rate—were too low. There is, for

---

[7] *Adult Education in Illinois,* Research Department Illinois Legislative Council, Springfield, Ill. Publication No. 72, November, 1945, p. 35.

example, the fact that a subcommittee of the Senate Committee on Education and Labor reported that almost 1,000,000 men had been rejected for military service because of illiteracy. This figure would indicate a much higher rate of illiteracy for the population as a whole than had been estimated by the Census Bureau.

Conflicting estimates of the extent of illiteracy probably grow out of failure to define precisely what is meant by illiteracy. The Census Bureau terms as illiterate those over twenty-five years of age who have had less than one year of schooling. Persons having less than five years of schooling, however, commonly are presumed to have insufficient literacy skills to enable them to meet the ordinary reading needs of adults. If such a standard of literacy is accepted, and it seems reasonable to think that it should be, then it should be clear that there is an enormous task ahead of us before we can call ourselves a literate people. When we consider the fact that most of our illiterates have voting privileges, it can be seen that illiteracy is a most serious problem. Our experience in the war, when effective manpower was at a premium, highlighted the problem. The success of some states and communities in dealing with it, and the concern exhibited on the part of the Federal Government over this problem, provide good reason for believing that substantial progress will be made in its solution.

c. *Apprenticeship and foreman training.* There was a time when most trades and industries provided apprenticeship training for all beginning workers. The new worker learned his trade in that manner. For the past fifteen to twenty years we have been developing rather complete vocational and trade-training programs in public schools. This development took some of the edge from the apprentice program in industry. The tendency today is for the industry to provide technical and general education schools, which the workers frequently attend on the company's time, the idea being to provide a chance for the worker to qualify for a better position or to understand better the processes with which he is working.

d. *Continuation schools.* In general, the work of continuation schools was interrupted by the war. There is good reason for believing that the continuation school will serve a useful purpose in the future, although its function will be more broadly conceived than in the past. As its name indicates, the continuation school provides an opportunity for the student to continue his education after accepting a remunerative job. It seems probable that the continuation school of the future will be provided for older boys and girls, including high school graduates, and that the curriculum will be vitally related to their vocations and interests. The gradual eliminaton of child labor will remove the need for the continuation school as it formerly existed.

e. *Extension classes.* Thousands of person have been able to continue their education through the facilities of the extension departments of colleges and universities. Sometimes the work is organized into classes that provide systematic instruction in courses that lead to degrees or diplomas; sometimes the instruction is offered quite informally, as in the case of agriculture and home economics. Whatever the plan, extension instruction has come to be a very prominent type of educational activity, covering nearly all fields of learning, engineering, mining, law, commerce, teaching, and the academic subjects.

f. *Correspondence or home study courses.* Closely akin to the extension work is the home study or correspondence study, the essential difference being that in the latter the student pursues his work as an individual and not as a member of a class. Many of our leading universities provide extensive offerings of this sort and there are numerous private agencies devoted entirely to this work. Uncounted hundreds of workers have been able, through these advantages, to qualify for better positions or to go forward with the educational program they were not privileged to complete in school. Home study has been steadily gaining respect and standing in academic circles and holds much promise for the future.

The greatest impetus that correspondence study has ever received was that provided by the United States Armed Forces Institute during the war. Personnel in any branch of the Army, Navy, Marine Corps, or Coast Guard were eligible to take Institute courses. In addition to other types of educational opportunity, the Institute offered correspondence courses in which the student was furnished with textbooks and lessons. The text was studied and lessons were completed and returned to the Institute, where a teacher was assigned as the student's educational counselor. The counselor graded the lessons and wrote suggestions. The fee for the course was $2.00, and this fee admitted the student to any number of additional courses without further cost. Those who preferred to do so were permitted to take correspondence courses directly from any one of eighty-three colleges and universities. The government paid half the cost of tuition for these courses. It would be difficult to overestimate the value of these courses to service men and women during the war.

g. *State programs of adult education.* In recent years the states have increasingly recognized their responsibility for developing and helping to finance programs of adult education. It has become clear that local districts alone will not be able to meet adult education needs. State and Federal financial support are needed. A study made by the United States Office of Education disclosed that the following states have comprehensive adult education programs: California, Michigan, Pennsylvania, New York, Connecticut, Delaware, Maine, Minnesota, Nebraska, New Jersey, North Carolina, Oklahoma, Oregon, Rhode Island, South Carolina, Utah, Virginia, and Wyoming. It was found that the four states first named had gone much further than the others in the development of such programs.

California pioneered in the development of a comprehensive state program of adult education. The legislature of that state has been dealing with adult education legislation since 1920, when a Division of Adult Education was established in the state Department of Education. The following year a law was enacted requiring school boards to provide instruction whenever twenty-five or more applicants for naturalization papers petitioned for such instruction. In 1923 school boards were required to provide classes upon the application of a minimum of twenty adults unable to speak, read, or write the English language with sixth-grade proficiency.

In 1931 the California Legislature provided for state aid to be furnished for schools and classes of adults in substantially the same manner as it was furnished for the regular public school program. Provision was made for the establishment of special day and evening classes in a variety of subjects in all local school districts, the number of these classes to be limited only by the demand for such instruction.

In 1939 a Community Recreation Act was passed authorizing school districts and other civil units to promote and conduct such programs of community recreation as would contribute to the attainment of general recreational and educational objectives for both children and adults. With the extension of the adult education program to include recreational services, California now makes available, through the public schools and under the supervision of the state Department of Education, educational services to meet the needs of adults and out-of-school youth, as well as of those eligible to attend the regular schools. The adult education program for the state include classes in the fields of agriculture, business and commerce, homemaking, trades and industries, arts and crafts, social civics and Americanization, health and physical education, recreation, and parent education.

3. Recreation and Leisure-time Activities

Organized society seems about ready to embark upon a program that would place greater emphasis upon the leisure time and recreational activities of adults. What we have done for the children in public playgrounds maintained by municipalities and school districts we are about to attempt on a larger scale for adults. The government is acquiring vast areas that are to be developed as recreational centers, with directors and nature guides to assist people to take full advantage of them. The projects are almost limitless in scope, including better facilities for camping, hunting, fishing, hiking, golf courses, tennis courts, and swimming pools. This program offers not only splendid outlets for people to enjoy their increasing leisure time, but excellent vocational opportunities for recreational leaders and directors.

a. *School camps.* Some may object to the inclusion of school camps under recreation and leisure-time activities. Unquestionably the school camp should have objectives that go beyond those that could be termed recreational. Yet it can scarcely be argued that the average boy and girl will not regard the camping experience as recreational, in contrast to his regular school experience. This is as it should be, and teachers should be careful not to introduce so many "educational" features to the camp as to destroy that joyous anticipation with which boys and girls look forward to going to camp.

Camping has long been the prerogative of the children of well-to-do families and of families so poor that charitable institutions undertook to provide a camping experience for them. All too often neither type of camp was of truly good quality. In the expensive private camps the profit motive frequently weighed far more heavily than all others, including educational outcomes.

The development of public school camps is still in its infancy in the United States. A promising beginning was made during several years preceding the war, and although the war interrupted that program, it now is being resumed. Both day camps and full-time camps are being provided by forward-looking school systems to supplement the regular school experiences.

Every city school system should make provision for full-time, all-year camping as an important and vital part of the educational program for children and youth. The camping experience should be introduced to children at about age ten, and should continue to be provided through high school. The camp program should be built around the interests and needs of children and youth, rather than around the traditional and academic objectives of the school. Certainly the camp situation provides many opportunities for the attainment of important objectives related to personal development: learning to get along with others, coöperation, initiative, health, and resourcefulness. It is these and other aims that can be attained better in the camp situation than in the classroom that should be emphasized.

If teachers are to work effectively in the school camp program it will be necessary to include camping as a part of the curriculum in teacher education. Some teachers colleges are already doing this. In the absence of such training, there is grave danger that many teachers might ruin the camping experience for the pupils under their direction. For the present it probably would be wise to put camping on a purely voluntary basis for both teachers and pupils.

For older students, of high school and college age, work camps are becoming increasingly popular. The opportunity to live and work with others of one's own age at socially useful tasks in a stimulating and challenging situation is one that has a great appeal for many young people. It should become a recognized part of the educational opportunity that is provided to American youth.

B. Curriculum Innovations

Our conception of the curriculum is expanding and evolving, to permit the teaching of subjects that were formerly not regarded as the function of the school. The rigid subject-matter boundaries are disappearing, and, as was indicated in Unit I, the acquisition of knowledge as a goal is being replaced by pupil activity. In this section it is our purpose to discuss several activities in which pupils are now taking part. They are termed curriculum innovations because they represent new departures in school offerings that cannot be readily classified under existing departmental groups.

1. Safety Education

One of the most pressing problems of our day is safety education, particularly with respect to safety on the public highways. Last year nearly 40,000 persons were killed in automobile traffic accidents and ten times that number were quite seriously injured. The toll of traffic accidents has been mounting at an appalling rate, keeping pace with the improvement in highway construction and the refinement of automotive engineering. Only recently have we begun to realize that traffic regulations and motor patrols do not furnish the solution to this problem. A safety campaign conducted in several cities furnishes a potent suggestion for more con-

scientious observance of traffic rules.   In this campaign a squadron
of five white automobiles, all equipped with loudspeakers and
manned by city police cruised about the streets and stopped at
strategic points to broadcast safety talks.   Criticisms were made
at the time when pedestrians and drivers were in the act of breaking
rules or taking risks.   The term "voice of safety" was applied to
this extraordinary safety education device.

For years industrial and commercial organizations have carried
on extensive campaigns to prevent accidents.   For example, an
Associated Press dispatch carried the story that in one state 1,688
out of 4,492 concerns had perfect no-accident records during the
preceding year.   The state industrial inspectors reported also
that accidents were reduced 17.5 per cent in frequency and 6.5
per cent in severity despite a 10 per cent increase in working hours
and 2.8 per cent rise in number of employees.   Industry has undoubtedly reduced the losses from accidents through its safety
campaigns.   We might also cite the life-saving campaigns of the
Red Cross.   Innumerable lives have been saved at bathing pools
and beaches through the effort of persons trained in the Red Cross
instruction programs.   Such effective programs point the way
for persons who are interested in highway safety.

The efforts thus far might be divided into four main groups.
First, we should name the promotion campaigns carried on by the
state and city departments in control of vehicular traffic.   Bill-
board posters and newspaper publicity and catchy slogans, such
as "Spare our Children," and "Children should be seen, not hurt,"
have been employed with beneficial results.   When coupled with
close supervision of the highways and punishment of flagrant offenders, the results are even more satisfying, despite the difficulty
in securing a sufficient number of patrolmen.

A second type of attack is that of the research worker.   Dr.
H. R. DeSilva, while an instructor in psychology at Massachusetts
State College, devised a number of tests to measure the reaction
time, distance perception, and color vision of operators and pros-
pective operators of motor vehicles.   Professor Alva Lauer, of
Iowa State College, has also devised similar instruments and de-

veloped techniques for discovering and eliminating persons lacking the necessary physiological equipment among those who apply for a driver's license.

The third approach is a training program. Professor A. E. Neyhart, of the Pennsylvania State College, is a pioneer in the movement for better training of automobile drivers. He conceived the notion that many accidents were due to faulty manipulation of the car, which was, in turn, traceable to inaccurate and inadequate learning in the beginning. He published a basic textbook [8] to be used in teaching high school and college students how to drive automobiles safely. His experiments attracted the attention of the National Safety Council and the American Automobile Association and other safety experts, all of whom are exceedingly hopeful and optimistic about this training approach to the solution of our highway safety problems.

As a fourth method of attack we should mention the instruction in public schools and the efforts of safety patrols who function at dangerous intersections used by children passing to and from school. In localities where these boys and girls have received encouragement and aid from the local police authorities, the program has been particularly effective in preventing accidents. Whatever the approach to the problem, we may expect increasing attention to it, in and out of school, in the future.

2. Speech Education

The boy who stuttered or stammered was formerly the object of pity or ridicule among his classmates and associates. These unfortunates receive better treatment today because the public schools are carrying on speech education programs, the objective of which is to study and remove the causes of speech defects. Scientists have discovered that a very large proportion of speech defects are correctable, many of them being due to faulty speech habits. Numerous other defects that are caused by malformations of the speech organs may be corrected by comparatively minor

---

[8] A. E. Neyhart, "How to Drive," published by American Automobile Association, Washington, D. C., 1941.

operations.   The net result of this research is that teachers now have at their disposal expert knowledge that enables them to locate at a very early age the children with speech difficulties.   Many of the cases they are able to deal with themselves; others they refer to the speech education specialists as clinical cases.   The services of these specialists are now so readily available in school districts, state departments of education, or in universities, that there is little excuse for children being doomed to unhappiness and humiliation throughout their school careers because of unfortunate speech defects, or careless speech habits.

3.   Consumer Education

Judging by the amount of attention given to the consumer in recent years, one would think that he was the proverbial "forgotten man" who had suddenly been rediscovered.   Several books similar in purpose and theme to the pioneering volume, *Your Money's Worth*,[9] have focused attention upon the need for sales resistance against the high-powered national advertising in the daily press and current periodicals and particularly on the radio.   "Consumer's Research" [10] was established as a nonprofit enterprise to inform its clients regarding the relative merits of various nationally advertised products.   The buying public suddenly became "quality conscious," and wary; they became suspicious that they had not been buying what they thought they were buying.   At about the same time, there was a shift in emphasis in thrift education from mere saving to wise spending.   Many people had seen the savings of a lifetime wiped out in bank failures.   It was natural that these problems should be called to the attention of the school, and we are now entirely justified in including consumer education among the promising curriculum innovations.

We find these discussions of the problems of the consumer introduced as practical units in courses in home making, social studies,

---

[9] Stuart Chase and F. J. Schlink, *Your Money's Worth* (New York: Macmillan, 1927); Gaer, J., *Consumers All* (New York: Harcourt, Brace, 1940); Tonne, Herbert, *Consumer Education in the Schools* (New York: Prentice-Hall, 1940).

[10] Consumer's Research, Inc., Washington, N. J.

and science, and a few high schools have organized new courses of study for consumers. The girls in home economics departments learn how to identify and test fabrics and to be critical in appraising the claims of advertisers and salesmen. Science classes conduct simple experiments testing the strength of materials or the durability or efficiency of machines and appliances, and they make chemical analyses of food or drug products. Students of social problems collect data on the price of raw materials compared with that of the finished product, study transportation and distribution of commodities, and investigate the conditions that seem to warrant legislation to protect the interest of consumers.

"The Consumer's Cooperative," which has been described as the "economic embodiment of the principles of brotherhood," offers a progressive but, as yet, visionary solution to the problems of the consumer. The following three statements illustrate the contribution of this particular social agency to education:

Next to free public schools, the consumer's cooperative movement is the greatest social invention of modern times; it is of the people, by the people, and for the people. . . . When studied and practiced in school, the cooperative movement gives young people a new life and sense of responsibility for their own destinies. . . . The cooperative movement is the practical application of the golden rule; it is the ultimate democracy.[11]

High school students show great interest in these tendencies, which is ample excuse for including them in the curriculum. It seems reasonable to hope that this new venture in social science will produce more critical and intelligent buying.

4. Character Education

Educational leaders have always placed great emphasis upon the development of character as one of the first objectives of the school. Frequently, there has been lack of agreement concerning the methods to be pursued in reaching this objective, but virtually

---

11 J. E. Morgan, "The Ultimate Democracy," *Consumer's Cooperation*, 22:69, May, 1936.

everything that was done in school was supposed to make a direct contribution to character development. During the late twenties and early thirties we experienced a renewal of interest in character education. There were several factors responsible for this awakened interest, chief among them being the "flaming youth" era and the crime wave of the years following World War I. The schools were told that they had failed in their task, and criticisms came so frequently and from so many sources that school leaders felt obligated to examine their program with a view to improving their practices.

Among the resulting changes in character training there are two developments that stand out in bold relief when compared with former procedures. First, we find educators attempting to approach the problem of character from the point of view of the John Dewey philosophy. This point of view may be paraphrased as follows: Character is developed in genuine life situations in which the pupil acquires desirable traits through the satisfaction he finds in doing the right thing. There is nothing mysterious about character. An individual learns to acquire traits and habits as he learns anything else; it is a psychological as well as a moral problem. In pursuance of this view, learning how to be self-analytical and self-directing individuals in practical life situations has replaced the teaching of morals and abstract virtues by precepts, preachments, and prohibitions. The second development lies in the application of scientific research techniques to the study of conduct. Research programs have been set up to evaluate objectively the results of our instruction methods. This is a rewarding type of endeavor. Such investigations substitute objective evidence for guesswork and supposition. These studies represent a new approach to character training, and they give promise of attainment that will be beneficial to the school program. The work of Hartshorne and May [12] is a good illustration of this type of investigation.

---

[12] Hugh Hartshorne and M. A. May, *Studies in Deceit,* 1928; *Studies in Service and Self-control,* 1929; *Studies in Organization of Character,* 1930 (New York: Macmillan).

5. Visual Education

The school has always suffered from too much verbalism, too much emphasis upon verbal and abstract meanings. In spite of the influences that came down through the years from Pestalozzi, we have found great difficulty in bringing objects, specimens, models, and concrete experiences into the classrooms. In recent years we have experienced a pronounced trend toward visual education and the use of other sensory aids. Visual education is now one of the most promising of the curriculum innovations. A few states even require that a teacher complete a course in visual education before a permanent certificate is granted. · Projectors and other apparatus for showing slides and motion pictures, both silent and with sound accompaniment, are now considered standard equipment for schoolrooms. Several companies are manufacturing comparatively inexpensive portable projectors that may, on short notice, be pressed into use in any type classroom. Vast sums of money have gone into research and the preparation of teaching films that are designed especially for classroom use. There is abundant scientific evidence [13] that the use of pictorial materials not only enriches the study of any topic, but also contributes positively to the acquisition of fundamental skills and knowledges.

The findings of psychological research furnish ample justification for the increased use of visual or other sensory materials. Learning will be easier and more permanent if the impressions are received in a variety of ways. A word will be more easily recalled if, while learning it, the student sees it, hears it, writes it, speaks it, and handles the object represented by the word, if there be such an object. Words represent ideas or concepts and it is logical to assume that meanings will be clear and useful only to the extent that words may be recalled when needed. The use of objects and models in laboratory situations and of pictorial representations and charts and graphs in conjunction with all types of procedures adds materially to the enjoyment and enrichment of the learning

---

[13] A good illustration of a scientific study is *Motion Pictures in the Classroom,* by Ben D. Wood and Frank N. Freeman (Boston: Houghton Mifflin, 1929).

experience. Subject matter may be more easily integrated. The day has passed when such materials were looked upon as frills or sugar-coating; they have come to be regarded as an integral part of the instructional program.

Closely related to the classroom use of visual materials is the school journey. This affords opportunities to take pupils on field trips and excursions where they may visit factories or industrial plants or commercial establishments and observe the processes by means of which raw materials are prepared or distributed. Or they may visit governmental agencies at work, such as courts or legislatures or executive departments. Social problems may be studied by visiting welfare agencies, missions, recreation centers, penal institutions, and the like.

The use by the armed services of a large quantity and variety of training aids during the war has served as a great stimulus to the further development of auditory and visual aids in the schools and colleges. Men who participated actively in the development of training aids for the armed services are now making their experience available to the schools. We may confidently expect a great increase in the development and use of auditory and visual aids, for the extensive utilization of these materials by the armed forces will cause them to be less condemned as mere fads by tax-conscious citizens.

6. Liberal Curriculum Tendencies

Most of the topics discussed in this section were presented also in Unit I as current tendencies in American education. They are repeated here for two reasons. First, we desire to indicate that these tendencies are among the most promising ones, in the sense that they are in the direction of the greater usefulness of the school in society. Second, we are defining the curriculum in broader terms. We formerly thought of the curriculum wholly in terms of subject matter, whereas we now place the emphasis upon pupil activity. We are coming to regard the curriculum as including anything that the school attempts to do.

a. *Socialized classroom procedures.* The school is undoubtedly a happier place than it was a generation ago, largely because of the socialization that is developing. We find less and less of artificiality and strained relations in the schoolroom. The teacher is no longer a domineering taskmaster, but is more of a guide and co-worker, assisting the pupils to attain goals that they propose and accept as desirable. The creation in the classroom of genuine, natural social situations is entirely in harmony with the sociology and psychology of learning. We are not referring at this point to any particular form or type of socialized recitation or to anybody's plan. Rather we are referring to the harmonious coöperative relations that exist between teachers and pupils. With such relations as a basis there are much greater opportunities for challenging the students to think for themselves and to participate in discussions that will encourage them to ask questions and reach sound conclusions. The memorizing and reciting of a former day are gradually disappearing. Of course, there are many able students of education who are not in sympathy with this tendency, being fearful that it leads to scrappy and superficial learning. Caution is necessary on this point and teachers need to be mindful of the danger. On the whole, however, it seems reasonable to expect a genuine social situation to contribute more than formal procedures to the development of habits of constructive thinking.

b. *Treatment of contemporary controversial issues.* People cannot think constructively and vote intelligently about contemporary issues unless they have an opportunity to know about them. They cannot really know and understand unless they hear and consider all the arguments and points of view concerning a given problem. They cannot see and hear all sides of a story if the school is content merely to serve in small doses what some of its leaders have prescribed as a safe diet. There seems only one answer in a democracy; any other procedure suggests a dictatorship with the accompanying blind acceptance of dictums and interpretations handed down from above. The school must expose to the light of critical examination and evaluation all contemporary social, economic, and political questions. This is being done today as we have never dared attempt it before, and it is submitted here as one of the most hopeful indications that the school of the future will be able to make a definite, positive contribution to the preservation of the democratic ideal.

We have been too fearful of indoctrination. We need to realize that there is just as much indoctrination in permitting pupils to think only about the safe, harmless questions before society as there would be in bringing before them discussions that are certain to lead to controversy. It should be remembered that holding no point of view is, after all, really holding a point of view. All this suggests two developments. First, teachers will have to become more aware of and more interested in social problems. Second, there are strong indications that the social studies will become the core of the curriculum and that everything the school attempts will be based upon that social substructure. This is a challenging thought, indeed, and one worthy of the best efforts of those already in the profession and those who contemplate entering it.

c. *Breaking down departmental lines.* The only hope that we can attain the goals indicated in the foregoing paragraphs lies in the current emphasis upon integration of subject matter, which leads ultimately to a breaking down of the departmental lines. We cannot continue to think in terms of water-tight subject-matter departments. Life's problems are not departmentalized; they cut across all subject-matter lines. What we need is an instruction program that permits students to seek the truth concerning a problem and to pursue it in whatever direction the solution lies, regardless of the subject matter required. This procedure calls for an entirely different organization of curriculum materials, and, it should be added, a much broader outlook on the part of teachers.

The Eighth Yearbook of the John Dewey Society faced this issue in the following statement: "Improvement of the curriculum usually is retarded by the feeling prevailing in many schools that the conventional daily schedule with its five to eight equi-length periods and regular passing periods in between is a 'must'. . . . If the schedule can be changed from day to day for football rallies, for overlong assemblies, or to provide more time for administrative work in the homeroom, it can be changed to suit the needs of a different kind of curriculum. Teachers report that as they move toward a more life-centered type of curriculum they need a more flexible daily schedule, with longer and fewer periods and with more time for pupil-teacher conferences." [14]

The arguments are supported by educational philosophy and by the findings of educational psychology. The committee points out, among other arguments, that the probability that what is learned will later be recalled for use when needed increases in proportion as the learning situation resembles that in which the learning is used or applied. Nowhere outside the schoolroom do we find the solution of problems being approached in terms of subject-matter divisions. It is, indeed, a hopeful sign when we see efforts being made to integrate subject matter. A broad category such as Recreation, including as it would sports, reading for pleasure, the drama, art, and music, is undoubtedly more consistent with life situations than a department of Physical Education. We may, with confidence, expect curriculum reorganizations to move in that direction in the future.

d. *Opportunities for creative activities.* The emphasis in recent years upon creative activities holds much promise for the future. We are using "creative" here in a very broad sense. We do not confine the term to original compositions, themes, and poems in English, and creative efforts in music, art, shop, or home economics. Those activities all have their place, and we are justified in taking pride in the progress we have made in these areas in recent years. In addition to all this, we include those activities and experiences that furnish opportunities for expression of the individual's impulses, attitudes, ideals, and aspirations. An experience is creative for an individual if it provides a chance for him to put himself into it wholeheartedly. It will be creative for him because it affords him a means of expressing himself. That is the thing the kindergarten does so well, and it is challenging to note that we are attempting to retain this spirit all the way through

---

[14] *The American High School, Its Responsibility and Opportunity,* Eighth Yearbook of the John Dewey Society, Hollis L. Caswell, Editor, pp. 242, 243. New York: Harper, 1946.

the grades and to take advantage of it as the pupils become more able to plan and think for themselves. Many of these opportunities present themselves in systematic classwork, and teachers are becoming increasingly alert in recognizing them. Some of the best possibilities are found in extra-class activities, which we shall present more fully in the next section.

Photo from Black Star

Fig. 20.—This Young Man Is Expressing Himself Creatively

e. *Organized student life.* One of the most conclusive arguments in favor of interpreting the scope of the curriculum more broadly is seen in the fact that many activities that were formerly regarded as extracurricular are now termed curricular and frequently carry credit toward graduation. They are now organized and directed, with citizenship and character development as important goals. Home rooms are organized as civic units of the school community and student councils as representative legislative bodies, both of them providing an opportunity for coöperative participation in the life of the school. Assemblies serve as a clearing house for all the activities of the school, by means of which is developed a spirit of unity and solidarity, the "group consciousness" of which the sociologist talks. A wide variety of clubs, and varsity and intramural participation in athletics and other activities, take into consideration the gregarious tendencies of the adolescent and furnish opportunities for those creative impulses that we discussed in the foregoing section. Being president of a student council, managing an athletic team, preparing a stage set for a play, and being a member of a band or orchestra are undoubtedly creative experiences. Dr. E. K. Fretwell [15] expresses the point we desire to emphasize when he insists that extracurricular activities should "grow out of the curricular activities and return to them to enrich them." One of the most hopeful and fruitful of current tendencies is to be seen in the merging of curricular and extracurricular activities; in bringing into closer relationship the in-school and out-of-school interests of boys and girls.

C. Guidance and Personnel Work

For forty years an increasing amount of attention has been given to guidance and personnel work in the public schools. It represents one of the developments incident to the shift from subject matter to pupil activity. Teachers have been encouraged to study the children, to know their home and community backgrounds, and to deal with them as individuals in terms of their capacities and interests. "To learn the pupil" is weak grammar, but it is sound pedagogy.

The guidance movement is due to several factors that are operating in and upon our schools. The first impetus came from the rapidly increasing numbers of students, particularly in the secondary schools. As the numbers increased, the school population became increasingly heterogeneous and unselected, and the need of many students for assistance in choosing an occupation became

---

15 E. K. Fretwell, *Extra Curricular Activities in Secondary Schools* (Boston: Houghton Mifflin, 1931).

more and more apparent. The movement began in 1908 with the efforts of Frank Parsons to assist the youth of Boston in the pursuit of a vocation. About the same time, we ran into an era of specialization. Industry and commerce and the occupational world generally were calling for more specialized training as a product of the public schools. Students, in turn, called for much advice concerning their choices. The junior high school appeared on the scene with its emphasis upon "guidance as the keynote." All this called for a counseling program. The larger schools added advisers or deans of boys or girls to their staffs, persons who devoted all or a part of their time to counseling. Nearly all cities have well-organized guidance and personnel departments. Smaller schools that are unable to employ deans or counselors appoint directors or committees in charge of guidance programs; but in either case, the major responsibility for counseling falls upon the teachers, usually in their capacity as home-room sponsors.

1. Pupil Counseling

The primary aim of the guidance program is to establish sufficiently cordial and intimate pupil-teacher relationships to enable pupils to get the help they need in preparing for the work they want to do. In the beginning the emphasis was upon vocational guidance, which was concerned primarily with choosing the right vocation. That involved an analysis of the occupation to ascertain its possibilities and limitations and an analysis of the individual in terms of the requirements of the job. After choosing an occupation, moreover, there comes the problem of preparing for that occupation. That task calls for some sort of educational guidance, which embraces choosing courses or curricula and which, for many students, necessitates selecting and preparing for college or technical school. Another problem that counselors encounter may be referred to as social-civic guidance, the emphasis here being upon social and civic attitudes; that is, getting along with other people in social and civic relationships. The need for attention to these problems is seen in the fact that nearly as many people fail in their work because they are unable to make the social adjustments as fail because they lack the required skills and abilities. The National Vocational Association, which is the official agency representing the varied interests of guidance workers, has formulated a definition that states the objectives of the guidance movement quite completely: "Vocational guidance consists of giving experience, information and advice with respect to the choosing of an occupation, preparing for it, entering upon it, and securing satisfactory status in it." [16] The guidance program opens up new avenues of service for the schools and fine opportunities for teachers.

2. More Flexible College Entrance Provisions

Most of the developments we are discussing here are being manifested at all school levels. A few of them are primarily secondary school problems, and their success and effectiveness are being brought close to us by the tendency toward more liberal and more flexible college entrance requirements. Ever since the establishment of high schools and academies, the college has exerted a degree of domination over the secondary school curriculum. Traditionally students have been given few choices of subjects in the typical high school because the college entrance requirements prescribed very narrow limitations. It was also quite general for everybody connected with schools to believe that a college entrance curriculum was also the best education for all students, whether they were going to college or not. At the present time, the pendulum is swinging in the other direction. The colleges are less interested in the particular subjects studied and are more interested in knowing the type of work a student is able to do and his aptitude for the work for which he wishes to prepare. To be sure, the College Entrance Board and the New York Regents examinations still exert a sort of standardizing pressure in the areas where they are operative, but even there the tendency is to try to find capable people and to pay less attention to particular subjects. For ex-

---

16 Accepted definition of the National Vocational Guidance Association, Fred C. Smith, Executive Secretary, University of Tennessee, Knoxville, Tenn.

ample, the University of Chicago openly invites students to come whether they have finished high school or not. The only test is ability to do college work successfully. The Progressive Education Association [17] in 1941 completed with a selected group of high schools and preparatory schools throughout the country an experiment that looks forward to more flexible entrance standards and closer relations between colleges and secondary schools.

Thirty public and private secondary schools of all types were engaged in the experiment, and more than two hundred colleges and universities agreed to coöperate to the extent of admitting the graduates without reference to the usual entrance requirements. The students in the so-called "progressive" groups pursued a modified curriculum that placed greater emphasis upon more continuity and better integration of subject matter that was selected because of its vital and functioning value, rather than in terms of traditional requirements. Systematic efforts were made to adapt the work to the individual capacity, needs, and interests of the students, to learn more about them, and to discover better methods of recording their progress. The results of the experiment are very well summarized in the following extract from a report of its Director, Dr. Wilford M. Aikin, Ohio State University:

In the comparison of the 1475 matched pairs, the College Follow-up Staff found that the graduates of the Thirty Schools
1. earned a slightly higher total grade average;
2. earned higher grade averages in all subject fields except foreign language;
3. specialized in the same academic fields as did the comparison students;
4. did not differ from the comparison group in the number of times they were placed on probation;
5. received slightly more academic honors in each year;
6. were more often judged to possess a high degree of intellectual curiosity and drive;

---

[17] Commission on the Relation of School and College of the Progressive Education Association, Wilford M. Aikin, Director, Ohio State University, Columbus, Ohio.

7. were more often judged to be precise, systematic and objective in their thinking;
8. were more often judged to have developed clear or well-formulated ideas concerning the meaning of education—especially in the first two years in college;
9. more often demonstrated a high degree of resourcefulness in meeting new situations;
10. did not differ from the comparison group in ability to plan their time effectively;
11. had about the same problems of adjustment as the comparison group, but approached their solution with greater effectiveness;
12. participated somewhat more frequently, and more often enjoyed appreciative experiences, in the arts;
13. participated more in all organized student groups except religious and 'service' activities;
14. earned in each college year a higher percentage of non-academic honors (officership in organizations, election to managerial societies, athletic insignia, leading roles in dramatic and musical presentations);
15. did not differ from the comparison group in the quality of adjustment to their contemporaries;
16. differed only slightly from the comparison group in the kinds of judgments about their schooling;
17. had a somewhat better orientation toward the choice of a vocation;
18. demonstrated a more active concern for what was going on in the world.[18]

The experience of the colleges with returning service men and women is providing still further evidence that maturity and significant life experiences are more important than Carnegie units and College Entrance Board examination results as determinants of fitness to undertake college work. The more than one million GI's enrolled in American colleges in 1946–47, many of them with irregular patterns of academic work, have, through their excellent records, made a great contribution toward liberalizing college entrance requirements.

---

[18] Wilford M. Aikin, *The Story of the Eight-Year Study* (New York: Harper, 1942).

D. Intercultural Education

One of the most promising and most significant educational activities today is the concerted effort that is being made to lessen, if not to eradicate, intolerance and bigotry in American life. No thoughtful person would believe that this can be accomplished in a short time. Most would agree that it is basically an educational problem. One can look at the considerable amount of intolerance in our society and be tremendously discouraged and depressed. Or one can look at the constructive efforts to correct it that are under way and find cause for encouragement.

During the war there was a kind of enforced truce in the extent to which intolerance and discrimination could be carried. To a degree, at least, we subordinated our prejudices and worked unitedly to win the war. It was freely predicted, however, that with the end of the war there would come a greater wave of intolerance than ever before. There was some justification for this belief. Certainly there were enough manifestations of intolerance during the war to confirm suspicions that the evil had not disappeared. Following World War I there was the revival of the Ku Klux Klan. Many persons believed that even worse consequences would follow the end of hostilities in World War II. It can be stated that to date these have not occurred. It would appear to be true that the credit for averting a new outbreak of intolerance and bigotry, to the extent that it has been averted, should be given largely to those many thoughtful individuals and groups that have sought valiantly to educate the people to the evil and futility of such outbreaks.

The Bureau for Intercultural Education, the National Conference of Christians and Jews, and the Council Against Intolerance in America are only some among many organizations and groups that have been working on this problem. Supporting their efforts are many thousands of individuals representing all racial and religious groups in our society. State and municipal governments have contributed greatly through the establishment of committees of representative citizens officially appointed to deal with the problem at local and state levels. In New York and in many other cities there is a Mayor's Committee on Unity.

The short-time effort has been to avoid immediate violent outbreaks. In the main that effort has met with success. The somewhat more remote goal has been to educate our present generation of adults to subordinate their prejudices, at least to the point of recognizing the right to exist and to work of those groups that they do not like. There has been the further effort to persuade adults that hate groups can serve no constructive purpose. These efforts to date have been more than moderately successful. The long-term effort is the acceptance in actual practice and without discrimination of the great American democratic ideal of equality of opportunity for all persons, regardless of race, creed, or sex. And finally, there is the long-term effort to gain acceptance and practical implementation of the concept of the Brotherhood of Man. Admittedly, this last is indeed a long-term objective, but the world will not be safe until it has been achieved. Each step we succeed in taking toward that objective, both in our relations with our fellow citizens and in our dealings with other countries, will increase the likelihood that we and our children will be able to live out our lives in peace. No greater task confronts American education.

E. Problems and References for Collateral Study

Problems for Students

1. From a limited sampling of the population, estimate the need and the demand for nursery schools or kindergartens in your community.

2. Prepare a digest of the research studies that throw some light on the relationship between kindergarten attendance and the later school achievement.

3. Prepare a brief description of all the adult education activities in your home community.

4. Collect information relative to the amount of illiteracy in different nations and the measures employed to reduce illiteracy.

5. Prepare a list of various projects being sponsored by Federal, state, and local governments to provide recreational facilities.

6. What were the values (or weaknesses) of your own participation in the student life of high school?

7. What are your qualifications or lack of qualifications to be a successful school camp counselor?

8. Analyze your prejudices. What are you doing about them?

Selected References

Aikin, Wilford M., *The Story of the Eight-Year Study*. New York: Harper, 1942.

Allers, R., *Character Education in Adolescence*. New York: J. F. Wagner, 1940.

Allport, Gordon W., *ABC's of Scapegoating*, Central YMCA College, 19 South La Salle Street, Chicago, Ill., 1944.

Baruch, Dorothy, *Parents and Children Go to School*. Chicago: Scott, Foresman, 1940.

Benedict, Ruth, and Gene Weltfish, *The Races of Mankind*, Public Affairs Pamphlet No. 85, New York, 1943.

Bryson, Lyman, *Adult Education*. New York: American Book Company, 1936.

De Lissa, L., *Life in the Nursery School*. New York: Longmans, Green, 1939.

Forest, Ilse, *The School for the Child from Two to Eight*. Boston: Ginn, 1935.

Gaer, J., *Consumers All*. New York: Harcourt, Brace, 1940.

Gesell, Arnold, and others, *First Five Years of Life*. New York: Harper, 1940.

Koos, Leonard V., *Integrating High School and College*. New York: Harper, 1946.

Laubach, F. C., *Toward a Literate World*. New York: World Literacy Committee, 1938.

Olsen, Edward G., and others, *School and Community*. New York: Prentice-Hall, 1946.

Powdermaker, Hortense, *Probing Our Prejudices*. New York: Harper, 1944.

Raubicheck, Letitia, *Teaching Speech in Secondary Schools*. New York: Prentice-Hall, 1935.

Slavson, S. R., *Character Education in a Democracy*. New York: Association Press, 1939.

Stiles, Dan, *High Schools for Tomorrow*. New York: Harper, 1946.

Thorndike, E. L., *Adult Interests*. New York: Macmillan, 1935.

Tonne, Herbert, *Consumer Education in the Schools*. New York: Prentice-Hall, 1940.

Updegraff, Ruth, and others, *Practice in Pre-School Education.* New York: McGraw-Hill, 1938.

Vickery, William E., and Stewart G. Cole, *Intercultural Education in American Schools.* New York: Harper, 1943.

INDEX

A

A. & M. colleges, establishment of, 74
Academic freedom, question of, 261–268
Academic preparation for teaching, 33
Academies:
 military and naval, 81
 or Prep Schools, 59, 64, 115–116
Achievement, measurement of, 115–116
 standard tests of, 156
Adams, J. T., *On Jeffersonian Principles,* 112, 205
Adler, adherence to psychoanalysis theory by, 149
Administration, school:
 and supervision, 9–11
 democratization of, 284–285
Administrative organization for public education, 77–82
Adult education:
 and part-time education, 312–319
 state programs of, 318–319
Advertising as an educative agency, 191–192
Age norms:
 and grade norms, 157
 use of, 156–157
Agencies of education, 177–193
Agriculture, instruction in, 74, 81, 279
Aid and grants for education, 48, 74, 78, 81–82, 189, 295–299, 310, 318–319
Aikin, W. M., *Story of the Eight-Year Study,* 336–337
Alaska, Federal supervision of schools in, 81
Aldermann, L. R., Director of Education Division of W.P.A., 48
Alexander, Thomas, *Prussian Elementary Schools,* 101–103
Allport, G. W. and F. H., *A-S Reaction Study,* 154
Alschuler, R. L., *Two to Six,* 308
American Association of School Administrators, 216

American Association of Teachers Colleges, 264
American Association of University Professors, 264, 266
American Automobile Association, safety drives of, 323
American education and schools:
 changes in organization of, 49
 chronology of significant events in, 118
 conflicting tendencies in, 119–120
 current tendencies in, 82–98
 evolution of trends in, 94–98
 historical and traditional influences affecting, 107–119
 historical résumé of developments in, 114–119
 ideals of, three basic, 110–114
 influences affecting, 107–174
 necessary and impending changes in, 271–305
 need for larger units of administration in, 273–280
 needed administrative changes in, 272–288
 number of teachers in, 2
 organization of, 43–82
 philosophical influences affecting, 119–174
 scientific or psychological influences affecting, 141–174
American Federation of Labor, 241
American Legion, 298
American School of the Air, educational value of, 184
American school system, 43–104
 comparison of, with foreign, 98–104
 divisions of, 45–76
 elementary education in, 50–57
 graded ladder organization of, 45–50
 higher education in, 65–76
 local control in, 76–78
 national organization in, 81–82
 secondary education in, 57–65
 state administration in, 78–81
Americanization education, 314–315

345